THE AMERICAN HORTICULTURAL SOCIETY

COMPLETE GUIDE TO

WATER GARDENING

THE AMERICAN HORTICULTURAL SOCIETY

COMPLETE GUIDE TO
WATER
GARDENING

PETER ROBINSON

A DK PUBLISHING BOOK

PROJECT EDITOR Cangy Venables
PROJECT ART EDITOR Gillian Andrews

MANAGING EDITOR Louise Abbott
MANAGING ART EDITOR Lee Griffiths

US CONSULTANT James A. Lawrie
US EDITORS Barbara Ellis, Mary Sutherland

DTP DESIGNER Chris Clark
PRODUCTION Ruth Charlton
PHOTOGRAPHY Peter Anderson, Steven Wooster
ILLUSTRATIONS Karen Cochrane, Valerie Hill, John Woodcock

First American Edition, 1997

Published in the United States by
DK Publishing, Inc.,
95 Madison Avenue,
New York, New York 10016

Library of Congress Cataloging-in-Publication Data
Robinson, Peter
American Horticultural Society Complete Guide to Water Gardening
Peter Robinson. – 1st American edition.
p. cm.
Includes index.
ISBN 0-7894-1478-3
1. Water Gardens. I. Title. SB423.R585 1996
635.9'674-DC20   96-30989
                                        CIP

Color reproduction by Bright Arts, Hong Kong
Printed and bound by A. Mondadori, Verona

KEY TO PLANTING PLANS

In planting plans accompanying
water garden designs, color
coding indicates whether plants
are growing in water, in moist
soil, or in ordinary garden soil.

▢	WATER PLANTS
▢	MOISTURE-LOVING PLANTS
▢	OTHER PLANTS

KEY TO SYMBOLS

The following symbols accompany plant descriptions, indicating
the type of plant and its cultivation requirements.

✳	Prefers a sunny position	◓	Tender perennial grown as an annual in the North
�ള	Prefers partial shade	◊	Well-drained but moisture-retentive soil
✳	Tolerates full shade		
⬇	Submerged plant	◖	Moist soil
⬇	Floating-leaved plant	●	Wet soil
⬇	Free-floating plant		
✿	Water Lily		
❀	Lotus		
⬆	Marginal Plant		

CONTENTS

CREATING WATER FEATURES

STOCKING & MAINTENANCE

PLANT CATALOG

Author's Foreword

THE CURRENT RISE in popularity of water gardening is not difficult to understand. This most beguiling element can be introduced to every size and style of garden. Perhaps surprisingly, water features are one of the most practical and least wasteful ways of transforming a garden into a cooling retreat with lush and varied plant growth.

However, without adequate care being given to the design and construction of a water feature, its full potential may be tantalizingly elusive. The intention of this book is to inspire and inform gardeners at every stage. For the garden owner contemplating a new water feature, it provides a complete practical guide to design and siting, construction, planting, stocking, and maintenance. This book is designed to have equal value to the owner of an existing water feature, offering ideas for improvement, care, and introduction of new plants. In common with so many other aspects of ornamental gardening, a careful mix of science and art is required to make sure that a water garden achieves, then maintains, visual harmony and ecological balance. The aim here has been to explain and overcome all of the myths and problems so often associated with water features.

Throughout this book, particularly in the section on water garden design, photographs and plans show how water features in a variety of styles may be integrated into overall garden plans. My thanks are due to the designers and owners of these gardens. The practical step-by-step sequences, showing exactly how features are built and equipment installed, were also photographed in private gardens. In order to provide realistic guides to construction, the projects shown were actually built as permanent features, and continue to provide considerable pleasure. I am especially grateful to the owners of these gardens for their help in producing a book that will, I hope, be both a visual and practical inspiration to its readers.

Peter Robinson

PETER ROBINSON

INTRODUCTION

Throughout history, water has been valued and even revered all around the world – in some cultures rivers, springs, and streams possessed their own deities. The name of France's Seine River, for example, comes from that of the Celtic goddess Sequana. The earliest tradition of building structures that conserved and channeled water is seen in areas where water was scarce – canals that conducted water away from reservoirs to irrigate fields and settlements have been found dating back as far as the 6th century BC.

But even in these very early times, water gradually assumed roles beyond strictly practical uses. Water features became centers for community life and ornamented the pleasure gardens of the rich and powerful. In the Far East, water assumed symbolic significance in the private garden of the philosopher. The decorative possibilities of combining water with plants and ornamental materials were explored in ever greater depth. Because it can add such atmosphere and visual beauty, water has had a profound influence on the development of garden design.

FORMAL ORIENTAL WATER GARDEN
Artful naturalism in Oriental gardens was often balanced with the formal use of water, as in this contemporary interpretation of a straight-edged pool with symmetrical plantings and pergolas.

It is surprising to discover just how central the use of water features is to gardens worldwide at all times in history.

WATER GARDEN DESIGN AS AN ART FORM

The Oriental style is one the oldest and most influential in water gardening. The Chinese strove to imitate their natural landscape: like poetry or painting, gardening became an artistic emulation of nature. Great care was taken in designing gardens in which water and rocks represented the central principles of *yin* and *yang*. Their placing was crucial in attaining harmony. By the 3rd century AD, the pattern for the Oriental garden, with a lake, island, arched bridges, and subtle planting, was established. By the early 15th century, this had become an art form that was a source of inspiration worldwide.

In Japan, garden design was first influenced by Chinese culture; then the philosophies of Buddhism and Shintoism introduced a strong element of religious symbolism. While Japanese design is much admired and imitated in the West, few Westerners have succeeded in understanding the delicate precision that governs the placing and combining of plants, water, and rock based on religious, historical, and romantic associations.

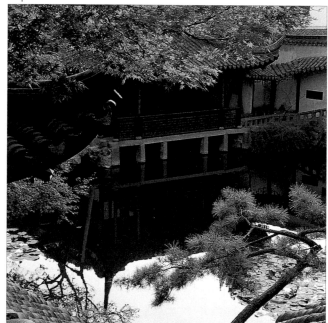

ENCLOSED CHINESE POOL
The traditional Chinese courtyard garden was an enclosed, intimate space for scholarly contemplation, often heightened by the tranquil presence of still, reflecting water.

THEMED LANDSCAPE
The planting around this pond at Coombe Wood in Dorset, England, appears informal, yet is a skillful composition of all the components of Oriental designs – Japanese maples, rhododendrons, and other evergreens. A fountain animates the elegant statues of cranes and the two Oriental bridges. In Japanese style, all is immaculately well kept.

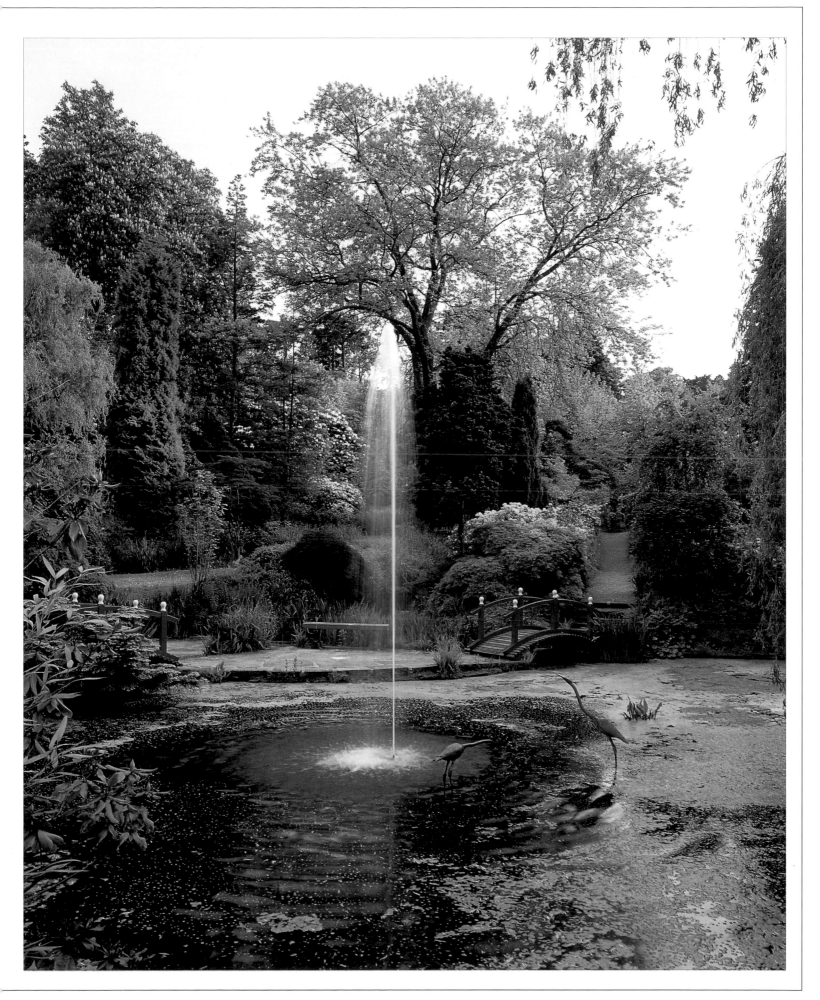

THE EARLY ISLAMIC WATER GARDEN

In addition to containing water essential for practical uses, early Islamic water gardens provided the serenity of still water and the refreshment of gently splashing fountains. Like the early Egyptians, they created enclosed, walled gardens designed to provide relief from the relentless heat of the sun. Unlike designs from the Far East, Islamic gardens were formal and non-representational, with tiling and elaborate stonework often taking the place of plants that would have used up precious water reserves. Gardens were often arranged in four divisions, intersected by canals representing the four rivers of Paradise.

THE SPREAD OF ISLAMIC INFLUENCE

From the conquest of the Middle East, Islam spread through Egypt and North Africa and from there into southern Spain. Here too, the arid climate necessitated that water be transported to gardens for both decorative and practical purposes. Among the most outstanding water gardens are those at the fortress palace of Alhambra, in Granada, where Moorish gardens and surrounding buildings are subtly integrated. Water for the Alhambra, built in the mid-13th century on a hillside, had to be elevated by aqueduct from the Darro River.

CANAL AT GENERALIFE, GRANADA
This narrow canal, with its arching jets and a brimming dish fountain at its head, highlights the beauty of the stone and ceramic tiling used in this 13th-century Moorish garden.

FORMAL COURYARD
The talent for creating perfect gardens with limited water resources is found throughout the Islamic world. The interrelationship of restrained planting and architecture is enhanced by the gentle movement of running water. This small fountain and shallow basin and pool, central to the garden's design, is surprisingly economical with precious water.

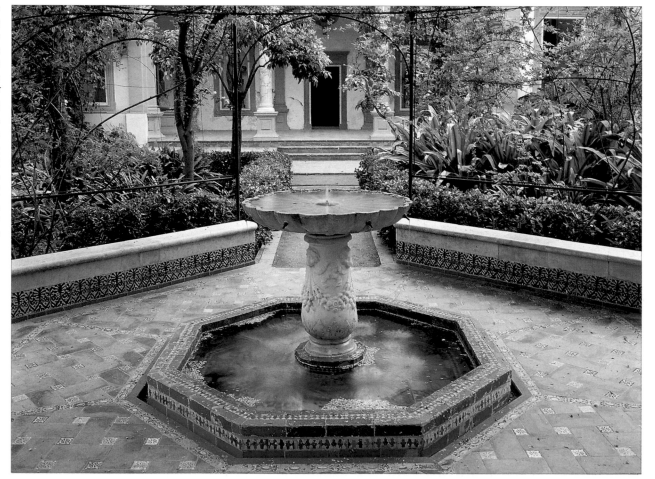

The Islamic use of water in the garden was to make a significant impact in the gardens built by the Mogul emperors in northern India between the 15th and 18th centuries. Again, fountains and large sheets of still water were introduced to provide refreshment from the continual heat. Similarly, the gardens were divided into four by canals, which were surrounded by sunken flower beds and raised paths. Gardens such as those of the Taj Mahal and at Nishat Bagh took traditional Persian design to new heights, associating water with spectacular architecture and harnessing water pressure for aesthetic effect.

ANCIENT ROME

In contrast to the crisp simplicity and decorative function of Islamic gardens, records reveal that the Romans were early pioneers of the modern concept of using water for ornament. Water was brought into the garden solely for the pleasure it gave, especially when associated with lavish, well-tended plantings. Many affluent Roman citizens became early "gentleman gardeners," taking a keen interest in cultivation techniques and in new plants brought back from far parts of the Empire. Statuary, not permitted in the Islamic world but central to the Roman system of beliefs, was often used to ornament gardens and water features.

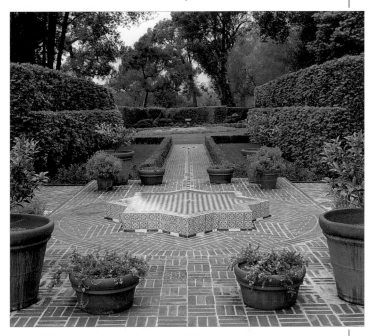

MOORISH INFLUENCE IN MODERN AMERICA
The use of decorative materials rather than plants to frame water is equally practical in this dry Californian garden. A tiled pool is surrounded by brick terracing, whose abstract patterning is typical of Islamic art and architecture.

THE WATER GARDEN IN RENAISSANCE ITALY

Rome also became a center for the exuberant use of water that characterized the gardens of the Renaissance. The hilly terrain north of the city provided ample water pressure, making it an ideal location for water gardens that rapidly became ever grander in scale. Movement and sound could be exploited to the fullest, and fountain design was spectacular, often incorporating statues of human figures, animals, or mythological creatures to create dramatic tableaux. The Villa d'Este remains the most outstanding and imaginative example of the technical brilliance and extravagance of the period: ingenious hydraulics produce a pathway of 100 fountains, a water organ, and a spouting dragon.

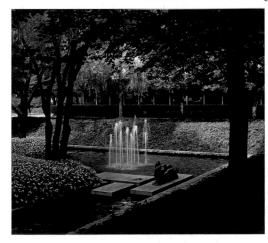

PEPSICO GARDENS, NEW YORK
Throughout the world designers now realize the benefits, long recognized in the Arab world, of introducing water as a cooling and refreshing element in public spaces.

POST-RENAISSANCE EUROPE

The influence of the Italian Renaissance reached France in the latter part of the 15th century, when Charles VIII invaded Italy. However, it was not until

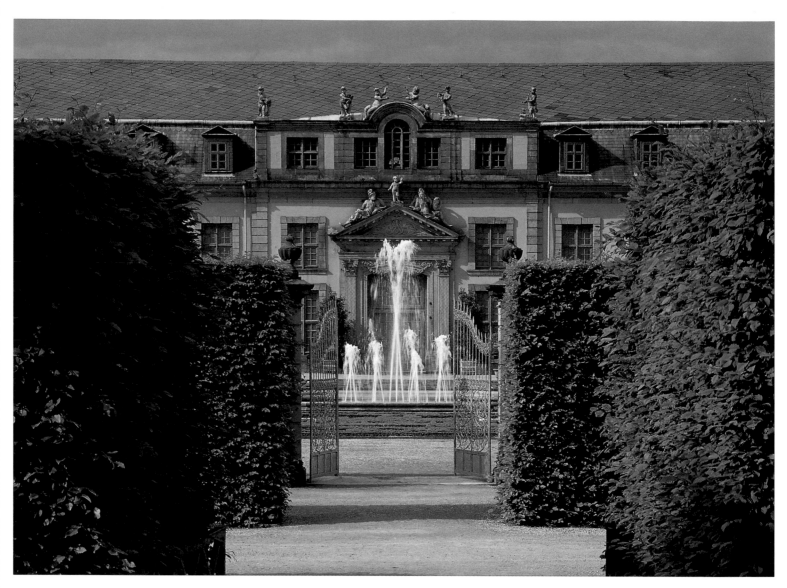

the 17th century that classical formality in France really came to the fore. Louis XIV's Versailles, designed by Le Notre, exemplified tasteful flamboyance and was the model to which garden designers all over Europe aspired for the next century or so. No expense was spared to create an extravaganza of water in a garden setting. It was combined with sculpture and architecture and in many cases with the creation of broad, elaborate parterres in order to achieve grand formality.

Le Notre's work inspired other grandiose schemes in Europe. In Russia, his disciple Le Blond created a garden with water tumbling down marble stairways into a huge marble basin. In Spain, Louis XIV's grandson Philip V created a magnificent water garden at La Granja with impressive fountains and cascades. At Herrenhausen, in Germany, water was used to animate and link formal areas within a strictly geometric pattern that epitomizes the more rigid contemporary German and Dutch styles.

A MORE NATURALISTIC APPROACH

During this period many formal water features were brilliantly executed in England, notably at Chatsworth, in Derbyshire. The break with the formal use of water came toward the middle of the 18th century, with the

STATELY STYLE
For centuries in Europe, ornamental gardening was practiced purely for the pleasure of the wealthy. As technical and mechanical skills developed, water features became more powerful and elaborate, reflecting the status of their owners. By the mid-19th century, few large houses were without awe-inspiring jets and cascades to welcome and impress the visitor, as here at Herrenhausen in Germany.

landscape movement in Great Britain. William Kent (1685–1748) was one of the great pioneers of the movement, using Classical buildings in the landscape to great effect. His management of water was his greatest skill; he replaced formal features such as fountains with three-dimensional compositions of woodland, lawn, and water. Contrasts of light and shade superseded tight architectural form. Craggy waterfalls, grottoes, and other follies became popular, taking their cue from the Romanticism evident in Germany during the 18th century. Monet's garden at Giverny, in France, is a landmark in the movement toward planting rather than architecture, which was to gather momentum in the 20th century. It combines extensive informal planting and stretches of water on which reflections, light and shade, and floating water lilies interplay.

WATER GARDENS IN NORTH AMERICA

Water features began to make an impact in America at the turn of the 19th century after the upheaval of the Civil War in a period known as the "Country Place Era." Private wealth enabled ornamental gardening to surge in popularity. Islamic features were incorporated with the styles of the Renaissance and the French gardens of the late 16th to early 18th centuries, dominated by still pools and fountains. The "Country Place Era" came to an end as planting became more significant. Gardens filled with bulbs, perennials, and annuals appeared as the domestic garden developed. Between the two world wars, North American gardens developed their own sense of identity, often based on abstract form and landscaping.

ENGLISH VERSATILITY
At Shute House in Dorset, a formal vista with statue is seen beyond a foreground of dense, informal waterside planting in a brilliant and inventive blending of styles.

CONTEMPORARY WATER GARDENS

As ornamental gardening has become more accessible to a wider section of society, the average garden size has decreased. Modern materials and techniques allow water features to be used in gardens on a small domestic scale. Perhaps the most essential development in the 20th-century water garden, though, has been the breakdown of the traditional differentiation between formal and informal styles. Elements may be freely borrowed from other cultures and eras, then combined and adapted to today's gardens in individualistic and innovative style, making water gardening one of the most exciting aspects of garden design.

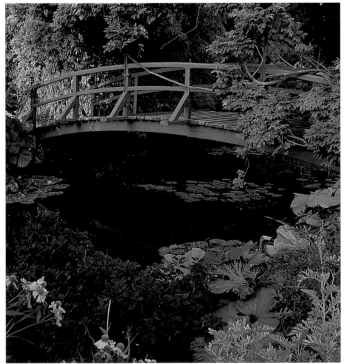

MONET'S GARDEN AT GIVERNY
This naturalistic pond with rustic bridge epitomizes the move toward informality that now characterizes most domestic gardens, where water serves to enhance the beauty and color contrasts of luxuriant plantings.

WATER GARDEN DESIGNS

DESIGNING WITH WATER
RAISED DOUBLE POOL • LARGE FORMAL POOL
CONTAINER GARDENS
ORIENTAL-STYLE WATER GARDEN
COURTYARD POOL • INFORMAL POND WITH
PEBBLE BEACH • MILLSTONE FOUNTAIN
WILDLIFE POND WITH BOG GARDEN • STREAM
FOR CITY OR COUNTRY GARDEN

ORIENTAL-STYLE WATER GARDEN (*LEFT*)
*The careful placement of water, plants, rocks and other materials, the
subtle use of color and foliage, and the contemplative atmosphere of
the Oriental garden make it a popular landcaping style.*

DESIGNING WITH WATER

WATER FEATURES CAN BE accommodated in any garden, whether in an urban, suburban, or country setting. Although the site may dictate certain constraints, it is surprising how flexible these limits are. The following pages feature examples of excellent water design in gardens large and small, in formal or informal style – some combining elements of both. All are different, yet all exemplify the exceptional role water can play in a garden setting. Water features can animate and transform a landscape or garden corner with movement and sound or with stillness and reflection. Above all they create settings for new and beautiful plants.

DECIDING ON A DESIGN

To be really satisfying, a water feature requires an initial and quite searching appraisal of what you intend it to bring to your garden. Unlike lawns and borders, which are relatively easy to enlarge, reduce, or alter in shape, a water feature is less easy to change once installed. Each of the features here succeeds through a mix of elements that relate, above all, to the satisfaction of the owner. Some use water to enhance the colors and textures of decorative materials, while in others the water is there to lure wildlife. Some reflect an advanced sense of plantsmanship, while others use plantings simply as a textural element, to break or highlight line and color.

FORWARD PLANNING

A new garden provides the perfect opportunity to incorporate water in a new and complete design. There is an enormous advantage constructing a pond if mechanical equipment is able to maneuver freely, for example. It can achieve in a few hours of

REFLECTING FEATURE
Waterside areas open up exciting planting opportunities: Gunnera manicata *is ideally placed where its huge leaves can be seen reflected in the water surface.*

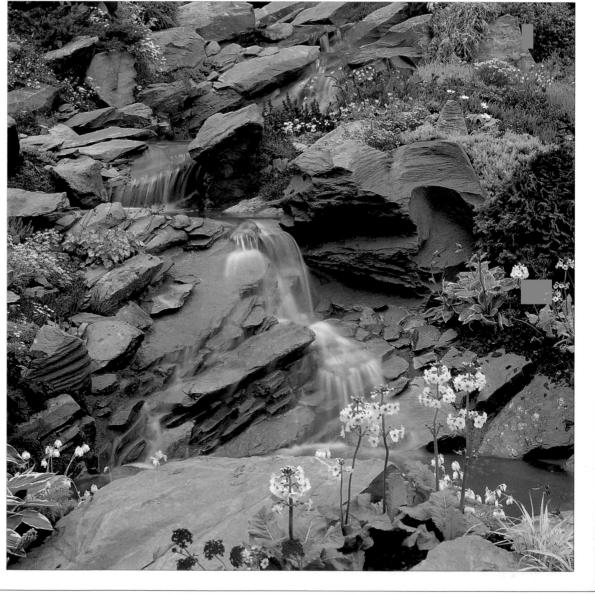

ROCKY STREAM
A level garden can be landscaped to create a cascading stream; the new generation of small, self-contained submersible pumps are much easier than older models to install and maintain.

ATTRACTING WILDLIFE
For many, the sight of wildlife around a pond is one of the most rewarding features of a water garden. Providing a feature that is attractive to insects and other creatures needs thought at the planning stage.

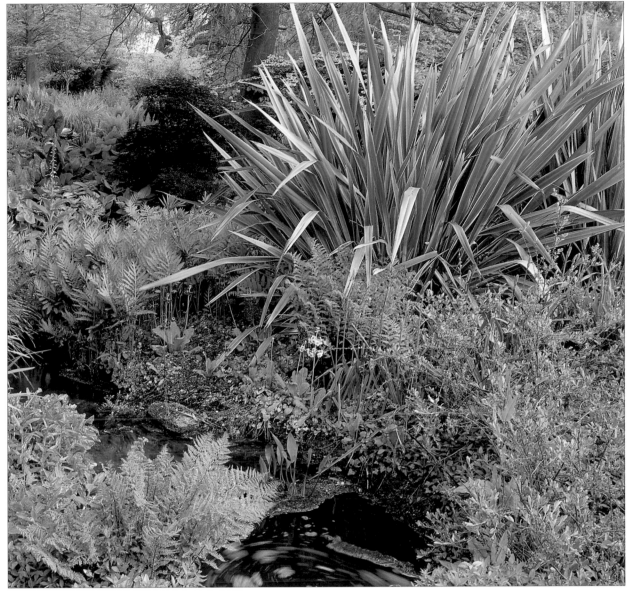

LUSH LANDSCAPE
A dedicated area of moist or boggy ground, where moisture-loving plants can thrive is especially satisfying. Such plantings are very practical in areas with dry summers.

excavation what would take days of hand digging. Placing large boulders by mechanical means, such as those used in the Oriental-style garden *(see pp. 28–31)*, would be extremely difficult once the surrounding garden had been made, but they are an essential ingredient if the design is to work well.

But while a new garden is an ideal blank canvas, it is more common to want to add a water feature to an existing garden. There is no reason why this should not work well, provided care is taken to integrate it well into its surroundings; a pond that suddenly appears in a border or lawn invariably looks like an afterthought or impulse decision. Try, therefore, to envision and plan your water garden in its entirety from the start. A feature that is built and added to piecemeal over the years never has the style of one designed and installed as a whole.

LOOKING FOR INSPIRATION

Visits to garden centers and water garden specialists pay dividends when planning a design, although you may not be ready to purchase. They often have demonstration gardens where new materials and the latest technology can be seen in action. Also visit as many gardens containing water as you can in search of ideas. Do not be daunted by large gardens, where abundant resources and protection from mature trees will have made it easy to create and maintain beautiful compositions. Scrutinize the detail, looking for attractive materials and the way these are juxtaposed with water and plants, then relate these to your own site and requirements.

DESIGNING WITH CONFIDENCE

When designing, bear in mind the limitations of your site and climate, and keep the skills needed to install and maintain the feature comfortably within your capabilities. While designs should not be overambitious, there is no need for them to be timid either. Successful designs demonstrate a strong theme, and when executed with confidence, they are satisfying from the day the last stone or plant is in place and improve with time as plants grow. The designs on the following pages have become expressions of their owners' individuality or interest, be it plants, wildlife, or a combination of elements. Their success reflects the thought, investment, and interest the owner has put into them.

RAISED DOUBLE POOL

I N THIS MATURE, STYLISH garden the two interlinked pools in turn link the paved terrace area to the rest of the garden. More skillful connections are made in the plantings, with leaf shapes and colors echoed and blended perfectly in and around the water and beyond.

INTERPLAY OF SHAPES AND COLORS
The general impression here is of calmness and continuity. The double pool, its formal edges softened by plants, is well built using materials that are in keeping with the paving and other stonework. Containers filled with alpines and tender perennials continue the gradation toward ground level. A pump sends water from the lower to the upper pool via a conduit in the shared wall and up through a millstone fountain. The upper pond features double waterfalls of exactly the same height. This requires skillful bricklaying. The slabs over which the water spills can be filed or ground down to perfect the effect. Flowering plants are few; harmony is created by bold positioning of complementary foliage – spiky irises, for example, are echoed by the white-variegated grass to the right, the red cordyline on the left, and the spikes of foxgloves and delphiniums in the bed beyond.

THE GARDEN PLAN
Seen from the house and terrace, the pool is surrounded by plantings that have largely been kept low to avoid blocking views of the lawn and borders beyond. Paving stones leading to the garden continue the theme of the terrace and stonework. The plantings use plenty of bold greenery to capitalize on the backdrop of trees in neighboring gardens.

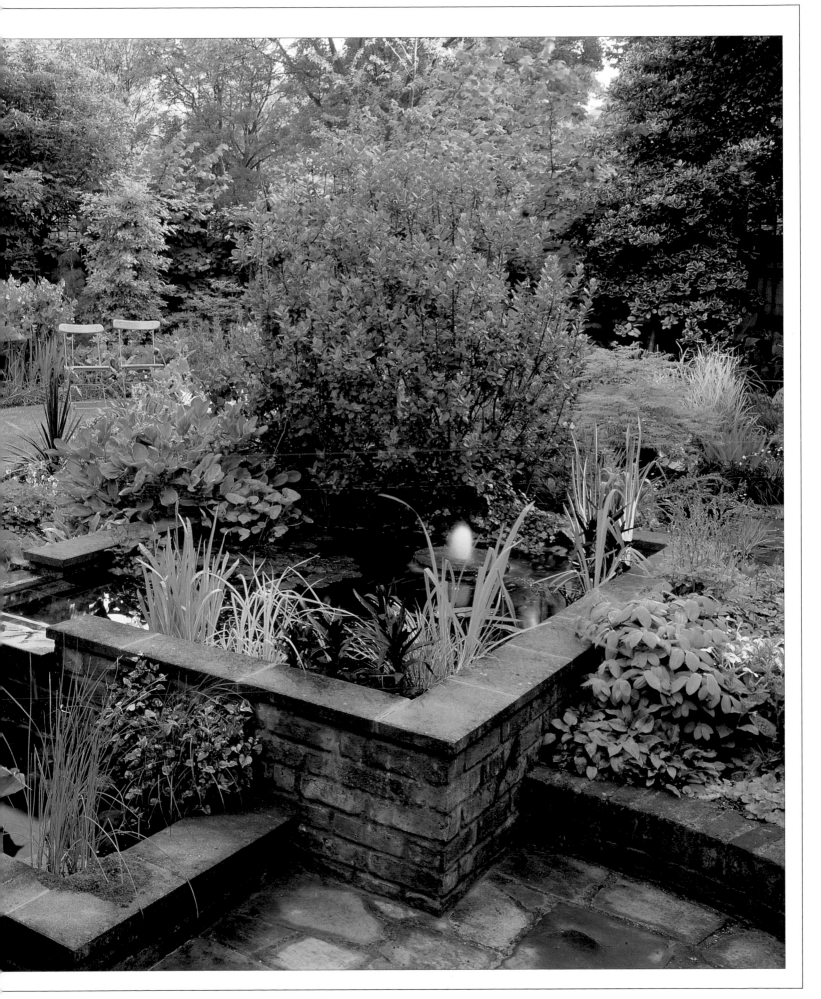

PLANTING PLAN FOR THE RAISED POOLS

WITHIN THE POOLS, restrained planting leaves areas of open water, displaying gleaming pebbles on the pool floor. These are heaped up around planting baskets positioned in the lower pool, helping to disguise them and preventing soil from being dislodged. Small clumps of submerged plants (*Lagarosiphon major* and *Potamogeton crispus*), together with the splashing action of the fountain and waterfalls, keep the water oxygenated and clear. The soil surrounding these contained pools is not wet, but by using plants in these beds that are often seen in moist ground – willow, astilbes, hostas, ferns – and keeping them well watered for lush growth, the illusion is created of natural waterside planting.

DYNAMIC PLANTING WITH FORMAL POOL

This design is dominated by foliage: contrasting shades of green interspersed with bright patches of red, yellow, and purple. Water bubbles and trickles in the pools just enough to add movement, while not disturbing plants. A non-return valve prevents the upper pool from draining through the delivery pipe when the pump is turned off.

SOFTENING LINES
Plants are positioned informally, so that they do not look too regimented against the rectangular shapes of the two pools. Vertical-leaved plants such as irises give height and break the lines of straight edges well.

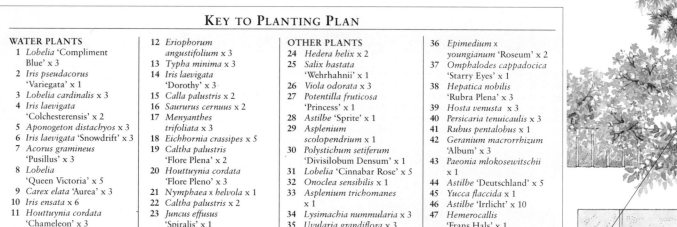

KEY TO PLANTING PLAN

WATER PLANTS
1 *Lobelia* 'Compliment Blue' x 3
2 *Iris pseudacorus* 'Variegata' x 1
3 *Lobelia cardinalis* x 3
4 *Iris laevigata* 'Colchesterensis' x 2
5 *Aponogeton distachyos* x 3
6 *Iris laevigata* 'Snowdrift' x 3
7 *Acorus gramineus* 'Pusillus' x 3
8 *Lobelia* 'Queen Victoria' x 5
9 *Carex elata* 'Aurea' x 3
10 *Iris ensata* x 6
11 *Houttuynia cordata* 'Chameleon' x 3

12 *Eriophorum angustifolium* x 3
13 *Typha minima* x 3
14 *Iris laevigata* 'Dorothy' x 3
15 *Calla palustris* x 2
16 *Saururus cernuus* x 2
17 *Menyanthes trifoliata* x 3
18 *Eichhornia crassipes* x 5
19 *Caltha palustris* 'Flore Plena' x 2
20 *Houttuynia cordata* 'Flore Pleno' x 3
21 *Nymphaea* x *helvola* x 1
22 *Caltha palustris* x 2
23 *Juncus effusus* 'Spiralis' x 1

OTHER PLANTS
24 *Hedera helix* x 2
25 *Salix hastata* 'Wehrhahnii' x 1
26 *Viola odorata* x 3
27 *Potentilla fruticosa* 'Princess' x 1
28 *Astilbe* 'Sprite' x 1
29 *Asplenium scolopendrium* x 1
30 *Polystichum setiferum* 'Divisilobum Densum' x 1
31 *Lobelia* 'Cinnabar Rose' x 5
32 *Onoclea sensibilis* x 1
33 *Asplenium trichomanes* x 1
34 *Lysimachia nummularia* x 3
35 *Uvularia grandiflora* x 3

36 *Epimedium* x *youngianum* 'Roseum' x 2
37 *Omphalodes cappadocica* 'Starry Eyes' x 1
38 *Hepatica nobilis* 'Rubra Plena' x 3
39 *Hosta venusta* x 3
40 *Persicaria tenuicaulis* x 3
41 *Rubus pentalobus* x 1
42 *Geranium macrorrhizum* 'Album' x 3
43 *Paeonia mlokosewitschii* x 1
44 *Astilbe* 'Deutschland' x 5
45 *Yucca flaccida* x 1
46 *Astilbe* 'Irrlicht' x 10
47 *Hemerocallis* 'Frans Hals' x 1

PLANTING PLAN

Salix hastata 'Wehrhahnii'
Deciduous shrub for free-draining or moist soil. White catkins are borne in early spring. Oval green leaves then appear. Propagate from cuttings, semi-ripe in summer or hardwood in winter. Zones 6–9. H and S 5 ft (1.5m).

MILLSTONE FOUNTAIN
Millstones are attractive
accents for fountainheads.
They can be used within
pools or over concealed
reservoirs *(see p. 114)*.

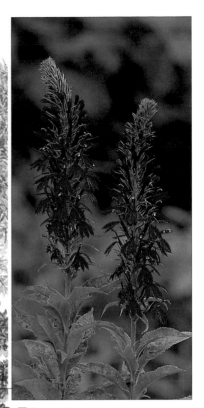

✳ ◖

Lobelia cardinalis
(cardinal flower)
Herbaceous, short-lived, clump-
forming perennial producing tall
spikes of two-lipped, scarlet
flowers from mid- to late summer.
Stems are usually smooth, and the
lance-shaped leaves either green or
reddish bronze. This plant dislikes
very wet winter conditions and, if
grown in boggy soil, must be
lifted before the onset of winter.
Propagate from seed or by
division in spring. Zones 4–8.
H 3ft (1m), S 10in (25cm).

✳ ⬚ ◖

Houttuynia cordata 'Flore Pleno'
Vigorous, deciduous, spreading
perennial marginal plant that grows
well in shallow water or moist soil
where the foliage is not submerged.
The leaves are leathery and aromatic.
Small white flowers are produced in
summer. It is extremely invasive,
and its spread is best contained by
planting in containers sunk in the
soil at a pool's edge. Separate new
plantlets that root from spreading
stems in spring. Zones 5–9.
H 4in (10cm), S indefinite.

LARGE FORMAL POOL

FLOWERHEADS AND SPIKY LEAVES around this formal pool are lit up by late afternoon, late summer sunshine. While earlier in the day the water was a mirror for the sky, now it assumes mysterious depths, with glimpses of submerged plants and fish. Weathered stone, a trickling fountain, and plants that tumble over path edges combine to give an air of faded grandeur.

CLASSIC SIMPLICITY

This is a design that perfectly combines the surfaces of water and stone and the soft color palette of plants that are suited to both aquatic and arid conditions. The large, concrete-lined pool was built some time ago using the skilled and laborious forming method *(see p. 91)*. Today, one option for a formal pool like this one is to build a concrete block shell and line it with a flexible liner – preferably butyl, since this is extremely hard wearing. (For other options, *see pp. 90–91*.) The small, gently brimming fountain sits within its own small concrete pool, completely independent of its larger neighbor.

THE GARDEN PLAN

Classically European yet suitable for a range of climates, this design echoes that of grand country houses, where a formal pool was often situated near the house. Regular paths, trimmed lawns, and an enclosing screen of well-kept formal hedging contribute to the "stately home" illusion.

PLANTING PLAN FOR THE LARGE FORMAL POOL

IN THE DRY BEDS surrounding the small pool, a planting palette of pinks and grays is set off by natural stone, water, and the refreshing greens of the aquatic plants. All the plants chosen for these beds tolerate arid conditions and enjoy the reflected heat from the paving. In the large pool, fish may take refuge in the shade of several water lilies. Together, beds and pool form a feature that is easy to maintain, and where the plants thrive even in the hottest summer. Plants in the dry beds and the submerged plants in the pool have been allowed to spread informally, while the water lilies and marginal plants are contained in planting baskets. Marginal shelves are easy to incorporate in concrete pools, providing a shallower planting depth. Plants in baskets can also be perched on stacks of bricks, which allows more flexibility in moving plants around; this can be convenient when perfecting the final look of a pool. In cool climates, planting baskets also allow tender plants such as cannas to be lifted from the pool and stored over winter to protect them from freezing water temperatures.

INFLUENCE OF THE PAST

Flat terraces make excellent settings for formal pools and beds surrounded by wide paths, traditionally sited near the house in large country-house gardens. Here more relaxed, low-maintenance plantings have replaced the labor-intensive, formal parterres of the past. This arrangement of pool and planting beds could also easily be reduced in scale for a smaller, similarly sheltered patio or terrace, using plants either singly or in groups of two or three instead of the larger, intermingling drifts planted here.

REGULAR SHAPES
A small, square, unplanted pool echoes the shape of the pavers yet forms a small oasis in the middle of the dry beds and pathways.

Iris laevigata 'Snowdrift'
Deciduous perennial forming upright clumps of smooth, swordlike leaves and sparsely branched, erect stems that each bear two to four beardless white flowers in early to midsummer. All cultivars of *Iris laevigata* will also grow well in permanently moist soil. Propagate by dividing rhizomes in late summer. Zones 4–9. H 2–3ft (60cm–1m), S indefinite, water depth to 3–4in (7–10cm).

PLANTING PLAN

KEY TO PLANTING PLAN

WATER PLANTS
1 *Iris laevigata* 'Snowdrift' x 1
2 *Nymphaea* 'Escarboucle' x 1
3 *Schoenoplectus lacustris* x 2
4 *Lagarosiphon major* x 2
5 *Iris laevigata* 'Variegata' x 1
6 *Pontederia cordata* x 1
7 *Iris sibirica* x 3
8 *Nymphaea* 'William Falconer' x 1
9 *Myriophyllum verticillatum* x 1
10 *Menyanthes trifoliata* x 2
11 *Iris ensata* x 1
12 *Lysichiton camtschatcensis* x 1
13 *Nymphaea* 'Marliacea Albida' x 1
14 *Orontium aquaticum* x 1
15 *Caltha palustris* x 1

16 *Canna flaccida* x 3
17 *Canna glauca* x 1
18 *Glyceria maxima* var. *variegata* x 2
19 *Juncus effusus* 'Spiralis' x 1

OTHER PLANTS
20 *Lychnis coronaria* Oculata Group x 1
21 *Dianthus* 'La Bourboule' x 6
22 *Lavandula angustifolia* x 5
23 *Colchicum speciosum* x 1
24 *Allium christophii* x 7
25 *Saxifraga cotyledon* x 5
26 *Iris* 'Matinata' x 1
27 *Ptilostemon afer* x 1
28 *Erodium manescaui* x 3
29 *Centaurea hypoleuca* 'John Coutts' x 1
30 *Diascia flanaganii* x 4

31 *Dianthus* 'Pink Jewel' x 1
32 *Silene vulgaris* subsp. *maritima* x 1
33 *Allium giganteum* x 3
34 *Artemisia alba* 'Canescens' x 1
35 *Iris* 'Brannigan' x 1
36 *Iris* 'Langport Wren' x 1
37 *Dierama pulcherrimum* x 1
38 *Dianthus* 'Old Square Eyes' x 4
39 *Iris sibirica* x 1
40 *Diascia rigescens* x 3

🗲 🌱 🌢 🌢

Iris laevigata 'Variegata'
Deciduous perennial forming
clumps of smooth, swordlike leaves
and erect stems. In early to midsummer two to four blue, beardless
flowers appear. This cultivar has
variegated leaves; there are others
with different flower colors. Will
grow in permanently moist soil.
Propagate by dividing rhizomes in
late summer. Zones 4–9. H 2–3ft
(60cm–1m), S indefinite, water
depth to 3–4in (7–10cm).

☀ 🌱 🌢

Canna glauca
Rhizomatous perennial with
straplike leaves and showy, pale
yellow flower spikes. Given full sun,
it grows well in shallow water. In
cool climates (where it is also a
popular summer bedding plant) it
must be lifted in fall and stored in a
frost-free place. Thrives in a rich,
loamy planting medium. Propagate
by dividing rhizomes in spring.
Zones 10–11. H to 4ft (1.2m),
S 2ft (60cm).

CONTAINER GARDENS

A MINIATURE POND in a pot, barrel, trough, or sink can be the central feature on a terrace or balcony, or can be tucked into a corner of a garden. A wide variety of plants thrive in containers, and combining them can yield surprising and satisfying effects. Consider using a watertight container to make an indoor pool for tender plants. There are both tropical and hardy dwarf water lilies small enough for containers. When combining plants, include tall ones to prevent a squat appearance; papyrus (*Cyperus papyrus*), for example, adds an attractive vertical accent. Containers also restrain the growth of some beautiful floating-leaved plants that are invasive in open water such as *Eichhornia* and *Azolla*. Remember that submerged plants will still be necessary.

FIBERGLASS PLANTER

This small, lightweight tub is the centerpiece of a sun room used to grow and display frost-tender plants. Warmth and the humidifying effect of the water intensify the scent of the water lily and other flowers. *Myriophyllum* is a good choice of oxgenator, as it also contributes some visible, attractive foliage.

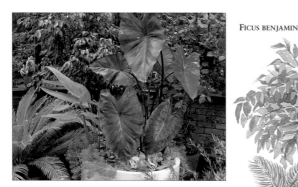

PLANTER IN ITS SETTING
A backdrop of glossy ficus leaves and vivid bougainvillea heightens the tropical look of this container planting. Asparagus fern and a cycad blend with the trailing, feathery stems of Myriophyllum.

PLANTING PLAN

CYCAS REVOLUTA

FICUS BENJAMINA

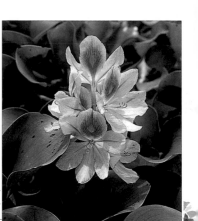

Eichhornia crassipes (water hyacinth)
Evergreen or semi-evergreen free-floater forming rafts of foliage on spongy stalks. It flowers only in warmer conditions and is a menace in tropical areas. Separate new plantlets in spring or summer. Zones 8–11. S indefinite.

ASPARAGUS SCANDENS

Nymphaea mexicana (banana water lily)
Free-blooming species with fragrant, deep yellow flowers opening around noon. Leaves, olive-green when young, are splashed with purple or brown. Can spread rapidly in ponds. Zones 8–11. S 3–4ft (1–1.2m), water depth 18–24in (45–60cm).

KEY TO PLANTING PLAN

WATER PLANTS
1 *Colocasia esculenta* 'Fontanesii' x 1
2 *Myriophyllum aquaticum* x 2
3 *Pistia stratiotes* x 1
4 *Nymphaea mexicana* x 1
5 *Eichhornia crassipes* x 1
6 *Thalia dealbata* x 1

HALF-BARREL

Prepared barrels *(see pp. 94)* make excellent miniature ponds. They can be freestanding, surrounded by other plants and perhaps a few stones at the base, or partially or completely sunk into the ground, which gives some frost protection. A variety of planting depths has been achieved here by standing planting baskets on brick stacks of various heights, enabling both marginal and deeper-water plants to be grown. To maximize space, tall, slender plants with attractive straplike leaves or unusual stems have been used, including *Juncus*, *Isolepis*, and *Equisetum*, leaving room for a miniature water lily and free-floating plants; these should be thinned regularly.

BARREL IN ITS SETTING

In this sunny corner, cheerful plantings with colourful flowers surround the barrel. Bidens and plumbago enjoy the sun, while a golden grass lights up the shadier side and echoes the variegated leaves of the Acorus.

PLANTING PLAN

KEY TO PLANTING PLAN

WATER PLANTS
1 *Azolla filiculoides* x 1
2 *Acorus gramineus* 'Variegatus' x 1
3 *Juncus effusus* 'Spiralis' x 1
4 *Isolepis cernua* x 1
5 *Myriophyllum aquaticum* x 2
6 *Hydrocharis morsus-ranae* x 1
7 *Equisetum japonicum* x 1
8 *Acorus calamus* 'Variegatus' x 1
9 *Nymphaea x helvola* x 1

Juncus effusus 'Spiralis' (corkscrew rush)
Evergreen, tuft-forming perennial that grows well in shallow water or moist soil. Its semi-prostrate, dark green, leafless stems twist and curl. Dense, greenish brown flower tufts form in midsummer. Propagate by division in spring. Zones 7–9. H 3ft (1m), S 2ft (60cm).

Myriophyllum aquaticum (parrot's feather)
Deciduous perennial for any water depth, with stems covered in finely divided leaves. These can grow to up to 6ft (2m), becoming woody at the base, and will extend above the surface of shallow water, scrambling and softening water edges. Thin regularly. Propagate from cuttings. Zones 6–11. S indefinite.

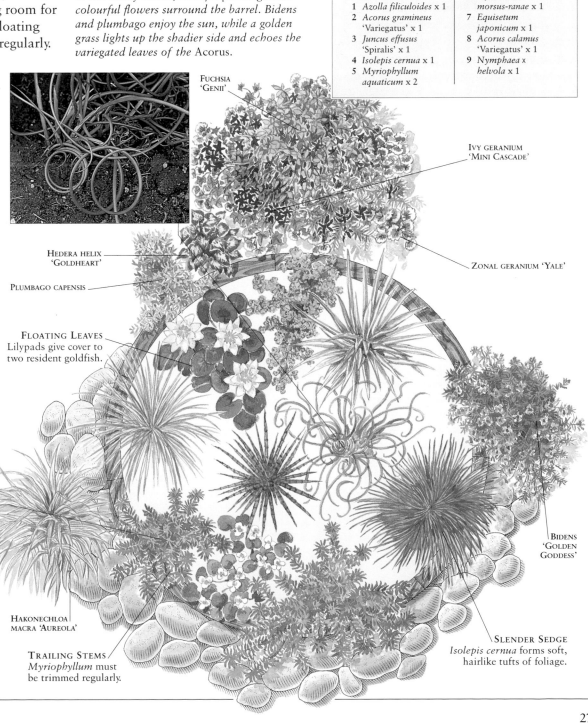

FUCHSIA 'GENII'

IVY GERANIUM 'MINI CASCADE'

HEDERA HELIX 'GOLDHEART'

PLUMBAGO CAPENSIS

ZONAL GERANIUM 'YALE'

FLOATING LEAVES
Lilypads give cover to two resident goldfish.

BIDENS 'GOLDEN GODDESS'

HAKONECHLOA MACRA 'AUREOLA'

TRAILING STEMS
Myriophyllum must be trimmed regularly.

SLENDER SEDGE
Isolepis cernua forms soft, hairlike tufts of foliage.

ORIENTAL-STYLE WATER GARDEN

T HE ORIENTAL-STYLE GARDEN is probably the most popular exotic landscaping style in the West. Moving and still water, rocks, and gravel surfaces have major roles to play in its representation of nature. There is great subtlety in the layout and planting; space, light, shadow, subtle harmonies and contrasts of color, and viewing angles are all given great consideration.

BALANCE AND HARMONY

In this garden, although all the elements seem artlessly placed, a perfect balance exists between the simplicity of the partly raised formal pool and the more naturalistic pond. It is an ambitious design involving rock terracing and heavy boulders that need foundations and plenty of padding beneath to protect the butyl liner. While the liner extends under rocks in the foreground to create an informal outline with planting pockets, the gravel terrace on which the bonsai sits needs a rigid edge for support; a solid retaining wall lies behind the liner on this side. The liner extends under the deck *(see pp. 130–131)*, so that it seems to overhang the water. The garden can be lit up at night.

THE GARDEN PLAN

The overall plan demonstrates the importance placed on views from the windows and deck around the house. Although the areas of clear water are small, they open up this enclosed garden by bringing reflections of the sky and surrounding trees into a very private domain.

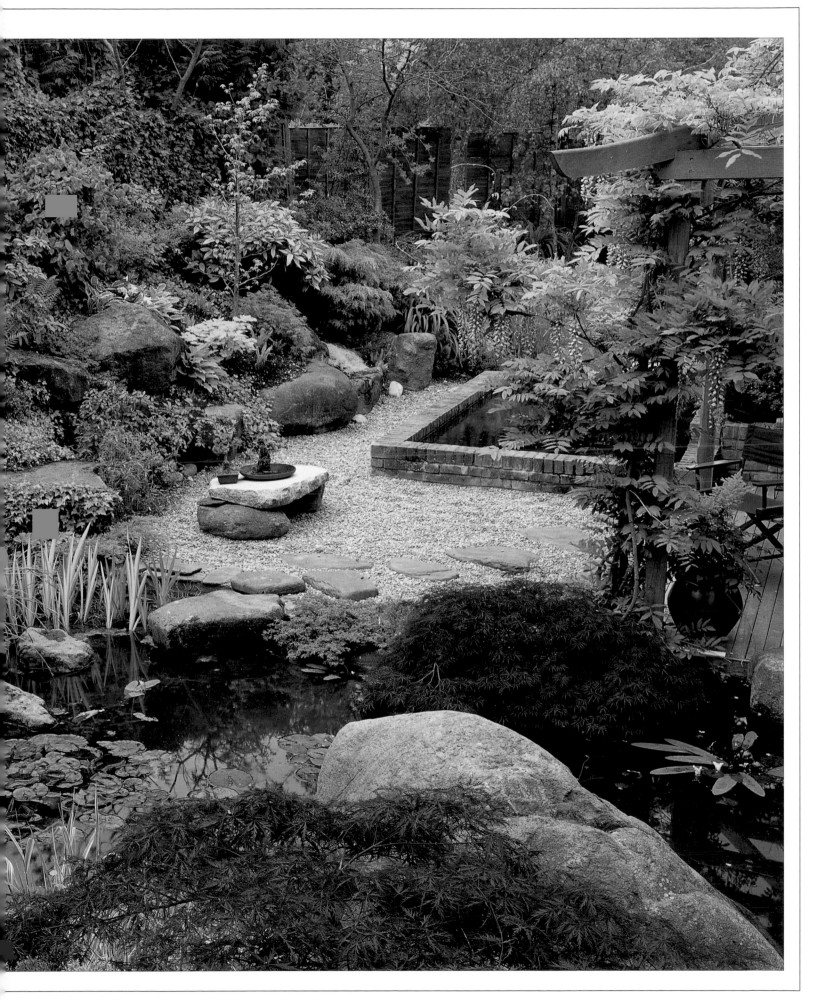

PLANTING PLAN FOR THE ORIENTAL POND

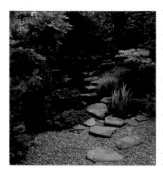

THE PLANTS FOR this garden are low key, with occasional bursts of bright color. Trees and plants are set out asymmetrically in order to imitate the wildness of nature. Planted terraces slope up to tall trees at the perimeter of the garden, providing both privacy and shelter. Soft greens and browns predominate, harmonizing with the colors and textures of the brick, gravel, and boulders, as well as the wooden fences, deck, and pergola. The permanency of the large rocks and the evergreens is given greater impact by the scattering of occasional flowers that help highlight the passing of the seasons. Rocks lead the eye across the pool to the plantings beyond. This line of stepping stones also extends across the gravel, which is kept free of plants because, in Japanese gardens, these carefully raked dry areas are a symbolic representation of water.

PLANTING FOR EFFECT
Mountain ash and silver birch trees look appropriate among the upper rocks, while the elegant foliage of the Japanese maples gives a classically Eastern feel. A dry island (see pp. 80–81) in the pond near the pergola pillar enables one of the maples to be planted so that it appears to float on the water surface.

Foliage color is critical in achieving the subtle variations essential to Oriental designs, where flower color is traditionally limited. The red and pinkish purple tones provided by azaleas, rhododendrons, and a Chinese wisteria are complemented by the maples. The oxygenating plants here are all completely submerged, leaving the water surface clear for the clean outlines of lilypads and the leaves of water hawthorn (Aponogeton distachyos).

ENCLOSING OPEN SPACE
The formal pool is clear of plants to give a still, reflective surface, complementing the flat, raked gravel. However, around the informal pond and leading up the rock terracing and on the fences, dense plantings enfold the open space.

Polystichum setiferum 'Divisilobum Densum'
Evergreen or semi-evergreen fern with soft, spreading, finely divided fronds that are white-scaled when young and unfurling, then mature to a matte mid-green. Remove faded fronds regularly. Propagate by division in spring. Zones 5–8. H 24in (60cm), S 18in (45cm).

Hosta undulata var. *albomarginata,* syn. *H.* 'Thomas Hogg'
Clump-forming, shade-tolerant perennial grown chiefly for its foliage. The leaves have irregular cream or white margins, sometimes extending to produce a streaked effect running toward the midrib. Slender-stalked, pale violet flowers are produced in summer. Prone to slug and snail damage. Propagate by division in early spring. Zones 3–8. H 30in (75cm), S 3ft (1m).

CLEAR CONTRAST
The brick-edged formal pool is unplanted, emphasizing its simplicity and clear lines.

PLANTING PLAN

APONOGETON DISTACHYOS
Water hawthorn is near the deck so that its scented flowers can be appreciated.

CREEPING PLANTS
Prostrate plants such as ivies (Hedera) soften rock edges and make the boulders seem more permanent.

SETTING THE STYLE
Japanese maples spreading over large boulders create a classic Oriental effect.

KEY TO PLANTING PLAN

WATER PLANTS
1 *Hottonia palustris* x 5
2 *Aponogeton distachyos* x 3
3 *Nymphaea* 'Escarboucle' x 5
4 *Iris laevigata* x 7
5 *Carex pendula* x 3
6 *Iris pseudacorus* 'Argentea Variegata' x 9

MOISTURE LOVERS
7 *Lysimachia nummularia* 'Aurea' x 15
8 *Juncus ensifolius* x 1

OTHER PLANTS
9 *Betula pendula* x 3
10 *Aucuba japonica* 'Variegata' x 1
11 *Juniperus* x *media* 'Pfitzeriana Aurea' x 1
12 *Soleirolia soleirolii* 'Aurea' x 5
13 *Liquidambar styraciflua* x 1
14 *Gleditsia triacanthos* 'Sunburst' x 1
15 *Rhododendron* 'Hinode-giri' (azalea) x 5
16 *Hedera helix* 'Buttercup' x 4

17 *Polystichum setiferum* 'Divisilobum Densum' x 7
18 *Sorbus aucuparia* x 2
19 *Hosta undulata* var. *albomarginata* x 11
20 *Hedera helix* 'Green Ripple' x 12
21 *Dryopteris filix-mas* x 9
22 *Cornus controversa* 'Variegata' x 1
23 *Rhododendron* 'Elizabeth' (azalea) x 1
24 *Rhododendron* 'Mother's Day' (azalea) x 1
25 *Juniperus* x *media* 'Plumosa Aurea' x 1
26 *Camellia* 'Adolphe Audusson' x 1
27 *Wisteria sinensis* x 2
28 *Acer palmatum* var. *dissectum* Atropurpureum Group x 1
29 *Juniperus* x *media* 'Pfitzeriana Glauca' x 1
30 *Hedera helix* 'Angularis Aurea' x 1
31 *Vitis coignetiae* x 1
32 *Rhododendron* 'Palestrina' (azalea) x 1

COURTYARD POOL

THIS SMALL GARDEN has been transformed by a pond that dominates the limited ground space, yet opens up the vertical dimension of the courtyard, adding another planting level to the surrounding beds and trellises. A pool such as this, where the edging doubles as a path, must have solid walls; since the pool is small, a concrete block shell waterproofed with flexible liner *(see pp. 78–79)* is the easiest construction method. The floor need not be concreted, but a central patch of crushed stone foundation enables strong concealed brick pilings to be built *(see pp. 120–121)* to support an archipelago of "floating" stepping stones. A unified color scheme and continuity in the materials used prevents a fussy look, always a danger in small spaces. The pavers are softened by marginal plants in the water. Careful maintenance, removing faded or untidy foliage, and thinning and dividing plants whenever they threaten to crowd the pool will preserve the clean lines of this cooling retreat.

PLANTING PLAN FOR THE COURTYARD

Courtyards are often warm and sheltered, which allows for growing a wide range of plants, but it is a good idea to keep the planting restrained in such a small space. Plan for areas of clear water and paving to open up the design. In this garden, vertical-leaved plants enhance the clean, straight lines of the paving and the still water surface, while the lilypads echo the stepping stones and the curved contours of the Ali Baba pot. The stepping stones also make the water plants accessible and easy to maintain.

PLANTS IN BASKETS
Marginal plants in baskets are placed on brick stacks to obtain the correct planting depth. The water lily is set on the bottom of the pool.

REPEATED PLANTS
Repeating clumps of a small selection of plants helps tie the design together.

Typha minima (dwarf cattail)
Deciduous perennial forming tufts of slender elegant foliage at the water's edge. Rust-brown flower spikes in late summer mature into decorative, rounded seed heads. It is happy in shallow water, but also grows well in wet soil. Propagate in spring by seed or by division. Zones 6–11. H 2ft (60cm), S 12in (30cm), water depth to 6in (15cm).

Myosotis scorpioides
(water forget-me-not)
Deciduous, marginal perennial wildflower with a creeping rhizome. Stems are first prostrate, then erect, forming sprawling mounds of narrow, mid-green leaves. Loose clusters of small, bright blue flowers with a central eye of pink, yellow, or white appear in early to mid-summer. Zones 4–10. H 6–9in (15–22cm), S 12in (30cm), water depth 0–6in (0–15cm).

POTENTIAL FOR VARIETY

While the strong design of the formal pool with its stepping stones is permanent, the plants in their baskets could be moved around or substituted to vary the effect and extend the season of interest. Changing the color of the trellis and the color-washed pot would also dramatically alter the mood.

KEY TO PLANTING PLAN

WATER PLANTS
1. *Iris sibirica* x 3
2. *Nymphaea* 'Gladstoneana' x 1
3. *Lobelia cardinalis* x 1
4. *Myosotis scorpioides* x 1
5. *Iris pseudacorus* x 1
6. *Schoenoplectus lacustris* subsp. *tabernaemontani* 'Albescens' x 1

7. *Iris pseudacorus* 'Variegata' x 1
8. *Typha minima* x 1
9. *Carex elata* 'Aurea' x 2

OTHER PLANTS
10. *Cryptomeria japonica* 'Spiralis' x 2
11. *Anthemis punctata* subsp. *cupaniana* x 1

12. *Sisyrinchium striatum* 'Aunt May' x 3
13. *Hosta fortunei* var. *aureomarginata* x 1
14. *Elaeagnus* x *ebbingei* x 1
15. *Hosta* 'Hadspen Blue' x 1
16. *Iris pallida* 'Variegata' x 1

PLANTING PLAN

INFORMAL POND WITH PEBBLE BEACH

THIS SMALL SUBURBAN GARDEN has been transformed into a green paradise by an informal pond surrounded by lush and varied plantings. While drifts of plants seem to spill down from the veranda to the poolside and merge around it, the tended lawn and clean lines of the well-scrubbed pebbles and decking prevent any sense of neglect.

A VIEW FOR ALL SEASONS

Planting opportunities have been maximized at the waterside by using a flexible liner to form not only a pool with a variety of planting levels, but also wide areas of damp ground for planting around it *(see p. 78)*. In summer, the graduated heights of aquatic plants and vigorously growing moisture-lovers combine to produce a verdant oasis. Lighting *(see pp. 124–125)* allows the feature to be enjoyed as the long evenings darken. However, on winter days, the view from the house windows skips over the poolside planting, now not at its best, to the more resilient trees and shrubs around the lawn and beyond.

THE GARDEN PLAN
Curving lines, distinct planting areas, and the matching weathered shades of decking, steps, bridge, and bench are crucial to making this garden seem much bigger than it really is. Steps on the right, with a gravel path leading to the utility area, give more practical access between house and garden.

PLANTING PLAN FOR THE INFORMAL POND

THIS WATER FEATURE derives its impact from the skillful placement of plants against the glassy, still water surface as well as the subtle colors and textures of the hard landscaping materials. Plants and pebbles leading gradually down into the pond, and the echoed roundness of the pebbles and lilypads, blur the distinction between land and water. Plants with striking foliage such as gunnera and hostas are interplanted with soft, feathery ferns, sword-like irises, and slender grasses. These form a predominantly rich green canvas persisting throughout the season on which vivid splashes of color appear: the yellows of irises, ligularias, and marsh marigolds, scarlet *Geum* 'Borisii' and the plumes of a crimson astilbe. In the water the color is continued with a sequence of white, red, and magenta-toned water lilies.

VIBRANT COLORS AND STRONG FORMS

This is a garden of textures, deriving its impact from the range of edging materials used and the clever choice of plants. To ensure that the plants complement rather than compete with one other, all but the very largest ones are in clumps of three or more, allowing the character of even the most delicate specimen to be clearly determined.

PEBBLE BEACH
The pebble beach *(see pp. 80–81)* gives wildlife access to the water's edge, to be viewed undisturbed from the veranda.

TERRACED BEDS
On the "dry" side of the steps, terracing brings the plants up to form a screen between the veranda and the neighboring garden.

PLANTING PLAN

KEY TO PLANTING PLAN

WATER PLANTS
1 *Hydrocharis morsus-ranae* x 3
2 *Callitriche hermaphroditica* x 3
3 *Nymphaea* 'Attraction' x 1
4 *Nymphaea* 'Firecrest' x 1
5 *Lagarosiphon major* x 7
6 *Nymphaea* 'Laydekeri Fulgens' x 1
7 *Nymphaea* 'Marliacea Albida' x 1
8 *Scrophularia auriculata* 'Variegata' x 3
9 *Iris laevigata* x 6
10 *Caltha palustris* x 3
11 *Iris pseudacorus* 'Variegata' x 5

MOISTURE LOVERS
12 *Glyceria maxima* var. *variegata* x 1
13 *Hosta ventricosa* 'Alba' x 3
14 *Hosta fortunei* var. *albopicta* x 3
15 *Geum* 'Borisii' x 3
16 *Astilbe* 'Fanal' x 4
17 *Lysimachia nummularia* x 10
18 *Rheum palmatum* x 1
19 *Filipendula ulmaria* 'Aurea' x 8
20 *Osmunda regalis* x 3
21 *Miscanthus sinensis* 'Gracillimus' x 6
22 *Carex pendula* x 3
23 *Miscanthus sinensis* 'Zebrinus' x 7
24 *Matteuccia struthiopteris* x 5
25 *Ligularia dentata* 'Desdemona' x 1

26 *Ligularia* 'The Rocket' x 2
27 *Gunnera tinctoria* x 1
28 *Onoclea sensibilis* x 3
29 *Hosta sieboldiana* var. *elegans* x 1
30 *Heuchera sanguinea* x 5

OTHER PLANTS
31 *Origanum vulgare* 'Aureum' x 7
32 *Juniperus* x *media* 'Pfitzeriana Aurea' x 1
33 *Fargesia murieliae* x 3
34 *Cedrus deodara* x 1
35 *Alchemilla mollis* x 3
36 *Dryopteris filix-mas* x 3
37 *Fatsia japonica* x 2
38 *Chelidonium majus* 'Flore Pleno' x 1

Matteuccia struthiopteris
(ostrich fern)
Deciduous rhizomatous fern that can be grown in normal soil or in moist ground. Dark brown, fertile innermost fronds stand erect in the center, surrounded by lance-shaped, sterile fronds, 3–4ft (1–1.2m) in length, that spread outward like feathers. Propagate by division in autumn or winter. Zones 2–8. H 3ft (1m), S 18in (45cm).

WOOD DECKING
Decking made from planks or preformed wooden slabs *(see p. 130)* is best set above the water surface rather than level with it to keep it from becoming wet and allow rain to drain away.

Nymphaea 'Attraction'
Hardy water lily with oval leaves that are light bronze when young, turning dark green in maturity. The cuplike, then star-shaped flowers have inner petals of a rich, deep garnet, and slightly lighter outer petals surrounding orange stamens. Zones 3–11. S 4–5ft (1.2–1.5m), water depth 15–36in (37–90cm).

Ligularia 'The Rocket'
Clump-forming herbaceous perennial with dark green leaves with deeply cut, jagged edges, supported on dark stems. Narrow spikes of small, lemon yellow flowers, also on dark stems, are produced in late summer. Prefers a site with deep, fertile soil, and a mulch around the base to help prevent moisture loss and wilting on bright, windy days. Propagate from seed or by division. Zones 4–8. H 4–6ft (1.2–1.8m), S 3ft (1m).

Caltha palustris (marsh marigold, kingcup)
Deciduous hardy perennial that grows freely along streams and ditches in the northern hemisphere. In spring it produces clusters of waxy, cup-shaped, bright golden-yellow flowers, 1in (2.5cm) across, held above smooth, deep green leaves. Propagate from seed or by division in spring or early autumn. H 24in (60cm), S 18in (45cm), water depth to 6in (15cm).

MILLSTONE FOUNTAIN

RESERVOIR FEATURES pump water from a sunken or concealed container up through a decorative outlet such as a millstone or pile of river rocks. The water then spills and drains back into the reservoir *(see pp. 112–115)*. Reservoir features are simple and effective for the smallest spaces, working well either as a tiny garden's main element or as an unexpected accent in a larger one. Here, in an area that is no larger than 6ft (2m) square, there is refreshment, sound, and movement. The unobtrusive informality is carefully crafted, using low-growing plants in the foreground that benefit from the misting effect of the fountain and the moisture-retentive "mulch" of rocks. While the dry millstone on the left is real, the one forming the fountain is of textured fiberglass. Such features are easy to maneuver and install, and place less strain on the reservoir structure beneath; they are sometimes available in kits, together with a suitable pump. The strength of the pump determines whether the water bubbles gently or spurts from its setting. Varying the depth of the water in the reservoir changes the volume and quality of the sound created.

A TRANQUIL CORNER
This carefully composed water feature does not require full sun; its charm lies in cool, restful greens and the contrast of the plants with the shapes and textures of the rocks, millstones, and seat. The transition of color from dry to wet rocks highlights even further the beauty of natural materials, particularly when wet.

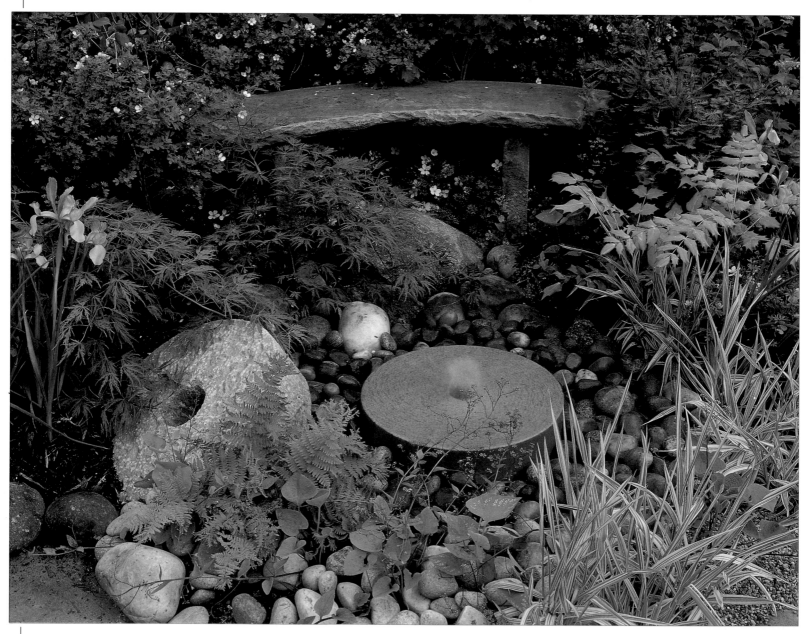

COMPOSITION IN GREEN

Unity has been achieved in this small and subtle planting plan by using similarly toned greens in a variety of shades. Darker color in the background graduates to brighter foliage in the foreground, creating an inviting rather than oppressive atmosphere in this shady corner. Variety has been introduced by using plants with differently textured foliage. There are no bright or showy flowers; instead, a simple and sparingly used palette of white, pale yellow, and mauve ensures that attention is not distracted from the delicate leaf shapes and the way in which they associate with the rocks and stone features.

✳ ◊ ◊

Dryopteris filix-mas (male fern)
Deciduous or semi-evergreen fern, usually well shaped with upright, then elegantly arching mid-green fronds. Grows equally well either in moist or in well-drained moisture-retentive soil, but prefers a shady site. Remove fronds as they fade. Propagate by division in autumn or late winter. Zones 4–8. H 4ft (1.2m), S 3ft (1m).

ORIENTAL TOUCH
Thriving in the shelter of the corner, a Japanese maple falls over the dry millstone.

LONICERA PERICLYMENUM
The scent of honeysuckle can be enjoyed from the seat.

DAMP AREA
Moisture from the fountain increases the humidity to help ferns grow in the damp rocks.

TEXTURED FOLIAGE
The distinctive pinnate leaves of *Mahonia japonica* are shown off to their full potential in such a simple composition.

LINKING PLANTS
Planting and pathway are beautifully brought together by the *Phalaris* in the foreground. A plant that needs keeping in boundaries, it is controlled here between the reservoir beneath the rocks and the path.

▨ ◊ ◊

Brunnera macrophylla
(Siberian bugloss)
Clump-forming, spring-flowering perennial that makes a good groundcover in a sheltered site when planted in groups . The delicate, star-shaped, bright blue flowers, on tall nodding stalks, are followed by heart-shaped, mid-green leaves. Propagate by seed in autumn or by division in spring or autumn. Zones 3–8. H 18in (45cm), S 2ft (60cm).

KEY TO PLANTING PLAN

MOISTURE LOVERS
1 *Dryopteris filix-mas* x 1
2 *Brunnera macrophylla* x 3
3 *Phalaris arundinacea* var. *picta* x 4

OTHER PLANTS
4 *Mahonia japonica* x 1
5 *Iris* 'Wedgwood' x 4
6 *Lonicera periclymenum* 'Belgica' x 1
7 *Heuchera* 'Painted Lady' x 3
8 *Viburnum opulus* x 1
9 *Potentilla fruticosa* 'Abbotswood' x 1
10 *Potentilla fruticosa* 'Elizabeth' x 1
11 *Acer palmatum* var. *dissectum* 'Ornatum' x 2

PLANTING PLAN

WILDLIFE POND WITH BOG GARDEN

N OT LONG AGO this coastal garden with dry, sandy soil was a completely open, windswept site. It now accommodates a sheltered, well-planted, informal pond surrounded by dense, vigorously growing, moisture-loving plants, making it a magnet for wild creatures from a wide surrounding area.

ENCOURAGING PLANT GROWTH

The plants around this pond are only in their second growing season, but the feature was so well planned to give plants good growing conditions that now little space remains for new specimens. The main pool area has a soil layer placed on top of the flexible liner, supplemented by nutritious waste from several fish. Wide, shallow edges – more than half the pond is less than 12in (30cm) deep – allow aquatic, particularly marginal plants to spread. Around the edges, the flexible liner has been extended under the soil to form a broad band of moist ground; behind the pond, more wet pockets of soil have been created by lining holes with polyethylene. Both these and the shallow, clay-lined depression that forms a boggy pool beyond the main pond must be independently watered. A pebble beach, randomly placed boulders, and a small island ideally suit the needs and habits of birds, amphibians, and water-loving insects. Together with the fish and plants, this sets up a rich food chain that keeps the water and its inhabitants in perfect ecological balance.

THE GARDEN PLAN
Most of this garden is open in plan to blend with the surrounding gently undulating farmland. On each side, and particularly around the pond (situated away from the house and main pathways to encourage shy creatures), a belt of trees and shrubs provides shelter from the damaging and, equally importantly, drying effects of sea winds.

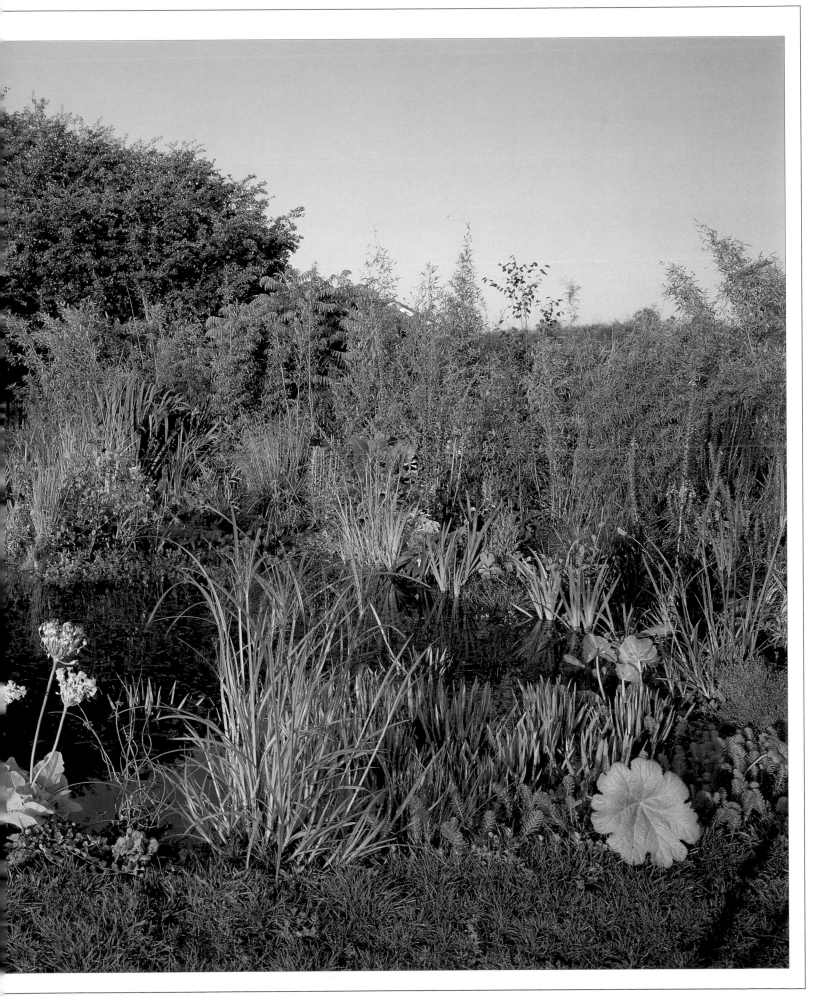

PLANTING PLAN FOR THE WILDLIFE POND

IN ORDER FOR A WILDLIFE pond to be accessible to the maximum diversity of creatures, it is of primary importance to provide ample cover nearby. This will enable birds and animals to approach the water in safety. Here, the side of the pond seen across the lawn is relatively open, so that the feature can be viewed and appreciated, and cover is provided on the far side. Taller, closely spaced plants to the rear of the pond lead right up into the clumps of bamboos (*Fargesia*) and trees such as English hawthorn (*Crataegus laevigata*) that may be used as nesting sites. For other creatures, shelter underwater is important: the underwater stems of submerged plants and a host of marginal plants in the shallows provide cover for fish and amphibians. Leaves of fringed water lily (*Nymphoides*) shade them from the sun – doubly important when water is shallow and heats up quickly.

INFORMAL, MIXED PLANTING

In any water feature designed to attract wildlife, the style should be informal and not too tidy: rigorously removing plant and animal debris deprives creatures of food and shelter. Allow plants to spread and mingle within reason – some lifting and dividing is essential to maintain their health. (Lythrum, because of its highly invasive nature, should not be planted near native wetlands or other ecologically sensitive areas.)

Here, while the planting is mixed, there are enough species to satisfy the dietary needs of a wide range of creatures. Common shrubs such as dogwoods (*Cornus*) and alder (*Alnus incana*) are pruned hard each year to keep them bushy. Perennials such as giant cowslips (*Primula florindae*) and water mint (*Mentha aquatica*) look appropriate and are often more attractive to insects than cultivated varieties. Adding wildflowers native to moist soil, like swamp milkweed (*Asclepias incarnata*) and swamp sunflower (*Helianthus angustfolius*) will attract a variety of creatures.

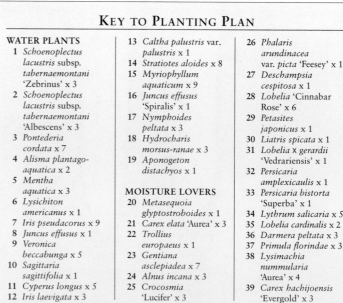

NATURAL STONE
Rounded sandstone boulders here blend in perfectly with the natural color and texture of the garden's soil.

READY FOR OCCUPATION

This large water feature is a virtual metropolis for insects, birds, visiting animals, and aquatic creatures, with every facility for sheltering, feeding, and bathing provided. Randomly placed boulders accentuate the mound between the main pond and an independent, boggy pool that enables yet more marginal and moisture-loving plants to be grown. The island, an ideal refuge for wildlife, further increases the planting opportunities by extending the area of shallow-water space available.

PLANTING PLAN

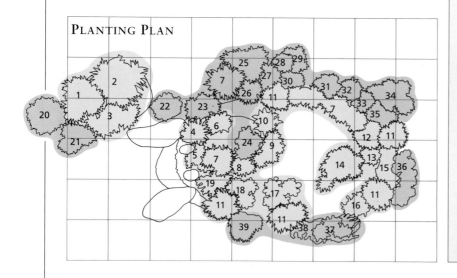

KEY TO PLANTING PLAN

WATER PLANTS
1 *Schoenoplectus lacustris* subsp. *tabernaemontani* 'Zebrinus' x 3
2 *Schoenoplectus lacustris* subsp. *tabernaemontani* 'Albescens' x 3
3 *Pontederia cordata* x 7
4 *Alisma plantago-aquatica* x 2
5 *Mentha aquatica* x 3
6 *Lysichiton americanus* x 1
7 *Iris pseudacorus* x 9
8 *Juncus effusus* x 1
9 *Veronica beccabunga* x 5
10 *Sagittaria sagittifolia* x 1
11 *Cyperus longus* x 5
12 *Iris laevigata* x 3

13 *Caltha palustris* var. *palustris* x 1
14 *Stratiotes aloides* x 8
15 *Myriophyllum aquaticum* x 9
16 *Juncus effusus* 'Spiralis' x 1
17 *Nymphoides peltata* x 3
18 *Hydrocharis morsus-ranae* x 3
19 *Aponogeton distachyos* x 1

MOISTURE LOVERS
20 *Metasequoia glyptostroboides* x 1
21 *Carex elata* 'Aurea' x 3
22 *Trollius europaeus* x 1
23 *Gentiana asclepiadea* x 7
24 *Alnus incana* x 3
25 *Crocosmia* 'Lucifer' x 3

26 *Phalaris arundinacea* var. *picta* 'Feesey' x 1
27 *Deschampsia cespitosa* x 1
28 *Lobelia* 'Cinnabar Rose' x 6
29 *Petasites japonicus* x 1
30 *Liatris spicata* x 1
31 *Lobelia* x *gerardii* 'Vedrariensis' x 1
32 *Persicaria amplexicaulis* x 1
33 *Persicaria bistorta* 'Superba' x 1
34 *Lythrum salicaria* x 5
35 *Lobelia cardinalis* x 2
36 *Darmera peltata* x 3
37 *Primula florindae* x 3
38 *Lysimachia nummularia* 'Aurea' x 4
39 *Carex hachijoensis* 'Evergold' x 3

LINKING PLANTS
Iris pseudacorus, which will grow in the shallows and in moist soil, links the aquatic and poolside planting.

INDEPENDENT BOGS
Separately watered planting pockets extend the moist area without depleting the pool's water in dry periods.

LIGHT COVER
Repeated clumps of graceful *Cyperus longus* give height and some shelter without obscuring the view.

Mentha aquatica
(water mint)
Low-growing, spreading perennial with fresh green leaves, fragrant when crushed. The creeping roots are useful for binding wet soil. In summer, it bears small, delicate clusters of flowers in a faded rose pink. Like all mints, it spreads rapidly and should be thinned if it encroachs on other plants. Can be prone to rust. Propagate by division in spring or autumn. Zones 5–9. H 8in (15cm), S 3ft (90cm), water depth 0–6in (0–15cm).

Iris pseudacorus (yellow flag)
Robust, vigorous perennial with sturdy, rhizomatous roots that can be grown in moist soil or shallow water. The broad, ridged leaves are green; those of the cultivar 'Variegata' are striped with yellow. Each tall, branched stem bears up to 10 beardless flowers with large, golden petals that often have a darker patch in the center of the falls. Propagate by dividing rhizomes in late summer to autumn or spring. Zones 4–9. H to 6ft (2m), S indefinite, water depth 0–12in (0–30cm).

STREAM FOR CITY OR COUNTRY GARDEN

WITH A LITTLE INGENUITY, even the smallest plot can accommodate a stream surrounded by lush planting. This small backyard garden is given enormous impact by being entirely devoted to one well-designed water feature, rather than trying to incorporate a number of necessarily scaled-down elements.

STREAMSIDE EDGING AND PLANTING

Water bubbles up slowly among rocks on the left, flowing into a deeper area on the right, where a small submersible pump sends it back to the start again; the stream flows along, rather than down the watercourse. The garden actually slopes upward toward the back and away from the house. The well-mortared bank of irregularly shaped rocks in the foreground acts as a retaining wall for the stream, while on the far side, boulders and the roots of many plants consolidate a bank of rich, moist soil. Since the feature is generally viewed from one side, like a stage set, the slope has been accentuated by planting low alpines in front, medium-height perennials in the middle area (on the far side of the stream), and to the rear, tall conifers and shrubs that also screen neighboring houses. The stream is lined with butyl and edged with a local red sandstone. Local stone, or reconstituted stone crafted to match it, usually complements the colors of local soil and bricks.

THE GARDEN PLAN

This slow-moving stream can be observed at leisure from a paved patio or, on less pleasant days, from the sun room built onto the back of the house; the slight upward slope brings the stream, plants, and visiting wildlife directly into view from the comfort of window seats. A stone bridge gives access to the far side and also provides a different viewpoint.

PLANTING PLAN FOR THE STREAM

SINCE THIS FEATURE is mainly viewed from only one side, the planting plan has been conceived to create three distinct areas, layered to provide an amphitheater of interest. The foreground plantings are low. With the exception of a planting pocket built to suit moisture-loving *Juncus ensifolius* (an extremely useful and attractive small, spreading rush), the soil is dry between the rocks and makes an excellent home for scrambling and creeping plants such as artemisia and barren strawberry *(Waldsteinia)*. On the near bank of the stream itself, small plants have been chosen that will not obscure the view of the water lilies. Although water lilies dislike fast-moving water, they thrive in this very gentle current. On the far side of the stream, the planting becomes denser and more diverse, with a variety of marginal and moisture-loving perennials dominated by the large leaves of the umbrella plant *(Darmera peltata)*. This moisture-lover forms long surface rhizomes that consolidate the soil, ideal for streamside plantings.

A BACKGROUND OF EVERGREENS

At the back of the garden, conifers, bamboos, and evergreen shrubs form an informal screen and provide natural protection for the lush growth of the marginal and moisture-loving plants. They are a permanent backcloth for the changing display of the perennial plants, although some also change with the seasons: *Pinus sylvestris* 'Aurea' will begin to assume yellow tints in time to echo the bold clumps of Bowles' golden sedge *(Carex elata* 'Aurea')*, which lasts well into the autumn. Yellow is an excellent color for bringing light into small enclosed gardens, and here there are splashes of yellow flowers or foliage to be seen all year. The darker greens of other shrubs and trees provide the perfect foil for the autumn's most striking display: the maroon tints taken on by the leaves of the umbrella plants *(Darmera)*.

INFORMAL BOUNDARIES
Plants have a softening effect that is well used here. The plantings give the illusion of continuity to this mock stream, breaking up the hard edges of stonework and, at the back, forming a natural boundary.

PLANTING PLAN

KEY TO PLANTING PLAN

WATER PLANTS
1 *Mentha aquatica* x 4
2 *Sagittaria sagittifolia* x 2
3 *Nymphaea* 'Escarboucle' x 2
4 *Menyanthes trifoliata* x 2
5 *Iris pseudacorus* 'Variegata' x 3
6 *Nymphaea* 'Gladstoneana' x 1
7 *Acorus calamus* 'Variegatus' x 1

MOISTURE LOVERS
8 *Polystichum setiferum* 'Divisilobum Densum' x 2

9 *Osmunda regalis* x 2
10 *Carex elata* 'Aurea' x 2
11 *Primula florindae* x 2
12 *Darmera peltata* x 5
13 *Mimulus luteus* x 3
14 *Phragmites australis* 'Variegatus' x 1
15 *Iris ensata* x 5
16 *Juncus ensifolius* x 6

OTHER PLANTS
17 *Metasequoia glyptostroboides* x 1
18 *Fargesia murieliae* x 3
19 *Griselinia littoralis* x 1

20 *Pinus sylvestris* 'Aurea' x 1
21 *Erica x veitchii* x 3
22 *Abies koreana* x 1
23 *Alchemilla mollis* x 2
24 *Erodium x variabile* 'Ken Aslet' x 1
25 *Waldsteinia ternata* x 2
26 *Artemisia frigida* x 1
27 *Persicaria affinis* x 2
28 *Hedera helix* 'Heise' x 2
29 *Thymus serpyllum* x 2

❄ ✿

Sagittaria sagittifolia
(common arrowhead)
Perennial marginal plant whose
leaves are strap-shaped at first,
then arrowhead-shaped. In
summer white, three-petaled
flowers are borne on spikes. It
flowers less readily in water
deeper than 6in (15cm). Propagate
by division in spring or summer,
or break off new plantlets in
spring. Zones 5–11. H 18in
(45cm), S 12in (30cm), water
depth to 9in (22cm).

❄ ◊

Darmera peltata
(umbrella plant)
Spreading, moisture-loving,
herbaceous perennial with creeping,
rhizomatous roots. In spring, while
the leaves are still small, white or
pale pink flowerheads appear. The
leaves then grow large and rounded,
on long stalks, resembling inverted
parasols. They turn copper and
maroon in autumn. Propagate by
division in spring or by seed in
spring or autumn. Zones 5–7.
H 4ft (1.2m), S 3ft (1m).

CREATING WATER FEATURES

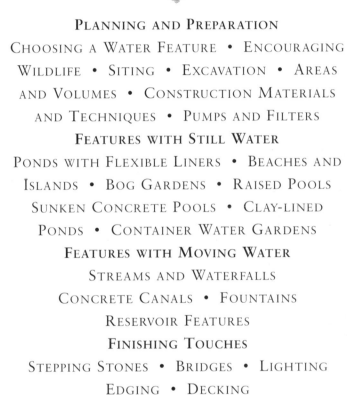

PLANNING AND PREPARATION
CHOOSING A WATER FEATURE • ENCOURAGING
WILDLIFE • SITING • EXCAVATION • AREAS
AND VOLUMES • CONSTRUCTION MATERIALS
AND TECHNIQUES • PUMPS AND FILTERS
FEATURES WITH STILL WATER
PONDS WITH FLEXIBLE LINERS • BEACHES AND
ISLANDS • BOG GARDENS • RAISED POOLS
SUNKEN CONCRETE POOLS • CLAY-LINED
PONDS • CONTAINER WATER GARDENS
FEATURES WITH MOVING WATER
STREAMS AND WATERFALLS
CONCRETE CANALS • FOUNTAINS
RESERVOIR FEATURES
FINISHING TOUCHES
STEPPING STONES • BRIDGES • LIGHTING
EDGING • DECKING

INFORMAL STREAM *(LEFT)*
*The irregular arrangement of sandstone rocks and the careful
but informal placing of plants gives a natural appearance to an
artificially constructed watercourse.*

PLANNING AND PREPARATION

CAREFUL PLANNING is the key to successful design and construction. Before making any decisions it can be useful to make sketches in order to clarify your ideas. Visit local garden centers specializing in water gardening: given information about your site and requirements, they may be able to offer advice on construction methods and materials that will save time and money.

SITING AND DESIGN

The first major decision to be made is where to site your water feature. There are many factors to be taken into account *(see pp. 56–57)*, and drawing up a simple scale plan of your garden can be an invaluable exercise. You may discover that your preferred location is impractical, so be open to the possibility of alternative sites. Consider views both outside and from within the house, especially from favorite garden seats and armchairs.

CHOICE OF MATERIALS
Concrete is one of the most versatile and economical of materials: in the right setting, even a concrete-lined stream can be attractive. Remember that setting times for foundations, floors, and walls must be incorporated when planning out construction schedules.

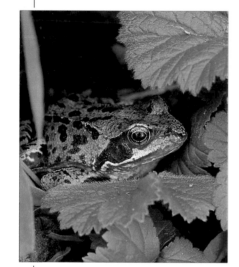

ENCOURAGING WILDLIFE
Wildlife enthusiasts need to take into consideration the needs and preferences of birds, insects, and amphibians from the earliest planning stages (see pp. 54–55) in order to provide an attractive and suitable environment.

SURPRISING SITES
In small spaces, bold designs can be surprisingly effective. In this narrow, enclosed courtyard, the sophisticated raised pool has been styled to complement its urban surroundings.

SAFETY PRECAUTIONS
Bridges (see pp. 122–123) add an extra dimension to a water garden, allowing access across water and providing visual interest. Their safety must be considered: hand-rails need to be sturdy but not obtrusive and can be softened by plantings.

A BOG GARDEN
A bog garden can adjoin a pond or, for plant enthusiasts who do not want to spend too much time on a pond's upkeep, can be a feature in its own right. They are cheap and easy to construct, and are an ideal way of growing moisture-loving plants where water conservation is of prime importance.

The design of the feature will depend very much on personal preference, but it should always be influenced by the site and its surroundings. You may not have the flexibility of incorporating water into a new garden plan, but with careful forethought, your feature will look naturally placed and as if it has always been an integral part of the overall garden design.

CONSTRUCTION AND MATERIALS

There are several methods of construction *(see pp. 64–69)* using a range of materials, each with advantages and disadvantages, so it is worth spending a little time thumbing through suppliers' catalogs. Compare the costs of liners and building materials, and work out how long construction will take. Also assess whether you are physically capable or skilled enough to carry out the work yourself and if not, whether you are prepared to pay someone to do the job for you. Remember to take into account the practicalities of transporting and working with materials. Concrete blocks and slabs, for example, are heavy, and large pieces of flexible liner are difficult to maneuver. If you decide to hire help or rent equipment, think about whether there

are other jobs in the garden that could also be accomplished with an extra pair of hands or piece of equipment available.

Of course skilled labor is expensive, and careful planning can save time and prevent costly errors. If taking on a challenging project yourself, it is worth having the name of a good builder available just in case you encounter unforeseen difficulties; struggling to complete the project yourself without the necessary skills may result in a feature that is never what you hoped it would be.

BRINGING ELECTRICITY TO WATER

The one area in which there is no substitute for professional expertise is the bringing of electricity to a pool, whether it be to power a pump *(see pp. 70–73)* or lighting. Even the installation of relatively risk-free, extra low-voltage equipment can be made easier and safer with advice on weatherproofing connections and how to route buried cable. Only use equipment especially designed for garden and pool use and always carefully follow the manufacturer's instructions. When in doubt, call in a professional electrician to set up the system for you.

CHOOSING A WATER FEATURE

BEFORE MAKING A CHOICE, it is essential to consider which type of water feature will accommodate your needs and situation. The enormous variety of shapes, styles, and materials now available makes this easier, but remember to take into account both the practicalities involved and where your priorities lie. First, see how much space could be made available, then consider the amount of time and effort you are able to spare, both in building and maintenance. Choose a style that will blend in with the existing surroundings. Remember, too, that some construction methods and materials are more costly than others – this may rule out certain features.

THE RIGHT POND FOR YOU

There are two basic styles of pond – formal and informal – and your choice will be influenced by the existing site. In formal design, where symmetry and geometric shapes are often strong elements, both the pond and its surroundings should be regular. A formal pond, for example, may look out of place in the middle of a lawn with sweeping curves of mixed perennials. Similarly, the popular kidney shape can look unsuitable in surroundings dominated by straight edges and formal plantings. For a natural look, bog gardens *(see pp. 82–83)* or wildlife ponds *(see pp. 54–55)* are popular options.

SIZE AND SHAPE OF FEATURE

There is a recommended minimum size for still ponds: the surface area should ideally be no smaller than 50sq ft (4.5sq m), with a minimum depth of 1½ft (0.5m) – deeper is better. This should reduce problems caused by green water, excessive temperature fluctuation, and inadequate water oxygenation. The larger the surface area, the deeper at least one area of the pond should be. If you only have a small space, consider alternative water features such as container gardens or wall fountains.

Square, circular, and rectangular ponds may be constructed with a concrete shell or preformed rigid liner; the latter also come in a range of small irregular shapes. Use a flexible liner for larger irregular shapes, but keep the shape as simple as possible to make installation easier *(see pp. 66–67)*.

FORMAL POND
This clearly defined, symmetrical pond would look out of place in an informal setting. Ambitious features such as this demand considerable resources both for construction and maintenance: the meticulously tended topiary here, for example, is a key element in the design.

STILL OR MOVING WATER

Still water is valued for its tranquility and reflective qualities; the light it brings into an enclosed garden can transform its atmosphere. Still pools are ideal for viewing water lilies and ornamental fish. When styled more informally, they can be a haven for wildlife *(see overleaf)*. To bring the sparkle of moving

ACCESS TO THE WATER
These informal steps are attractive, but not everybody would find them easy to negotiate. Always try to incorporate one easy point of access to the water's edge.

RAISED POND
Raised ponds have definite safety advantages over sunken features, but the walls must be solidly constructed to withstand the pressure exerted by the water. A well-built, wide wall doubles up as a seating area, making it more comfortable and convenient to tend plants.

CHOOSING WATER FEATURES

Any number of factors can influence the choice of water feature. Those categorized below can all be constructed following the step-by-step sequences that appear later in this part of the book.

	Formal	Informal	Suitable for small garden	Sunken	Raised	Rectangular	Square	Circular	Irregular	Still water	Moving water	Inexpensive	Easy to install	Needs building skills	Easy to maintain	Affected by seasonal change	Affected by soil condition	No areas of open water	Can be adapted for children	Suitable for wildlife	Suitable for creative planting	Suitable for fish
Simple pond with flexible liner *(pp. 76–79)*	•	•	•	•		•	•	•	•	•		•	•		•				•	•	•	•
Flexible liner pond with beach/island *(pp. 80–81)*		•	•	•					•	•		•	•		•	•				•	•	•
Flexible liner pond & stream *(pp. 98–103)*		•	•	•					•		•	•	•		•					•	•	•
Raised pool with flexible liner *(pp. 86–87)*	•		•		•	•	•	•		•			•	•	•				•		•	•
Bog garden *(pp. 82–83)*		•	•	•					•		•	•	•				•	•			•	
Rigid pond unit *(pp. 84–85)*	•		•					•						•					•		•	•
Rigid pond & stream units *(pp. 104–105)*		•	•						•		•			•					•		•	•
Raised pool using rigid unit *(pp. 88–89)*	•	•	•		•	•	•	•		•			•	•	•					•		•
Concrete-lined pool *(pp. 90–91)*	•		•				•			•				•					•		•	•
Concrete canal *(pp. 98–99)*	•		•	•	•	•	•	•		•					•				•		•	
Clay-lined pond *(pp. 92–93)*			•		•				•	•					•				•		•	
Container water garden *(pp. 94–95)*	•	•	•		•					•		•	•		•	•			•		•	
River rock fountain *(pp. 112–113)*	•	•	•	•					•	•		•	•	•		•	•	•	•		•	
Wall fountain *(pp. 116–117)*	•	•	•		•						•			•		•		•	•			

---

water into a garden without a natural spring or stream, it will be necessary to install a pump, and to bring electricity out into the garden *(see p. 72)*. However, the equipment now available makes pump installation relatively easy and, because splashing water contains more oxygen, features with moving water can be much smaller than still ponds yet maintain healthy water chemistry.

DIFFERENT CONSTRUCTION SKILLS

PLASTIC ART
Flexible liners allow you to create customized, irregular shapes, with the option to modify or extend designs in the future.

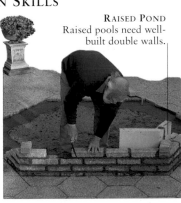

RAISED POND
Raised pools need well-built double walls.

DIY SKILLS
It is wisest not to attempt projects that involve bricklaying and symmetrical shapes and angles without some experience.

CONSTRUCTION METHODS

Building a water feature will be a satifying and enjoyable task if you choose construction techniques *(see pp. 64–69)* that are comfortably within your capabilities. Flexible liners and pre-formed units are easy to install and maintain, but preformed units do limit you to the designs offered by the manufacturer. Pouring concrete and laying bricks is not easy and requires some building experience to achieve an adequate result.

PERSONAL CONSIDERATIONS

The pond style will reflect the interests of the owner: the serious fishkeeper may well invest in a sophisticated filtration system *(see pp. 70–73)* in order to be sure that the water remains clear, whereas a pristine environment will not suit the purposes of the wildlife enthusiast. The design-oriented may see the feature as an opportunity to experiment with beautiful and unusual hard materials both in and around the water; the plant enthusiast may see the water in a secondary role, as a canvas for widening the range of plants that can be grown in the garden. Following the guidelines relating to shape, size, and siting *(see pp. 56–57)* will guarantee that the environment you create remains healthy and attractive, but it is the basic choice of feature and the way in which it is built and styled that ensures that individual preferences and creative expression are fully realized.

ENCOURAGING WILDLIFE

WATER WILL ALWAYS ATTRACT wildlife, whether birds, insects, amphibians, or mammals. The variety of wildlife will depend somewhat on the site and size of the water feature, but if you create a suitable environment, wildlife will be drawn to even the smallest pond. Careful planting is fundamental; plants should be chosen that not only sustain the water's ecosystem (see pp. 136–137) but also provide cover and food. Native plants and

flowers are usually more attractive to indigenous wildlife; natural streams and ponds in nearby countryside may suggest planting ideas (do not, however, take plants from the wild). In a successful wildlife pond, all plants and animals play their parts in complex food chains; never use choice plants around a wildlife pond, and do not stock it with costly decorative fish.

CONSTRUCTING A WILDLIFE POND

Natural or clay-lined ponds are ideal, but on a smaller scale, a well-planted pond with flexible liner can be a perfectly acceptable substitute. Make sure that the pond has plenty of variation in depth so that there are several different habitats that may support a wide range of plants and animals. The deep areas of the pond should be at least 18in (45cm), and preferably 36in (90cm), in depth. The sides of the pond should be gently sloping; both sunny areas and cool shade around the edges of the pond are important.

DIGITALIS PURPUREA
The flower spires of foxgloves (Digitalis) are magnets for bumblebees.

IRIS PSEUDACORUS

SAGITTARIA LATIFOLIA

SMALL MARGINALS
Grade plants by size, from trees to small marginals, right down to the water's edge to provide continuous cover. Plants with mat-forming roots, such as water forget-me-not (Myosotis scorpioides), spread well along the water's edge.

FLOATING LEAVES
Deep-water aquatics provide vital shade, and large, flat leaves also make landing pads for insects. Nymphoides peltata (here) and Nuphar are less formal-looking alternatives to water lilies for naturalistic settings.

PERCHING PLATFORMS
Flat stones provide perching spots; birds also clean their beaks on the surface of such stones.

SCHOENOPLECTUS LACUSTRIS

NOOKS AND CRANNIES
Hollows among rocks will allow amphibians to shelter during the summer heat and hibernate in winter.

GRASSES AND SEDGES
Evergreen and semi-evergreen grasses and sedges such as Carex and Schoenoplectus provide cover at the edge of the water for most of the year.

FOOD FOR WATER FOWL
Duckweed (Lemna trisulca) and duck potato (Sagittaria latifolia) are so called because they are favorite food plants of ducks.

WATER QUALITY
Submerged plants keep the oxygen level sufficiently high to support insect larvae, such as those of the dragonfly, that live on the bottom of the pond.

PEBBLE BEACH
A gentle slope ensures that amphibians, small mammals, and birds can approach the water safely.

LAGAROSIPHON MAJOR
Submerged plants play a practical role, releasing oxygen directly into the water and sheltering fish fry and other tiny creatures.

SALIX CAPREA
Willows are useful for moths and butterflies; several types of caterpillar feed on them.

INSECT-EATERS
Creatures that hunt on the wing, such as purple martins, swallows, and bats, are attracted wherever there are abundant flying insects.

RANUNCULUS LINGUA
Yellow flowers attract many winged insects.

TREES AND SHRUBS
The abundant flowers of hawthorn *(Crataegus)* and elderberries *(Sambucus)* attract insects, while the fruits that follow provide food for birds.

ACER CAMPESTRE
Plenty of cover with waterside plants, shrubs, and trees reassures animals that they may approach in safety. Taller trees provide safe havens where birds may nest.

BUTTERFLY BUSH
No wildlife garden or pond should be without buddleias, beloved of bees and butterflies.

BUTOMUS UMBELLATUS
The flowers of this rush attract pollinating insects, while the roots are a food source for small mammals.

CLUMPS OF COVER
Shyer birds such as warblers and some sparrows appreciate clumps of reeds, rushes, and aquatic irises.

NATIVE FLOWERS
Choose wildflower species rather than highly bred cultivars: cardinal flower *(Lobelia)*, meadowsweet *(Filipendula)*, and Joe Pye weed *(Eupatorium)* are more appealing to indigenous creatures.

PREDATORS
Be prepared for the arrival of predators; herons can wipe out fish and amphibian populations. Domestic cats may also develop a taste for hunting.

FILIPENDULA ULMARIA

SEED PRODUCERS
Plants that freely produce seed are valuable food sources for fauna.

ALISMA PLANTAGO-AQUATICA

BASKING PLACES
Rocks placed in sun and shelter near the water provide resting and sunning areas for small amphibians.

FURTHER INFORMATION

- Wildlife Pond with Bog Garden – pp. 40–43
- Simple Ponds with Flexible Liners – pp. 76–79
- Clay-lined Ponds – pp. 92–93
- Beaches and Islands – pp. 80–81

SITING WATER FEATURES

Siting considerations should be fully explored when making any design and construction decisions. The majority of water plants need plenty of light, but siting is much more than finding the sunniest spot. Locate a feature where it instinctively feels right and where it can be enjoyed to the utmost. There are also many practical factors that must be taken into consideration. If you already have a site in mind with luck it will indeed prove to be the ideal location once you have taken all factors into account. If you have yet to decide, using a process of elimination to remove all unsuitable sites from the available area can be helpful.

PRACTICAL CONSIDERATIONS

AREA AVAILABLE FOR SITING

First of all, you must establish the positions of any drains, pipes, and underground cables crossing the garden. Avoid excavating over or near any of these obstacles. The lay of the land, the position of the water table, and the soil composition (see Drainage and Excavation, pp. 58–59) will give you an idea of how much excavation work construction of the site will entail. Sloping sites, which can be exploited so well by streams and waterfalls, have their own design and building considerations. However, while the lowest point of a sloping garden makes a natural site for a pond, emptying the pond without a pump will be difficult. Low points can also be frost pockets, but more importantly, a rising water table may lift portions of a flexible liner to the pond surface or force a rigid liner out of the ground.

REFLECTIVE POTENTIAL

Place mirrors on the ground to see how much light the pond will reflect and to avoid "doubling" any eyesores. Even a small expanse of water that reflects sky and plants can transform a garden.

CHECKING REFLECTIONS IN A MIRROR

SHADED AREAS AT DIFFERENT TIMES OF THE DAY
Identifying areas of full sunlight, partial shade, and dense shade during the day and early evening is important. A pond in full shade will be visually dull, without character or reflective movement. It will also produce the kind of poor environmental balance that encourages algal growth because it will lack adequate sunlight to penetrate the water and promote plant photosynthesis. Partial shade can be acceptable: there are plants that tolerate these conditions, and dappled shade that produces contrasting patterns of light and dark can create effective mirror images on the water.

SOUTH-FACING GARDEN

PERMANENT SHADE
Do not site ponds where no sunlight will reach them during the day.

PARTIAL SHADE
Shade on part of the proposed pool or for part of the day need not rule out a site for a water garden. Dappled shade can also be attractive, as long as branches do not hang directly over the pool.

KEY TO DAILY SHADE PATTERN

Use string to mark out the areas that are shaded by planting and buildings in the morning, at noon, and in the afternoon.

	EARLY MORNING
	NOON
	EARLY EVENING

Consider, too, whether you will be able to see the feature from the house; this is particularly advisable in family gardens, so adults can keep an eye on children playing near the water.

LIGHT AND SHADE

Choose a sheltered but open site that will afford the feature the maximum amount of sunlight. Avoid extremely hot, sunny sites or you will increase problems with water evaporation in summer; also, fish will not be happy in baking heat. Although it may not be possible to find a spot completely free of shadows, the proximity of nearby tall plants and trees should be carefully considered: in addition to the shade they cast, falling leaves can become a problem. Site features as far as possible from trees with spreading root systems, such as poplars, which may damage foundations; from trees with toxic leaves and seeds, such as yew (*Taxus*); and from cherries (*Prunus*), on which water-lily aphids overwinter.

For the best visual impact, try to locate the pond where the reflective qualities of the water can best be enjoyed – a mirror is an invaluable aid (*see facing page*) for this. Experiment with various positions by marking the outline of the proposed pool with rope or hoses; study the direction and quality of light at different times of the day, and observe how well the pond can be seen from different vantage points.

PROVIDING SHELTER

Wind damages the soft, succulent stems of many bog plants, accelerates water evaporation, blows fountain spray out of the pool and, in some exposed sites, can result in the pond freezing over. Shelter can be provided by plantings, or by erecting a trellis or other screen on the windward side of the pool. You can use a windbreak to reduce the speed of the wind before it reaches the plants. A hedge, screen, or a fence with gaps (*see below right*) is a better windbreak than a solid structure, which simply deflects the wind to another part of the garden.

FINDING THE IDEAL SITE
Choosing the optimum location for a pond involves careful consideration of both aesthetic and practical factors.

ACCESS TO BORDERS Pond does not restrict access to other areas of planting.

AREA OF SHADE Pond is clear of shade cast by trees and overhanging branches.

SERVICES Pipes and cables are well clear of pond.

GAS MAIN

MANHOLE

SEWER PIPE

SEATING AREAS Patio area commands a fine view of the feature.

ELECTRIC OUTLET

PROXIMITY TO BOUNDARIES Space between pond and fence accommodates poolside planting and allows for future additions such as a rockery or stream.

CONSIDER VIEWPOINTS Ponds directly in front of large or French windows can clutter and obstruct views beyond.

VIEWING A WATER FEATURE ON A SLOPING SITE

Water features on sloping ground must either be cut into, or built up from, the slope (*see* Excavation and Drainage, *pp. 58–59*); the method will depend on whether you wish to view the feature from farther up, or from farther down, the incline. If you are constructing a retaining wall that extends above ground level, site it on the side of the pond that is farthest away from the house, seating area, or other ideal viewpoint. Otherwise, it will obstruct the view of the water surface.

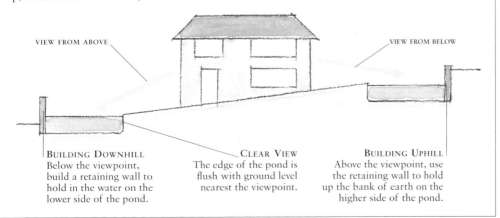

VIEW FROM ABOVE

VIEW FROM BELOW

BUILDING DOWNHILL Below the viewpoint, build a retaining wall to hold in the water on the lower side of the pond.

CLEAR VIEW The edge of the pond is flush with ground level nearest the viewpoint.

BUILDING UPHILL Above the viewpoint, use the retaining wall to hold up the bank of earth on the higher side of the pond.

REDUCING WIND SPEED

For maximum effect, a windbreak should be approximately 50 percent permeable; the gaps in the structure serve to break up the air currents as they pass through.

PREVAILING WIND

WIND-BREAK

FURTHER INFORMATION

- Choosing a Water Feature – pp. 52–53
- Excavation and Drainage – pp. 58–59
- Construction Techniques – pp. 64–69
- Soils and Containers – pp. 150–151

EXCAVATION AND DRAINAGE

EVEN IF YOUR GARDEN is reasonably well cultivated, you may never before have dug as deeply as you will to excavate a pond. Therefore, you may have little idea of the structure of the lower soil levels, and how easy they are to work with – for example, if a compacted or rocky layer exists that might mean extra labor or necessitate renting digging equipment. Since soil can vary from one site to another, dig test holes to determine its structure and composition. Another important consideration is the position of the water table. This, more often than not, does not present a problem; if it is high in your garden, temporary or permanent drainage may be needed.

EXCAVATING A SITE

If you do not have problems with wet ground *(see facing page)*, excavation is usually a reasonably simple, if laborious, task. Always stop if you feel any pain, and take breaks before, rather than when, you feel tired. If there is grass on the site, remove strips of sod and stack them upside down in an unobtrusive part of the garden; they will break down into a very good, fibrous loam planting medium. When excavating, first strip off the valuable topsoil to keep for planting areas. Place it separately from excavated subsoil. Use subsoil in the general landscaping of the feature, but always grade topsoil back over the subsoil when digging is complete. Dispose of excess subsoil, rather than dispersing it about the garden; it is of little use to plants.

TEST HOLE
Dig in the center of the proposed site, assess the situation, and adapt construction depending on results.

HIGH WATER TABLE
With water collecting spontaneously at this level, drainage or perhaps a shallower, but semi-raised, pond should be considered.

ESTABLISHING SOIL DRAINAGE AND THE WATER TABLE LEVEL
Dig a hole 18in (45cm) deep and fill it with water. If all the water does not seep away, you have poor drainage or a high water table. Remove the water and dig 18in (45cm) deeper. If the hole begins to fill with water, the water table is high: its level can be gauged when the water stops rising.

SOIL COMPOSITION

SOIL TYPE
The appearance of soil will tell you a great deal about its structure. Dry, sandy soil is firm and drains well, while wet, spongy soil has poor drainage. The upper levels of cultivated soil should be easy to dig.

RICH PLANT GROWTH

ACIDIC TOPSOIL

STONY LAYER

SANDY SUBSOIL

THIN PEATY LAYER

FERTILE TOPSOIL

SLATE AND SHALE SUBSOIL

SANDY SOIL   **CULTIVATED SOIL**   **WET BOGGY SOIL**

USING RETAINING WALLS ON SLOPING SITES

Unless you are leveling off the site *(see below)* a retaining wall on at least one side will be necessary to stabilize ponds built on a slope. If the wall is to be visible, pay careful attention to achieving a truly horizontal water surface, or the feature will always look askew.

HOUSE BRICKS

LINER AND UNDERLAY

RETAINING EARTH
This upper wall need not be obtrusive.

GRAVEL   CONCRETE

RETAINING WATER
A wall here creates the effect of a semi-raised pond. Viewed from below, it can obstruct views of the water surface.

LINER AND UNDERLAY

SLOPING GROUND
Plants with vigorous root systems will consolidate gently sloping earth banks.

LOWER SLOPE
Build up the lower slope first with excess subsoil and cover with topsoil.

LANDSCAPING USING EXCAVATION SOIL
The "cut-and-fill" method is a simple landscaping technique for leveling a sloping site (right), or for creating an earth bank using the soil excavated from a hole. It is essential, however, not to simply mound shoveled earth up as you dig to form the raised areas; sterile subsoil will then be brought to the surface and the valuable topsoil buried where plant roots cannot reach it. Strip off the topsoil first and replace it once you have created the basic contours.

LANDSCAPING
Always build gently sloping banks that will blend naturally into the terrain.

ORIGINAL SLOPE
Before excavation, the sloping ground would only have accommodated a very shallow pond.

CONSTRUCTION ON WET GROUND

You may know without digging a test hole that the water table is close to the ground surface or that drainage is poor. Telltale signs may provide ample evidence, including water pooling on lawns or the presence of water-loving plants such as rushes, sedges, and mosses. A site on a high water table may seem ideal for the construction of a natural pond, but in practice the water table is rarely high enough to create a pond that fills satisfactorily, so a water-retentive liner is still needed. The problem then is that the water in the soil will exert upward and inward pressure on the pond shell, placing structural stress on non-flexible materials such as concrete, and causing flexible linings, such as butyl or PVC, to balloon upward (see below, top).

There are a number of ways of dealing with this. One is to avoid digging down by building a raised pond (for which firm foundations are vital on unstable wet ground) – or, if you want a sunken effect, to raise ground level artificially so that the pond

SUBMERSIBLE PUMP. The pump expels the water through an outlet pipe.

TEMPORARY SUMP The water collects in the sump, which is situated below the lowest level of the excavation.

TEMPORARY DRAINAGE
A high water table leads to an accumulation of water in holes that makes further digging impracticable. To counteract this, dig a deeper hole to act as a sump; the sump will collect the water as digging continues. If necessary, use a pump with an outlet pipe to expel the water.

LAYING FLEXIBLE LINER ON A HIGH WATER TABLE

WATER TABLE

FLEXIBLE LINER

BALLOONING EFFECT Pressure of water makes the liner billow.

BALLOONING EFFECT
If flexible liner is laid below the water table, the accumulation of dissolved air from the ground water below the liner will push up, causing the liner to balloon up from the pool floor. With time, the the pond sides will slip down, causing further distortion.

POND SIDES Use topsoil to build up the area edging the pond.

FLEXIBLE LINER AND UNDERLAY

WATER TABLE

BUILDING A SUNKEN POND ABOVE THE WATER TABLE
To keep the floor of the pond above the water table, build up the surrounding ground until an adequate depth can be achieved for the pond. Unless you are paving around the pond, you must use topsoil, brought in if necessary, or plants around the pool edges will not thrive.

does not dip below the level of the water table (see left, center). To avoid a pond that resembles a volcano, however, it is essential to combine this with more general landscaping of the surrounding area.

The alternative is to install permanent drainage for the ground surrounding the pond. Trenches and pipes can vastly improve poor drainage; very few areas are so constantly rainy that a simple system cannot cope. But on a high water table, a pump will also be necessary (see left, bottom) so that water can be removed faster than it seeps back in again.

Even if you plan to build the pond so that it lies above the water table, when digging deeper to lay foundations, you may find that the accumulating water makes it extremely difficult to work. Dig out a small deep hole to act as a sump (see above) and, as water fills it, bail or pump it out. Make sure that the water is expelled in a place where it cannot seep back into the hole.

PROTECTED ELECTRIC CABLE

WATER TABLE

OUTLET PIPE

PUMP

WATERTIGHT SUMP

FLEXIBLE LINER   GRAVEL   PERFORATED PIPE

INTEGRAL FLOAT SWITCH

INSTALLING PERMANENT DRAINAGE
Before laying the liner, dig a trench below the base of the pond and place a perforated pipe between two layers of gravel; the gravel will reduce the risk of the pipe becoming clogged. Extend the pipe into a sump chamber containing a submersible pump. An integral float switch will activate the pump when the water in the sump reaches a certain level.

FURTHER INFORMATION
• Siting Water Features – pp. 56–57
• Construction Tools and Materials – pp. 62–63
• Construction Techniques – pp. 64–69
• Simple Ponds with Flexible Liners – pp. 76–79

MEASURING AREAS AND VOLUMES

FROM INITIAL PLANNING to the long-term care of a water feature it will at times be necessary to know its dimensions, including the surface area of the excavation and of the water and the volume of water the feature can contain. These statistics are necessary for estimating quantities and costs of construction materials. Flexible liners, for example, are priced per square foot or meter. They are also used when choosing appropriate pumps and filters, to decide the number of fish that a pond will house *(see p. 171)* and the quantities of submerged plants necessary for a healthy environment *(see pp. 152–153)*, and the dosage rates of chemicals, if needed.

STILL WATER FEATURES

Formal pools in symmetrical shapes such as squares and circles present the least difficulty in calculating dimensions, since they are easy to measure. Informal ponds can be more awkward. For simple informal shapes such as the kidney shape, the surface area can be easily approximated for most practical purposes by drawing a rectangle around its outline, using the width at its widest point and the length of its longest axis. The surface area of this rectangle can be multiplied by the depth to obtain the pool's volume. For more complicated shapes that cannot be "squared off" so easily, divide the pool into sections, each with a regular shape such as a rectangle or semicircle; their dimensions can be added together to give adequate approximate figures. When variations in depth occur, section the pool crosswise (as with the circular pool below). Remember that while marginal shelves make the volume of a pool smaller, they make the surface area of the hole bigger, and you will need to allow for extra liner.

The various formulas for calculating volumes will give measurements in cubic feet or meters. To convert cubic feet to gallons, multiply the figure by 6.25. To convert cubic meters into liters, multiply the figure by 1,000.

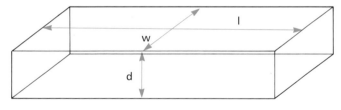

SQUARES AND RECTANGLES
It is easiest to calculate dimensions using measurements in meters or in decimal fractions of feet (e.g., 1.5ft for 18in). Multiply the length (l) of the pond by the width (w) to obtain the surface area. Multiply this figure by the depth (d) of the pool to establish its volume. For example, a pool 3ft (0.9m) wide by 4ft (1.2m) long has a surface area of 12sq ft (1.08sq m); with a depth of 18in or 1½ft (0.45m), the pool's volume is 18cu ft (0.486cu m).

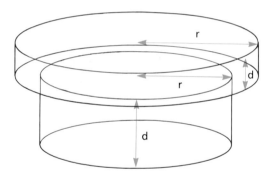

CIRCULAR SHAPES
Square the radius of the pool (r x r) and multiply this by the mathematical constant pi (π) – 3.14 – to obtain the surface area. To calculate the volume, multiply this figure by the depth (d). To calculate the volume of a circular pool with a marginal shelf, divide it transversely into two sections, as above, each with its own radius and depth, and add the volumes of the two sections together. To calculate the circumference of a circle, multiply the radius (r) by 3.14, then multiply this figure by 2.

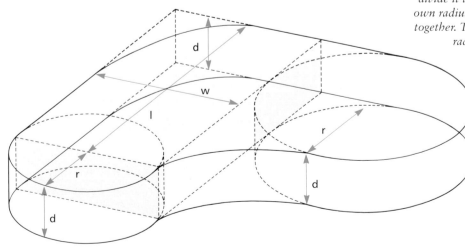

IRREGULAR SHAPES
For simple irregular shapes, use the maximum width, length, and depth to calculate surface area and volume as for a rectangle (above left). For more complex shapes (as right), divide the pond into approximate square, rectangular, or circular or semicircular sections and calculate the surface area of each. Add the figures together to calculate the total surface area. Multiply this figure by the depth of the feature to obtain the volume.

MOVING WATER FEATURES

A waterfall or stream less than 2ft (60cm) in drop or length generally makes little practical difference to surface area or volume and can be omitted from calculations, but longer streams and waterfalls should be added in. However, the height of the feature, from header pool or waterfall outlet to reservoir pool is always important: known as the "head," it is a factor in determining the power needed from a pump.

STREAMS

A gently meandering stream can be "squared off" like any other simple irregular shape. Multiply its length from top to bottom by the approximate maximum width (average out measurements taken at several wide points) to obtain the surface area. Multiply this figure by the depth (including any layer of gravel or rocks) to obtain the volume. To determine the length of a widely meandering stream more accurately, follow its curves with a tape measure or drape string along its margin, then measure the string.

WATERFALLS

Treat a waterfall as a vertical stream, measuring its width and "length" (the height of the drop). Multiply these to obtain the surface area (only one "face" of a free-falling waterfall should be counted in). For the volume of water in the fall at any given time, multiply the surface area by the depth of the outlet over which the water flows at the top of the fall. Add these figures to those of the feature's pool or pools to obtain total surface area and volume.

POOLS IN SERIES

These small waterfalls do not make a significant difference to calculations. Calculate the surface area and volume of each pool, then add the figures together. The distance from the water surface on the header pool to the bottom of the lowest pool is the "head."

CONSTRUCTION METHODS

A water feature with the same approximate surface area and volume, built in different styles, needs varying quantities of different materials; construction times can also vary. These five water features each have a surface area of 96sq ft (10sq m): as a rough guide, the formal pools could be 8ft x 12ft (2.5m x 3.7m) in width and length, and the informally shaped pools could be "squared off" to fit into a rectangle of these dimensions. Each has marginal shelf areas, and a volume of 144cu ft (4cu m): a water capacity of 900 gals (4,000 liters). To give some idea of the weight of water in the pools (and how strong the walls of the raised pool need to be), 1 gallon of water weighs 10lb; 1 liter weighs 1kg.

GUIDE TO REQUIREMENTS FOR DIFFERENT POOL STYLES

Style of pool	Digging time (with a helper)	Concrete, for foundations etc	Walling materials	Liner and underlay	Ready-to-mix mortar	Other materials	Coping stones/ edging
Raised oblong pool with double wall and flexible liner.	2 hours to dig foundations (but 20 hours' bricklaying)	110lb (50kg) cement, 1cu yd (1cu m) ballast	80 concrete blocks, 12 x 9in (30 x 22cm); 360 bricks 3 x 12in (8 x 30cm)	17ft x 13ft (5.2m x 3.9m): 221sq ft (20.5sq m)	12 x 55lb (25kg) bags	–	20 coping stones, 24in x 12in (60cm x 30cm)
Oblong concrete pool lined with reinforced cement	10 hours, plus removal of soil	1cu yd (1cu m) sand, 110lb (50kg) cement, 1cu yd (1cu m) aggregate	52 concrete blocks, 18 x 9in (45 x 23cm); 118 house bricks	–	6 x 55lb (25kg) bags	Reinforcing fibers for cement: 3 x 11lb (5kg) bags	20 coping stones, 24in x 24in (60cm x 60cm)
Informal pool with flexible liner and crazy-paving edge	10 hours, plus removal of soil	1½cu yd (1.5cu m) sand, 110lb (50kg) cement, ½cu yd (0.5cu m) aggregate	–	18ft x 14ft (5.5m x 4.3m): 252sq ft (23.4sq m)	3 x 55lb (25kg) bags	–	12sq yd (12sq m) crazy paving
Pool as above, 1ft (30cm) less wide, with small rigid-unit stream	13 hours (inc. bedding in units on soil-based mound)	1cu yd (1cu m) sand, 110lb (50kg) cement, ½cu yd (0.5cu m) aggregate	–	18ft x 14ft (5.5m x 4.3m): 252sq ft (23.4sq m)	2 x 55lb (25kg) bags	Two stream units, one header pool unit, sand for bedding in	10 sq yd (10sq m) crazy paving; 30 x 55lb (25kg) loose rocks
Wildlife pond edged with turf, planting, and pebble beach	10 hours, plus removal of soil	–	–	20ft x 16ft (6m x 4.9m): 320sq ft (29.4sq m) (for varied depths)	–	–	8 x 110lb (50kg) bags of rocks for beach area

CONSTRUCTION TOOLS & MATERIALS

THE TOOLS AND MATERIALS necessary for building water features vary from project to project, although some, such as a carpenter's level, are essential for any construction task. Do-it-yourself enthusiasts may be familiar with many of the techniques used in the step-by-step projects featured in this section and will have used the tools in other situations. It is important to choose the correct implement and materials for the appropriate stage of construction, and to use them with skill and care, in order to guarantee a structurally sound feature. If in doubt, seek professional help; sometimes it is worth the extra investment to obtain a good result.

CONSTRUCTION TOOLS

Using the appropriate tools for a job makes an appreciable difference in the ease with which the task can be accomplished, and in certain situations it is crucial to use the correct equipment. Consider borrowing or renting tools that you might never or rarely need again. If buying, it is well worth investing in good-quality tools if you can. They are usually longer-lasting and more comfortable to use.

BUILDER'S SQUARE

TAPE MEASURE

BAMBOO STAKES

STRAIGHTEDGE

CARPENTER'S LEVEL

SPADE

SHOVEL

MARKING OUT AND LEVELING
Tools for marking out and measuring, and for achieving true horizontals, are essential even for the smallest, simplest ponds. A builder's square, either bought or homemade, ensures accurate right angles.

BRICKLAYER'S TROWEL

POINTING TROWEL

PLASTERER'S TROWEL

RUBBER MALLET   MARKER PEGS

CLUB HAMMER

BOLSTER CHISEL

DIGGING TOOLS
Most gardeners will already own a good sharp-edged spade, but these generally have too small a blade to make large-scale excavation comfortable. Once the hole is big enough to stand in, use the spade to break the soil, then use a shovel, with its wide blade and inrolled edges, to scoop the soil out of the hole.

CORDLESS DRILL

MASONRY BITS

DRILLING HOLES
A cordless drill is much more convenient and safer to work with outdoors. Always use the correct drill bits for wood or stonework.

TOOLS FOR CONCRETE, CEMENT, AND MORTAR
A bricklayer's trowel has a better shape than a garden trowel for handling wet building mixes. Much more skill is required to use pointing and plastering trowels: to create an acceptable finish you will need plenty of practice, since you must work quickly with fast-drying mixtures.

CUTTING BRICKS AND SLABS
A hammer and chisel can be used to cut the odd brick or slab to fit a corner; however, if you have many pavers to cut into precise shapes, it is worth renting a brick-cutter.

MATERIALS FOR CONSTRUCTION

Unlike the decorative materials chosen for edging and other finishing touches, the basic materials used to build water features are often hidden from view. Most items will be available at any building supply store. A water garden specialist will stock a range of pool liners and is also the best source for delivery hoses and other piping: because they specialize in water-feature construction, they will be able to tell you exactly what you need to achieve the desired effect.

STANDARD
DELIVERY HOSE

WIDE DELIVERY HOSE

LIGHTWEIGHT PLASTIC PIPE

WIDE-GAUGE COPPER PIPE

NARROW-GAUGE COPPER PIPE

WIDE-GAUGE PLASTIC PUSH-FIT PIPE

NARROW-GAUGE PLASTIC PUSH-FIT PIPE

COPPER ELBOW JOINT   COMPRESSION JOINT

SOLDERED T-FITTING   SOLDERED ELBOW JOINT   PLASTIC ELBOW JOINT

PIPEWORK AND JOINTS

Pipes conduct water and protect electric cables. If pipes have to be visible (for example, on a wall feature), copper piping is more attractive and will take on a weathered appearance. All flexible piping, even if reinforced, must have rigid elbow joints at sharp changes of direction, or the pipe will kink and restrict water flow.

HOUSE BRICK

CONCRETE BLOCK

BUILDING BLOCKS

Common house or clay bricks can be used to build everything from decorative walls to submerged plant bases. Concrete blocks can be used to build concealed walls more quickly and economically.

COARSE SAND

CEMENT

MORTAR

MORTAR

Mortar is a mix that consists of cement, coarse sand, and water. It is available as a ready-made mix, but this is economical only where small quantities are used.

LINING MATERIALS

Flexible liners are generally made of polyethylene, PVC, butyl, or EPDM *(see p. 67)*. It is advisable to use some form of underlay to protect the liner, especially on stony sites. Polyester matting underlay will be available wherever liner is sold and is not expensive. Used carpeting can also be employed. Clay-based bentomat *(see pp. 92–93)* is an attractive alternative to plastic liner with an unobtrusive, textured matt finish.

BENTONITE

BENTOMAT   UNDERLAY   FLEXIBLE LINER

STRENGTHENING ADDITIVES

GRADES OF BALLAST

Adding small stones and sand to cement creates concrete. The larger the size of stone, the stronger the concrete: for very solid foundations concrete is poured over compacted crushed stone.

REINFORCING FIBER

This commercial fiber, similar to fiberglass, makes a cement mix stronger and more flexible; a layer of this mix on a concrete shell (see pp. 90–91) forms a lining that is less susceptible to cracking caused by water pressure and small earth movements.

FURTHER INFORMATION

- Construction Techniques – pp. 64–69
- Pumps and Filters – pp. 70–73
- Edging Materials – pp. 126–129

CONSTRUCTION TECHNIQUES

SOME CONSTRUCTION METHODS are better suited to certain styles of water feature than others and also to the type of job you are prepared to tackle. Rigid units such as preformed fiberglass pools *(see below)* are an excellent choice for a small to medium size self-contained pool and are relatively quick and simple to install. For a freer hand with the size and shape of pool, plus the option of incorporating customized features such as islands and planting pockets, flexible liner *(see pp. 66–67)* is the obvious choice. With some basic building skills *(see pp. 68–69)*, formal and raised pools edged with brick, paving, and wood can be considered.

USING PREFORMED POOL UNITS

Installing a rigid container to hold water, whether a fiberglass pool unit or an improvised version such as a plastic tub, involves simply digging a hole of the correct size and shape to house it so that it is absolutely level, both for visual effect and to make sure that planting baskets sit securely on shelves or bases. Small, evenly shaped units with only one depth level may be installed completely above ground level, but it is very difficult to give a larger unit with irregular contouring the support it needs unless the unit, or at least its deeper zone, is sunken into the ground.

DIGGING TIPS

• Place two polyethylene sheets beyond the hole's proposed edges: one for topsoil, the other for subsoil.
• Dig with a straight back and bended knees *(see left)* to minimize strain on your back.
• Once the hole is big enough, work from inside it to avoid extra bending.
• You may find it easier to dig the hole down to the correct depth and enlarge it: chop at the sides with a sharp-edged spade, then shovel out the soil.
• Only shovel small quantities of soil at a time.
• If you are not accustomed to a lot of digging, wear gloves to prevent blisters; shoes with sturdy soles are also essential. Stop and rest as soon as you begin to feel tired or if you feel pain of any kind.

STAGES OF CONSTRUCTION

Rigid units must be firmly supported and cushioned against sharp objects. Make sure that the base of the hole is firm, level, and free of sharp stones. Make the hole slightly wider than the unit so that you can backfill with ease. Filling the pool partway with water as you backfill will let you make adjustments so that the unit remains level as the weight of water settles it into position.

MARKING OUT
Before digging, you may use bamboo stakes to mark the perimeter of a unit that slopes inward toward the base. Be very careful to avoid eye injury when digging close to stakes.

FIRM SUPPORT
Bed units into a firm layer of sand or sifted soil, free from sharp stones. Do not use coarse sand where plants are to grow.

MARGINAL SHELF
Some trial and error is usually necesssary to contour the hole for marginal shelves.

MARKING OUT

MARKER PEG
Tap marker pegs into the ground just beyond the proposed edge of the hole.

CARPENTER'S LEVEL
Check levels both around the perimeter and across the hole.

LEVELING PEG
Set one leveling peg at the ideal level, then match all the others to it.

CORRECT LEVEL

REFERENCE POINT

LEVELING

USING MARKER PEGS

Marker pegs are used to obtain level, horizontal pool edges on uneven ground. Once the first reference point is established, use a carpenter's level to make sure that the marker level on all subsequent pegs corresponds to that on the first peg, which should act as a reference point.

USING A CARPENTER'S LEVEL

To achieve correct levels across a hole, or across distances wider than the length of a carpenter's level, use a straightedge: a long, straight strip of wood on which the level can be balanced. Check levels frequently at every stage of construction.

TYPES OF PREFORMED POND UNIT

In many ways preformed units make ideal ponds: they are easy both to install and clean. They are generally made of fiberglass or various plastics in a range of shapes and sizes, the maximum size being approximately 12ft (3.5m) across, and are available from most nurseries or garden centers. Fiberglass units are light, strong, and durable; they are recommended for semi-raised ponds. Plastic units tend to be cheaper, and may only last two or three years. Shallow, square, and circular units make ideal small formal features; their bases can be disguised with gravel or pebbles. To accommodate plants and fish, a deeper unit, ideally with marginal shelves, is essential.

SIMPLE SHAPES
The simpler the shape, the easier to install.

MARGINAL SHELF
Shelf space is wide enough for planting baskets.

GRAY COLOR
Neutral colors are the least obtrusive.

DEPTH
Unit has a deep zone, essential for fish and for planted ponds.

STABILIZING THE POOL
Before backfilling, fill the pool with 4in (10cm) of water to increase its stability. Continue to slowly fill the pond with water as you backfill.

WIDE RIM
The rim prevents soil from falling into the pond. It can be disguised with plants *(see right)* or with mortared-down slabs.

SUPPORTING THE LIP
After backfilling, remember to press sand or soil firmly up under the lip of the unit to support it.

DISGUISING PREFORMED UNITS

SUNKEN POND
One disadvantage of preformed units is that their wide rims form an unnatural edge. Unless you are surrounding the pond with paving, planting is the best way to disguise and soften the rim. Use clump-forming plants, including some moisture-lovers to give a more natural effect.

BACKFILLING AND TAMPING

BACKFILLING
Shovel sand or soil into the gap between the unit and the excavation wall.

1 MAKE THE EXCAVATION slightly wider and deeper than the unit so that you can backfill and tamp easily. Always shovel out or rake back soil well clear of the hole so that it cannot slip back in. Shovel a small quantity of sand or sifted soil into the gap all around the unit.

TAMPING
Consolidate each layer of backfill so that the unit remains secure.

2 A SHORT LENGTH OF WOOD is an ideal tamping tool. Press the sand or soil down firmly all around the unit. Repeat the process, backfilling gradually around the sides. Do not tamp so hard that the unit is distorted; filling partway with water, and checking levels frequently, will help avoid this.

SEMI-RAISED POND
Semi-raised units must have a firm supporting wall of timbers or mortared stones to remain secure. Backfill with rich, moisture-retentive soil and keep well-watered.

USING FLEXIBLE POND LINER

FLEXIBLE LINER IS THE MOST versatile material available to the water gardener. It can be used as waterproof lining for a porous shell – for example, a brick-built reservoir pool or an old half-barrel. An old, cracked concrete pond or rigid pool unit can be instantly "repaired" with a new lining. However, flexible liner comes into its own in the construction of informal ponds, allowing considerable freedom with the design of pools and streams, and the inclusion of a variety of additional features. Liner materials vary in price and quality. Inexpensive polyethylene can be adequate: high-density polyethylene is the least expensive but is of the poorest quality and should be used only in double thickness. It will crack under prolonged exposure to the ultra-

violet rays in sunlight, and any exposed areas must be concealed. Low-density polyethylene is of a slightly higher quality; it is stronger and fairly flexible. For a substantial, durable feature it is well worth investing in good-quality PVC or, better yet, EPDM or butyl liners *(see facing page)*. The latter are far less prone to tearing, puncturing, and ultraviolet deterioration; top-grade PVC, EPDM, and butyl usually carry at least a 10-year guarantee.

Measure the size of your pond carefully using a flexible tape measure to determine the correct size of liner to purchase *(see below left for details)*. Do not join liners unless the joint is above standing water level. Otherwise, leaks are inevitable, and you will have to drain and reline the pond to eliminate them.

LINING AN EXCAVATION

You should ideally unroll liner prior to laying it (see p. 76), but do not then drag it over the hole or you will disturb the underlay. Instead, roll the liner up from both sides toward the middle, lift the roll into position across the center of the hole and unroll carefully, without stretching it.

EXCAVATING THE POND

MARGINAL SHELF
Flatten the top and sides of shelves with a spade to compact the soil well.

SLIGHT SLOPE
Pond and shelf sides slope at a 20° angle to prevent earth caving in.

UNDERLAY
Prolong the lifespan of flexible liner by using underlay to cushion and protect it.

TEMPORARY HOLD
Lift the bricks to allow movement of the liner as the pond fills.

FLAT, FIRM BASE
Roots and stones have been removed from the base. If soil is very stony, add a layer of sand. Gently tread the base down, then rake.

MARKING OUT AND DIGGING
Rope, hoses, pegs, or sand are perfectly adequate for marking out an informal shape. Excavate the hole, angling the sides slightly inward. Marginal shelves should be at least 12in (30cm) wide to accommodate planting baskets; wider is better. If you are not incorporating a beach, you may wish to leave a sloping ramp on one side as an easy access or exit point for wildlife.

LAYING UNDERLAY

CALCULATING THE AMOUNT OF LINER

First determine the maximum length, width, and depth of the pond. The liner should measure the maximum width of the pond plus twice its depth, by the maximum length plus twice its depth. Add another 18in (45cm) to both width and length to allow for a flap overlapping the edge, in order to prevent leakage. If the pond sides are completely vertical, or for additional features such as an island *(see pp. 80–81)* or integral boggy area *(see pp. 82–83)*, extra liner will be necessary.

1 SPREAD THE UNDERLAY (here, fiberglass insulation material) over the base and sides of the excavation. Press the material firmly over and into the contours of the hole.

2 KEEPING THE UNDERLAY in position, trim it neatly at or slightly overlapping ground level. Try not to put your full weight on any marginal shelves. Then unroll the liner over it.

FILLING A LINED POND

1 USING BRICKS AS temporary weights, fill the pond slowly, gradually moving the bricks to allow the liner to settle down into the hole.

2 ONLY WHEN THE pond is full and the liner has ceased to move, trim off the surplus with scissors or a craft knife.

SMOOTH FINISH
Gentle curving shapes are easy to line; pleat material at sharp angles.

FILLING THE POND
Gently fill the pond, so that the water slowly presses and molds the liner down into the contours of the hole.

EXTRA LINER
A generous margin will allow the liner to be taken up under soil or edging.

PEBBLE BEACH
A gentle slope with a slight rim makes an ideal beach area.

MORTARING STONE ON LINER

1 FOR A SIMPLE EDGING, mortar rounded or flat stones directly onto the liner. More formal paved edging requires foundations (*see p. 68*).

2 FLAT SLABS should overhang the pond by 2in (5cm) to disguise the liner. Do not drop mortar into the pond or it will have to be emptied.

GRADES OF LINER AND UNDERLAY

The more expensive pond liners come in different weights and thicknesses, and the larger the area you wish to cover, the thicker the material should be. Black is the most unobtrusive color, although others are sometimes available. If buying good-quality liner, always protect your investment by using underlay beneath it. There are some excellent products available that will prolong the liner's lifespan.

UNDERLAY MATERIAL
Polyester matting underlay comes in rolls up to 6ft (2m) wide. Underlay can also be improvised, using insulation felt or even old synthetic carpet. Newspaper is sometimes recommended, but it tends to disintegrate fast.

CARPET   POLYESTER MATTING

PVC POND LINERS (*BELOW*)
Liners made from PVC (polyvinyl chloride) are popular and are more flexible than polyethylene. PVC comes in a number of grades; the thickest grade available (32mils) usually lasts longer and should be sold with a guarantee. Do not use PVC swimming-pool liners. They contain herbicides and biocides that can kill aquatic life.

32 MILS
30 MILS
20 MILS
15 MILS

BUTYL AND EPDM LINERS
The two best lining materials are butyl and EPDM. Both have more elasticity than PVC, which allows them to be installed with fewer creases and folds than other types of liner. They also have greater UV resistance and remain flexible even in cold weather. Both are generally sold with a 20-year warranty. The standard grade of EPDM is 45mils; butyl is generally sold in 60- or 30mils thicknesses.

60 MILS
45 MILS
30 MILS
20 MILS

USING BUILDING MATERIALS

BETWEEN THE TWO EXTREMES of a simple hole lined with polyethylene and a raised pond with brick walls lie a host of water garden projects requiring some knowledge of basic building techniques. Structures that will be concealed, such as foundations, concrete-block shell walls as well as planting beds and shelves must be well built to be durable, but they need not be perfectly finished. Flat paving and edging are not difficult to lay, provided that you work quickly and clean off excess mortar before it dries (dry mortar is almost impossible to remove). However, brick-laying and pouring concrete are skilled tasks that must be done properly or the finished product will be both visually and structurally poor, with no remedy but to have the job redone.

MARKING OUT STRAIGHT-SIDED SHAPES

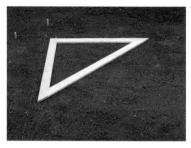

USING A BUILDER'S SQUARE
Formal shapes must be carefully staked out before construction begins. Check regularly for accuracy during construction. Corners must be perfect right angles or the walls and edging will not meet where they should: this can cause problems during construction whether you are using blocks, bricks, or pavers.

LAYING A FOUNDATION

1 FOR A SOLID FOUNDATION, spread a 4in (10cm) layer of crushed stone over the bottom of the hole before pouring in concrete.

2 CRUSHED STONE can be compacted with a mallet and block of wood, but if the base area is large, it is worth hiring a compactor. Its vibrating plate consolidates and flattens the stones, shaking smaller pieces into the spaces between larger stones.

CONSTRUCTING A STRAIGHT-SIDED POOL
Pools with straight edges and vertical sides are most effectively constructed using traditional building techniques and materials either beneath, or instead of, flexible pond liners. Firm foundations and solid walls are essential to prevent the soil from settling around the edges of the pool. Retaining walls of concrete blocks can be made watertight either with flexible liner (see pp. 78–79) or, as here, with a layer of cement made strong and flexible with special reinforcing fibers. With bricklaying skills, a low wall could be added around this pool to give a semi-raised effect.

CONCRETE BLOCKS
These holes in blocks make them lighter to handle. Once in position they can be filled with concrete for extra strength.

CONCRETE INFILL
Use concrete to fill any space between the blocks and the sides of an excavation, but the mortar between the blocks must first be *completely* set.

VERTICAL-SIDED HOLES
Use a plumb-line to make walls as vertical and even as possible; compensate for small irregularities by using concrete infill.

CRUSHED STONE AND CONCRETE FOUNDATION
A compacted, 4in (10cm) deep layer of crushed stone with concrete poured on top, makes firm footings for walls and structures such as stepping stones and bridge ends. For maximum stability, cover the entire base of a pool.

SAFETY PRECAUTIONS

• Even small bags of cement, mortar mix, and sand are heavy; take great care when lifting them. Always bend from the knees, rather than bending your back. Also, be careful to protect your back while digging *(see p. 64)*.
• Cement dust is an irritant: wear gloves when mixing mortar and concrete, avoid inhaling dust (wear a filter or cyclist's mask if possible), and never rub your eyes while working.
• String brightly colored or fluorescent tape at waist height between stakes around the hole when you leave it unattended.
• Never let children play alone near holes, tools, or materials.
• Unplug any power tools that you have been using, and never leave them unattended.

LAYING CONCRETE

1 POUR LARGE QUANTITIES of concrete from a wheelbarrow. For even coverage, try to pour the mix in gently overlapping folds.

2 LEVEL AND FIRM the concrete, both cross- and lengthwise, with a beam; use a carpenter's level to be sure the mix is level before it dries.

SIMPLE BRICKLAYING

STRING GUIDE

1 LAY BRICKS, frog downward, in staggered rows (a "bond" pattern). Apply a layer of mortar where the next brick will be placed.

2 "BUTTER" THE END of the next brick by drawing a trowel loaded with mortar across it. Do not overload the trowel.

TAPPING WITH TROWEL HANDLE

3 SET THE BRICK down firmly and squarely. Working with the guide and, after every few bricks, a level, tap the brick until it is level. Brush off surplus mortar with a wire brush.

COPING STONES
Bricks and pavers jutting over the pond edges must be securely mortared down for safety. Check edging regularly with a level.

ADDING WATER
Never fill a cement-lined pool unless its surface has been sealed to lock in harmful chemicals. Or, fill the pool and add potasssium permanganate crystals, leave for a week to "cure" the cement, then empty and refill.

SURFACE LAYER
A rendering of cement can be used on exterior walls as cladding, or to waterproof the interior of a pool.

MORTARS AND CONCRETE

Unless specific recipes are given, use a mix of 1 part cement to 3 parts coarse sand for bricklaying, or 5 parts sand for laying paving; for a general purpose concrete mix, use 1 part cement to 2½ parts coarse sand and 3½ parts aggregate.

- Before use, store ingredients in a dry place.
- Avoid cold weather when laying concrete; the cold will cause it to disintegrate before fully hardened.
- Always mix dry ingredients well before adding water.
- Add the water to a well in the center and fold the dry ingredients inward.
- Add water very gradually to avoid an over-wet mix.
- Work as quickly as possible once mixes are made up.
- Colorants can be added to mortar for visual effects.

WORKING WITH WET CONCRETE

A variety of items may need to be embedded into wet mortars and concretes before they set. Wall ties embedded at regular intervals will reinforce a double wall (*see pp. 86–87*). Steel brackets can be fixed onto bolts sunk into wet concrete to secure wood to a concrete base (*see pp. 122–123*). Reinforcing wire can be sandwiched between layers of wet concrete (*see p. 91*). Conduits for water overflows or for wiring can also be hidden between bricks or under coping (*see pp. 86–87*).

WALL TIE

BRACKET

WIRE MESH

OVERFLOW PIPE

CUTTING STONE SLABS

1 PLACE THE SLAB on a flat surface. Score a cutting groove on both sides and edges of the slab with the corner of a bolster chisel.

2 USING THE CHISEL with a mallet, carefully work along to deepen the scored line on both sides and at the edges of the slab.

3 BALANCE THE SLAB on a length of wood. Align the groove with the edge of the wood and tap with a hammer handle until the slab splits.

CUTTING BRICKS

Score the cutting line with the edge of a bolster chisel, then chisel an ⅛in (3mm) deep groove along this line. Raise onto a piece of timber, and tap with the handle of a hammer.

PUMPS AND FILTERS

PUMPS ARE USED IN conjunction with water features in order to recirculate water. An electric motor draws the water in through an inlet to which a strainer is fitted to prevent the system from being blocked by debris. Pressure pushes the water out through a pipe, which is attached to a waterfall, fountain, or filter. There are two types of pump – submersible and surface; submersible pumps run under water, and high-voltage surface pumps are housed above ground. Pumps come in a wide range of models to suit every type of water feature. They fall into two main categories – pumps to run a fountain or waterfall and solids-handling pumps to work a filter.

TYPES OF PUMP

A pump is required to move water either within a feature (through a fountain or filter) or to travel around a watercourse. To operate the pump, electricity will need to be brought to the vicinity of the pond water (see p. 72). Before choosing a pump, decide what you want it to do (see Points to Consider, p. 72) and consult a specialist with your requirements.

NOZZLE
OUTLET
FLOW ADJUSTER
T-PIECE
IMPELLER
STRAINER
NOZZLE
CASING
MOTOR

SUBMERSIBLE PUMP INTERIOR

SUBMERSIBLE PUMP
These pumps, with integral filters, are ideal for most small fountains and watercourses.

FOUNTAIN ATTACHMENT

STAINLESS STEEL BODY

PLASTIC BODY

PRE-FILTER
Sponge protects pump strainer.

SUBMERSIBLE PUMP AND STRAINER DETACHED

FOUNTAIN PUMP
A small fountain requires a submersible pump that has low output but high pressure. The pump may sit directly under, or away from, the fountain (see pp. 108–111).

PUMP FOR FILTRATION SYSTEM
A pump is not always installed to produce visible water movement; it may also be used to push or pull water through a filter. Heavily stocked fish ponds require this arrangement.

PUMP FOR WATERCOURSES
To move water any distance from a reservoir pool uphill to a header pool with waterfall requires a powerful pump with high output – in some cases, a surface pump.

SOLIDS-HANDLING PUMP *(left)*
Pumps that deliver water to filters (see facing page) are capable of handling small solids without clogging up the impeller. The rate of flow must be steady so that the filter works efficiently; if necessary, use a flow adjuster (see p. 72).

PROTECTED WORKINGS
Metal rotary blade within sealed casing chops up solid matter.

WATER INLET

SURFACE PUMP *(right)*
The advantage of a powerful surface pump is that it has high output and is useful for operating large watercourses or a group of fountains. Surface pumps require a dedicated electrical circuit and need to be housed in a chamber that is dry and well ventilated (see p. 73).

FILTRATION IN THE POND

Pond water may be filtered either before it enters, or after it is expelled from, the pump *(right)*. There are two types of filtration materials – mechanical and biological. Mechanical filters simply strain out solid particles; they are effective as soon as the system is switched on and can be run intermittently. Biological filters use materials with very large, complex surface areas on which bacteria collect and flourish; these break down and purify waste products and ammonia gas.

PRE-PUMP FILTER

POST-PUMP FILTER

EXTRA FILTRATION
A larger block of foam may be pushed over the pump inlet of self-contained submersible pumps.

ALL-PURPOSE POND FILTER
A filter chamber is normally housed outside the pond. A pump pushes the water through the filter's inlet pipe; it then passes through several layers of filter media. Once purified, the water returns to the pond via the outlet pipe.

FILTER BOX

OPEN-CELL FOAM

PLASTIC BIO-MEDIA

SPRAY BAR

FILTER LID

OUTLET PIPE

HEAVY-DUTY LID

INLET PIPE

SPRAY BAR

DOWNWARD FLOW

OPEN-CELL FOAM

PLASTIC BIO-MEDIA

OUTLET PIPE

FIRST STAGE OF FILTRATION
Water enters the inlet pipe and flows through the spray bar, which needs regular cleaning.

INTERIOR OF A FILTER
Mechanical and biological filtration is combined in this type of pond filter. Fine layers of open-cell foam and plastic bio-media purify the water, which then passes through the outlet pipe. An overflow system is provided, so that the filter is by-passed when it becomes blocked. The foam sheets should then be removed for cleaning.

OTHER FILTER MEDIA

BRUSHES AND PADS
Certain filters make use of brushes and pads arranged in the filter box, which catch any solids contained in the water before biological filtration.

ZEOLITES

RING MEDIA

LIGNASITE

BIOLOGICAL FILTERS
These materials are made of clays, glass, carbon granules, and other mineral compounds on which bacteria thrive.

SPECIALTY FILTER SYSTEMS

For crystal-clear water (for example, for a pond in which koi carp are to be displayed to best advantage), attach a UV clarifier and magnet to the existing system between the pump and filter. Ultraviolet radiation makes algae clump together, so that they may easily be strained out by the filter. The magnet is designed to prevent the buildup of minerals on which algae thrive.

UV CLARIFIER

ALL-PURPOSE POND FILTER

PUMP

MAGNET

SURFACE UV CLARIFIER
A surface UV clarifier and magnet work in conjunction with a filter and pump to combat algal growth.

HOSE TAIL

TEFLON SLEEVE

CABLE

BYPASS VALVE

LAMP

SUBMERSIBLE UV CLARIFIER
The newest extra low-voltage UV clarifiers can be placed directly in a pond. They are small, economical, durable, and have a high UV output.

ELECTRICITY AND WATER

All pumps are powered by electricity, either directly from a conventional circuit or passed through a transformer to produce an extra low-voltage current. Extra low-voltage pumps have a limited output and are only suitable for small waterfalls or a single fountain. A regular voltage system, used for large watercourses, must not be run without a circuit breaker and a ground fault interrupter (GFI), which makes electricity much safer to use in the garden. When buying a submersible pump, it should have enough cable attached to extend onto dry land, to avoid having to connect cables underwater *(see facing page)*.

WEATHERPROOF CONNECTOR

EXTRA LOW-VOLTAGE ELECTRICITY

An extra low-voltage system is used in conjunction with a transformer, and presents no danger from shock. The transformer should be located indoors, close to the wall socket.

FULL-VOLTAGE ELECTRICITY

If a pump is connected directly to a full-voltage circuit, the cable should be buried in rigid plastic pipe at least 2ft (60cm) underground.

TRANSFORMER • CABLE • SMALL FOUNTAIN • WEATHERPROOF CONNECTOR • PATH • PLASTIC CONDUIT • PUMP • SWITCH • GFI • LARGE FOUNTAIN • WEATHERPROOF CONNECTOR • PLASTIC CONDUIT • APPROVED UNDERGROUND CABLING • PUMP

PUMP FITTINGS AND CONNECTORS

Most submersible pumps can be obtained with a flow adjuster and a T-piece connector, which can easily be fitted between the pump's outlet and the delivery pipe. The T-piece makes it possible to send water in two directions, so that one pump can operate both a waterfall and a fountain. Two flow adjusters may be necessary to control each branch, as more water will go along the one that has the least resistance.

STANDARD FITTINGS
The T-piece and flow adjuster are secured to the delivery pipe with a hoseclip.

FLOW ADJUSTER • T-PIECE • HOSE CLIP

POINTS TO CONSIDER

When selecting a pump, it is advisable to seek help from a specialist. You will need to be able to answer the following questions, where relevant:
• Is the pump required to operate a watercourse, fountain, or filter, or a combination of the three?
• What is the volume of the reservoir pool *(see pp. 60–61)*? The flow rate per hour should not exceed the reservoir pool's volume.
• For features where water runs downhill, what is the height of the header pool above the reservoir pool (known as the "head")?
• What is the width of any streams and spillways?
• What type of fountain spray is required?
• How high do you want the spray to be?

1½ IN (3.5CM) • 1IN (2.5CM) • ¾IN (2CM) • ½IN (1CM)

DELIVERY PIPES
Delivery pipes come in a range of sizes. It is important to be sure that diameter and length are suitable for the pump. Delivery pipes are made of flexible plastic and run directly from the pump to the delivery point: a filter, fountain, or header pool. Always check the dimensions of pump outlets before buying a delivery pipe, and always overestimate the length of pipe you will need.

ROUGH GUIDE TO FLOW RATE
If you can achieve the desired flow of water over a fall or down a stream using a hose, then time how long it takes the hose to fill a container of known capacity, keeping the same flow rate. Use this to estimate the flow rate required of the pump. For example, if the hose fills a 100-gallon/liter container in 10 minutes, then a pumping rate of 10 gallons/liters per minute will be required.

POSITIONING PUMPS AND FILTERS

All submersible pumps should be placed on a base to raise it just above the bottom in order to reduce the amount of sludge being drawn into the strainer. Surface pumps need some kind of housing in order to protect them from the elements and disguise their appearance. Submersible pumps operate silently and do not require priming. Modern surface pumps are also self-priming, but are noisy when operating. A well-built pump chamber will help cut down the noise, or if necessary the pump may be sited some distance from the water feature.

SUBMERSIBLE PUMPS

The positioning of submersible pumps depends on whether a surface filter is being used. Without a surface filter, the general rule is to let the water take the shortest route between pump and outlet. The farther the water has to travel through a pipe, the more it will be slowed down by friction. To maximize use of a pump's power, delivery pipes should be as short as possible: site pumps directly below fountains or under waterfalls. However, if a surface filter is being used, the rules are reversed: the pump should be as far from where the filtered water enters the pond as possible, or pockets of water that are never drawn around the system, and hence never filtered, will develop.

FILTER IN SITU
Filters should be at the highest point of circulating features.

POSITIONING FILTERS

Surface filters need to be placed at the highest point in the circulation system. They can be disguised with rocks or plantings, or they may be hidden under raised decking or behind walls, the filtered water returning via a culvert *(see p. 103)*. Where it is difficult to site a large filter on dry land, a submerged filter may be used that relies upon the pump's suction to draw water through the filtering media: the drawback is that water circulation may be uneven, which will cause beneficial bacteria to die.

PLANTING
Submerged plants will anchor in the filter medium.

BUILDING BRICKS
Bricks are inexpensive and inconspicuous.

FLOATING-LEAVED PLANTS

MARGINAL PLANTS

FILTER MEDIUM

PUMP

A SUBMERGED BIOLOGICAL FILTER

A submerged filter allows the pump to suck water through the filter media, rather than pushing it through, as in a surface filter. This example is simple and economical to build, using unobtrusive clay bricks and a natural filtering medium (see p. 71), rather than plastic. It may be disguised with shallow-rooting submerged plants that take nutrients up through their stems, not through their roots; these will happily anchor themselves in the upper layer of the filter material.

PREVENTING BACKFLOW

WATERFALL ARRANGEMENT
The pipe should discharge above water level so that the water in the header pool cannot flow back down it.

DELIVERY PIPE
The end of the pipe is above water level.

DIRECTION OF FLOW

PUMP

NOZZLE

FOUNTAIN ARRANGEMENT
If the delivery pipe is submerged, a non-return valve will prevent the water from flowing back when the pump is off.

SPILL STONE

DIRECTION OF FLOW

PUMP

FOUNTAIN

ONE-WAY VALVE

SURFACE PUMP CHAMBER

This small, watertight pump chamber has been installed directly beside a pond. The inlet pipe is not visible, having been mortared to the poolside wall and then painted with a commercial sealant. The construction of the pump chamber must allow room for a ventilation brick, and for a large piece of rigid pipe to accommodate both the incoming electricity cable and the inlet pipe. As a precaution against flooding, there should be a drainage hole at the base of the chamber.

1 MARK OUT THE outline of the chamber and lay trench foundations. Build brick walls four courses high, incorporating a ventilation brick and a conduit for the inlet pipe and cable.

2 THREAD THE MAIN electric cord and inlet pipe through the conduit. Then connect these to the surface pump, situated on a small paving slab inside the pump chamber.

3 FIT A LIGHT, wooden lid over the chamber, which can be easily removed for pump adjustment. Paint the lid with exterior-grade paint in a color in keeping with the garden.

FEATURES WITH STILL WATER

STILL-WATER PONDS are ideal for any site and provide a superb setting for a wide range of water plants – in particular water lilies, which dislike water movement. The pond may be formal or informal, raised or sunken, small or large, and can be built using a range of methods and materials. Additional interest can be created with a boggy area for moisture-loving plants or with an island.

FORMAL POOLS

The main characteristics of formal pools are clearly defined edges and geometrical shapes; squares, rectangles, and circles are the most popular. The formal style gives an opportunity to use and display decorative edging material; a formal pond is also often associated with a paved area. Careful attention to measurements, angles, and levels is essential when constructing a formal shape. Water, of course, always finds its own horizontal level, and few things are more revealing of uneven or sloping edges and paving than still water.

REFLECTIVE SURFACE
Use the reflective surface of still water to mirror surrounding plants and the sky, bringing light into enclosed areas. Do not allow floating-leaved plants to spread too abundantly or the effect will be lost.

PLANTING SOLUTIONS
This small informal feature, part pond, part bog garden, transforms what was a difficult planting area of dry semi-shade. The vigorous, paddlelike leaves of Lysichiton and the brightly variegated irises are a welcome respite from the somber background of rhododendrons, whose flower colors are accented by candelabra primroses.

ALONG THE WATERSIDE
A long, narrow pond can create the illusion of a stream flowing across a garden. Use flexible liner to incorporate broad bands of damp ground on each side (see p. 78), so that plenty of moisture-loving plants can be used, such as Gunnera manicata.

FORMAL, SEMI-RAISED POOL
The still surface of this formal, partially raised pool provides an ideal contrast to the rich detail of the surrounding banks.

SLOPING BANK
Do not simply pile up soil from the excavation to create a bank sloping down to a pond. Instead, landscape the whole site, using nutritious topsoil that will help plants grow vigorously, allowing their roots to consolidate the sloping ground.

Concrete is in many circumstances the obvious choice for constructing formal pools, which require straight, solid sides. In the past, concrete mix was used to form a thick shell – a time-consuming task involving building expertise. Today, with the evolution of building materials, it is far easier to construct a simple shell of concrete blocks and line this either with tough flexible material (for the range of liners, *see p. 67*) or with a thin skimming, or layer, of cement to which special reinforcing fiber has been added (*see pp. 90–91*).

INFORMAL PONDS

Informal ponds generally have curving edges. Although clay-lined ponds (*see pp. 92–93*) are the least artificial of all, the majority of gardeners will need to use a waterproof liner, whose edges should be carefully disguised. A kidney-shaped preformed unit (*see pp. 88–89*) can be made to look quite natural if plants are used to cover and soften its hard edge. However, flexible liner (*see pp. 76–79*) gives a great deal more freedom in constructing irregular shapes. It is best to keep the general outline simple: it is far easier to create inlets and promontories using rocks on top of the liner than to excavate and line a complicated shape. Islands (*see pp. 80–81*) may also be added on top of the liner, but incorporating these at the construction stage gives the option of creating either a "wet" or "dry" planting environment. An informal pond that has well-planted, shallow margins is particularly appealing to wildlife (*see pp. 54–55*); formal ponds, with straight edges above the waterline and vertical sides, are less accessible.

AN APPROPRIATE SIZE

Still-water features can be built in any shape or size. In the examples illustrated on the following pages, each feature is given a specific size so that a practical guide to construction can be included. However, using simple calculations (*see pp. 60–61*), the pond size and quantities of materials needed can be adapted to your requirements. Within the limits of site and the available budget, it is advisable to have as large a pond as possible: the smaller the volume of water, the more difficult it becomes to maintain a healthy ecosystem (*see pp. 136–137*). Sufficient depth is particularly important; a large area of shallow water exposed to sunlight will suffer problems due to algal buildup, which are extremely difficult to control (*see pp. 140–141*).

STOCKING AND MAINTENANCE

Knowing the volume and surface area of your pond will enable you to determine the quantity of plants (*see pp. 152–153*) and fish (*see p. 171*) that it can support. This is a useful guide for initial stocking; however, a pond is a dynamic world full of life that must be kept in harmony. Regular attention to maintenance (*see pp. 140–141*) will keep major tasks to a minimum.

SIMPLE PONDS WITH FLEXIBLE LINERS

FLEXIBLE LINERS ARE the most versatile material to use in the construction of pond. When choosing a liner, however, bear in mind that they vary considerably in their quality and durability *(see p. 67)*. Inexpensive polyethylene liners have a life expectancy of only three to five years if exposed to sunlight, while the more expensive PVC, EPDM, and butyl liners will last up to 50 years. When installing liner,

INFORMAL POND

make sure that no part of the material is left exposed above the waterline. This will not only spoil the look of the finished feature, it will also leave an area of liner exposed to sunlight, which will cause cheaper brands to harden and crack, resulting in leaks and a drop in the water level of the pond. To prevent the liner from being punctured by sharp objects such as stones or rocks, always use good quality underlay *(see pp. 66–67)*.

LINING A SIMPLE POND WITH SHELF

CONSTRUCTION GUIDE

To build and line a 10ft x 7ft (3m x 2.2m) pond, you will need:

TOOLS
- Sand or string to mark out pond
- 10 wooden pegs
- Rubber mallet
- Carpenter's level
- Straightedge
- Shovel, spade
- Rake

MATERIALS
- Soft sand or sifted soil: ½cu yd (0.5cu m)
- Polyethylene, geotextile, or old carpet underlay
- Flexible liner: 15ft x 12ft (5m x 4m)
- Bricks to hold liner temporarily in place

1 MARK THE OUTLINE of the pond *(see inset)*. Position a peg at the edge of the outline to indicate the proposed water level *(see p. 64)*. Position the remaining pegs regularly around the pond. Use a carpenter's level and a straightedge to check that all the pegs are level.

USING FLEXIBLE LINER

Before buying flexible liner and underlay, calculate how much will be needed to line the pond *(see p. 66)*, including enough for a generous overlap. Preferably, unroll the liner and lay it flat in the sun for at least half an hour. The heat will increase the liner's flexibility and help to ease out any stiff creases. Roll it up again to make fitting easier. When fitting liner into an irregularly shaped pond, do not strain it tightly over the contours of the excavation, since this will reduce its natural elasticity and make it more likely to be punctured by sharp objects like stones or rocks.

2 REMOVE SOD 2in (5cm) deep and 12in (30cm) wide from the pond edge. Excavate the entire area to a depth of 9in (22cm). Rake the surface, then outline the proposed deep zone with sand. Leave marginal shelf areas that are at least 12in (30cm) wide to accommodate plants. (A separate bog garden or wide shelves are preferable where raccoons may visit ponds.)

3 EXCAVATE THE MARKED AREA to a depth of at least 18in (44cm). Excavate to a minimum of 30in (76cm) to overwinter goldfish; 3–4ft (90–120cm) for koi. Rake the floor of the hole and remove any large or sharp stones. Then spread a 1in (2.5cm) layer of soft sand at the bottom of the excavation, where the water pressure will be strongest. Remove the pegs.

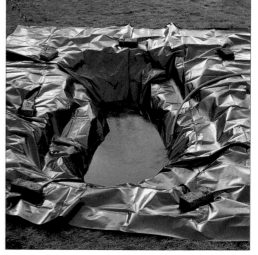

4 DRAPE THE UNDERLAY over the hole, then press firmly into the contours. Unroll the liner over the hole. Use bricks to hold the edges temporarily in place, and slowly fill the pond with water. The increasing weight of the water will settle the liner into the more difficult contours. Pleat any large creases as necessary. Adjust the bricks to allow the liner to settle.

5 THE POND IS NOW ready to be edged *(see pp. 126–129).* For an informal grass edging, trim the liner to leave a 6in (15cm) overlap. Replace the sod removed earlier; firm it down, and water well. For a formal, sharp-edged grass edge – or if the edge will take heavy traffic – make provision at the planning stage to dig out and add a foundation *(see right)* as for a paved edge.

INFORMAL AND FORMAL EDGINGS WITH FOUNDATIONS

There is a wide range of edging materials and styles to choose from *(see pp. 126–131).* For hard edging materials such as paving, or where earth may crumble under turf, foundations are advisable. This involves digging out a strip around the pond to a depth of 6–9in (15–23cm). The liner may be rolled over this outer shelf and the foundation laid on top of it *(left).* Bear in mind that the foundation will be visible, so choose attractive materials such as granite blocks, mortaring these together to prevent water leakage. To hide a brick and concrete foundation *(right),* lay the liner on top of it.

GREENER GRASS
Until it is ready to be put in place, roll back the sod *(as shown)* or stack it grass to grass.

BLOCKS
To strengthen the area closest to the water – and to disguise the liner – place sod on blocks mortared onto the liner. Once the mortar has set, backfill.

STABLE PAVING
Crazy paving should be carefully leveled, and laid flush with surrounding sod to prevent tripping and to ease mowing.

PERFECT DISGUISE
Sandwiching the liner and underlay between two layers of concrete serves to secure them and hide them from sight.

SOD

SOIL BACKFILL

LINER AND UNDERLAY

DEEP ZONE

BRICKS AND CONCRETE FOUNDATION

POND WITH CRAZY PAVING EDGE
Almost any artificially created pond can be transformed by strategic planting. Once the pond and its planted environs are established, it will be virtually impossible to distinguish it from a "natural" water feature. To make it easier for frogs and other water-seeking wildlife to climb out if they fall in, include at least one paving stone that slopes into the water. Overhanging paving stones provide fish with shade, and will help to disguise the liner by casting a shadow.

MULTIPURPOSE FLEXIBLE LINERS

The use of flexible liner has become increasingly popular; it is now so widely available that there is a good case for completing all the necessary pond or stream excavations before buying the liner. By finishing the excavation first, last-minute variations can be made to the depth and shape of the feature without having to take into account the width and length of a liner bought at the planning stage. When the excavation is complete, view it from a distance, or from a window in the house; a fresh perspective might suggest any number of variations and allow you to judge the effect that a differently shaped or enlarged water feature will have on the surroundings.

COMPLEX SHAPES

More complex shapes designed to enhance particular surroundings are easier to create with flexible liner than with materials that require building skills. Liner is generally sold in a wide range of precut sizes, although some dealers sell from rolls of various widths. One length of liner can be made to fit several shapes. If the liner is much too large for a narrow section of pond or stream, plan to use the excess to create peripheral features. It is best to avoid seaming together pieces of liner. For streams, use a separate sheet overlapped by the main pool liner, but only if the overlap is above standing water level.

ADDING PLANTING FEATURES

One of the greatest advantages in using flexible liner is the variety of depths and edges that can be incorporated in one pond (see below). By allowing adequate surplus liner around

NATURAL EDGING
It is much easier to disguise the edges of flexible liner than it is to disguise the edges of rigid units or concrete pools. Here, large, rounded stones, along with marginal and moisture-loving plants, make a perfect disguise.

the sides of the pond above the waterline, it is quite simple to incorporate features such as integral planting beds, boggy areas, or a stone beach (see pp. 80–81). If the flexible liner is buried beneath the soil, even if above the water level, plants in the surrounding soil will draw moisture from the pond; this is known as the "wick effect." In small planting areas, this is useful for moisture-lovers, as they will take the water they

CREATING PLANTING ENVIRONMENTS WITH FLEXIBLE LINER
This pond was designed to include several planting environments (see pp. 148–149), each of which allows plants to grow without the need for containers. The main pond is deep enough to support submerged plants, the shallower pocket beside it, marginals. A combination of marginal and bog plants grow in the pondside pockets made with surplus liner.

FILLING UP
A rain barrel equipped with a tap and buried hose leading into the pond is an ideal way to replace water lost through the "wick effect" of a large integral bog garden.

LIGULARIA

IMPERMEABLE BARRIER
Small rocks mortared onto the hump of the liner disguise the liner and create an impermeable barrier between the pond and a large bog garden.

HOSTA

SATURATED SOIL
For soil to be permanently wet for marginal plants, the water level must stay above the dividing hump of the liner.

PERMEABLE BARRIER
Rocks and sod allow water to constantly seep out of the pond to adjacent moisture-loving plants.

LYSICHITON

IRIS

CAREX

CALTHA

INDEPENDENT BOG GARDEN
Large bog gardens should be independent of the pond, or they will drain it of water.

STABILIZING BARRIER
Add a layer of stones or a weed mat under the liner to prevent the hump from leveling out.

SUBMERGED WATER LILY

VARIED PLANTING
The moisture content of the soil beyond the immediate edge of the liner will accommodate both marginal and moisture-loving plants.

need from the pond. If a large bog garden is not independent of the pond, however, the "wick effect" can quickly lower the level of water in the pond. To prevent this, the liner should come up out of the ground, or should have rocks or pavers mortared onto it to stop water from seeping out. Or, install a filling-up system using a rain barrel *(see facing page)*.

LINING FORMAL SHAPES

Liners are often used to waterproof old, damaged concrete pools or containers that leak, such as old barrels. Always use top-grade butyl or EPDM liner where there are sharp edges or corners to be covered; the cheaper PVC liners are liable to tear in these circumstances. However, using top-grade liner in a large pool can be expensive; it is more economical to use a layer of cement mixed with reinforcing fibers over the shell of large, regularly shaped formal pools *(see pp. 90–91)*.

FOLDING A LINER

Sharp curves in informal ponds and the angles of corners in formal rectangular pools, will inevitably result in large creases having to be made in the liner. Careful folding of the liner can, however, make these folds look less conspicuous; the folds may also be disguised with coping stones or, in the case of informal ponds, with stones mortared onto the liner *(see p. 67)*. Once the pond is filled, the weight of water should hold the folds down; alternatively, pleated material can be secured with two-sided

---

WATERPROOFING A BARREL

Old half-barrels make charming container water features, but they may leak. A lining of inexpensive polyethylene or PVC will make them watertight. Fold the liner neatly around the inside edges of the barrel, as shown here. Then wedge – and disguise – the liner under a small, thin wooden strip fixed to the inside top edge of the barrel with galvanized screws. Secure the strip as near as possible to the top of the barrel, so that the screws do not penetrate the liner and are clear of the water. Then trim back the excess liner.

LINING A BARREL

---

waterproof tape. When making folds, make sure that there is ample liner at your disposal, so that the material does not have to be stretched too much, as the sheer weight of the water may cause it to split. Whatever the shape of the water feature, formal or informal, always complete the task of folding the liner before releasing water into the pool; the weight of only a few liters/gallons of water will make further manipulation of the liner very difficult, and may cause it to rupture.

FLEXIBLE LINER IN FORMAL POOL

This cross-section of a formal pool demonstrates how basic contstruction materials and flexible liner can be used to accommodate a variety of planting environments. A marginal shelf, suitable for containerized marginal plants, is created by drawing the liner over loosely mortared bricks. Integral planting beds can also be built on top of the liner, either along the sides of the pool or free-standing in the center.

MAKING FOLDS
Create a neat corner fold by making a diagonal pleat in the liner. Use bricks to secure the liner until the weight of the water can keep the fold in place.

CORNER BED
Loosely mortared clay bricks allow water to seep into the soil of the marginal planting bed.

SUBMERGED PLANTING BED
This planting bed for water lilies, 2ft x 2ft (60cm x 60cm) in size, is built with loosely mortared clay bricks and filled with topsoil.

TOPSOIL

MARGINAL PLANTING BED
An integral marginal planting bed can be created by building a parallel wall with walling blocks and loosely mortared clay bricks.

FLEXIBLE LINER AND UNDERLAY

CRUSHED STONE

CONCRETE

FOLDING THE LINER
Always finish folding the liner before filling the pool with water.

BUILT-IN SHELF
Concrete blocks can be used beneath the liner to construct firm marginal shelves.

CONCRETE BLOCKS

FURTHER INFORMATION

- Siting Water Features – pp. 56–57
- Simple Ponds with Flexible Liners – pp. 76–79
- Beaches and Islands – pp. 80–81
- Raised Pools with Flexible Liners – pp. 86–87

BEACHES AND ISLANDS

ROCKS AND PEBBLES

MANY PONDS FAIL to attain their full potential as wildlife habitats (see also pp. 54–55) because their construction deters wild creatures who will not approach water they might fall into and not be able to get out of. Almost vertical side walls and large gaps between the water surface and overhanging coping stones or paved edges are common obstacles. A beach, gently sloping toward the water, is not only visually appealing but will also allow access for a great variety of wildlife. It is better to make provision for islands at the design stage, although it is possible to install a "wet" island in an existing pond (see facing page). Formal features tend not to have islands, but submerged formal beds can be built (see pp. 78–79) with retaining walls constructed from house or decorative bricks, and filled with topsoil.

MAKING A STONE BEACH
Before positioning the underlay and liner, dig a shallow shelf sloping down to the water. The shelf should be 4–6in (10–15cm) deep at its lowest point and, to achieve a gentle, "natural" gradient, at least 2–3ft (60–90cm) wide. Extend the liner over the prepared area. Build up a "lip" at the edge of the beach – as shown here – by mortaring stones in place.

PLANTING POCKETS
Soil between stones forms wet pockets for marginal plants.

STONE FLOOR
To protect the liner and underlay, use smooth, rounded river rock.

LINER EDGE
Make sure the edge of the liner extends well above the water level, and is concealed with stones.

NATURAL OUTCROPPINGS
Protruding stones provide birds and other creatures with stepping stones, as well as with basking and resting places.

FLEXIBLE LINER AND UNDERLAY

RETAINING WALL
Mortar a row of large river rocks onto the liner to prevent smaller rocks from slipping into deeper water.

GRAVEL BEACH
A simple, gently sloping pea gravel beach is an inexpensive, easy-to-install feature, which will be welcomed by small creatures attracted to the water's edge by the easily negotiable terrain. Only smooth, washed pea gravel should be used, since sharp stones could damage the liner. To stop the gravel from slipping into deeper water, mortar a retaining row of large river rocks directly onto the liner.

CHOOSING STONES

For the most natural effect, select stones local to your area; imported ones can look artificial. Rock collecting is prohibited on many beaches and in natural areas. If you are able to gather stones at the beach, wash them thoroughly before using them in the pond; residual salt on the stones may damage pondlife.

GRADED PEBBLE BEACH
Pebbles and rounded stones both small and large make a natural-looking covering for a shallow beach. Imitate nature by grading the stones, with the smallest nearest the water. Where the beach slopes away into deeper water, mortar down a row of stones to prevent the rest from slipping into the pond. The pebble floor will protect the liner from the claws of birds and animals, and from the damaging effects of ultraviolet light.

CONSTRUCTING ISLANDS

Ideally islands should be incorporated when the pond is built. To ensure stability, they should be at least 4ft (1.2m) across; anything smaller than this will limit the number and variety of plants the island can accommodate. As a result, it will not provide wildlife – primarily birds – with shelter, nesting sites, and protection from predators. The retaining walls can be constructed from sandbags, although polypropylene bags filled with smooth river rocks are longer lasting. Since an island will reduce the volume of water in a pond – thus affecting the pond's ecosystem (*see pp. 136–137*) – the surface area of the water should be a minimum of four times the surface area of the island (*see pp. 60–61*). The inclusion of both a "wet" and a "dry" island in one large pond will provide sites for a wide range of plants with differing moisture requirements.

MAKING DRY ISLANDS

Dry islands, which are designed to provide normal soil conditions, should be pre-planned and constructed at the same time as the pond. In a flexible-liner pond, dig a moat around a flat-topped mound of earth that extends 4–6in (10–15cm) above the proposed waterline. Fit the liner over the contours of the mound; then, to expose the topsoil of the mound for planting, cut away the liner covering the top of the mound above the waterline. Finally, disguise the edges of the liner with topsoil or sod. Remember that it may be necessary to water plants on dry islands in dry conditions.

MAKING WET ISLANDS

To incorporate a shallow wet island in a pond at the design stage, leave a flat-topped mound in the excavation that is at least 9in (22cm) lower than the proposed water level, covering the mound

CROSS-SECTION OF A WET AND A DRY ISLAND

The retaining walls of this shallow wet island (below, left) are constructed with layers of inverted sod. To prevent the topsoil from dispersing before the spreading roots of the plants can knit it together, use heavy soil high in clay content. The flexible liner on the dry island (below, right) extends above the waterline. It is disguised and protected beneath two layers of sod.

BUILDING A WET ISLAND IN AN EXISTING POND

First, drain the pond water, then build up inward-sloping retaining walls with sandbags or polypropylene bags filled with rubble. Once the first three bags are in place, fill the center with 10–12in (24–30cm) of rubble. Build up the walls and fill with topsoil. When they are within 4–6in (10–15cm) of the final water level, disguise them with two layers of inverted sod.

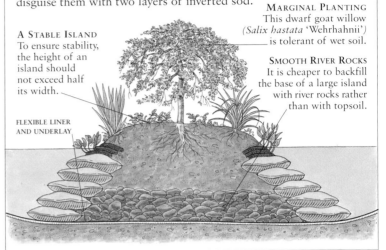

A STABLE ISLAND
To ensure stability, the height of an island should not exceed half its width.

MARGINAL PLANTING
This dwarf goat willow (*Salix hastata* 'Wehrhahnii') is tolerant of wet soil.

SMOOTH RIVER ROCKS
It is cheaper to backfill the base of a large island with river rocks rather than with topsoil.

FLEXIBLE LINER AND UNDERLAY

with the liner and underlay. Build up low walls around the edges of the mound with inverted sod (*see below, left*). Fill with heavy soil, which will not easily disperse. To build a "wet" island in an existing pond, the pond should have a level bottom and a stable base (*see above*). Marginal plants such as *Calla palustris* (hardy calla) will thrive in wet island conditions.

CREATING A WET ISLAND

Provided a flat-topped mound has been left under the liner to within 12in (30cm) of the final water level, a wet island is easy to build with a wall of inverted pieces of sod retaining the topsoil. Once the sod wall is in place, build up the center of the island for planting.

WET CONDITIONS
Moisture seeps through walls to provide wet planting conditions.

MARGINALS
Marginal plants with creeping root systems will consolidate the soil.

SUCCESSFUL DISGUISE
Inverted sod disguise the flexible liner lying above the waterline.

PLANTING MEDIUM
Use good-quality topsoil for the planting area.

RETAINING WALLS
For a shallow island, inverted sod make suitable retaining walls.

WATER LEVEL
The water is above liner level for the wet island, and below it for the dry island.

WATERPROOF LINER
To prevent water from seeping into the soil, flexible liner extends above the waterline.

FURTHER INFORMATION

- Encouraging Wildlife – pp. 54–55
- ConstructionTools and Materials – pp. 62–63
- Construction Techniques – pp. 64–69
- Simple Ponds with Flexible Liners – pp. 76–79

BOG GARDENS

BOG, OR MARGINAL, gardens may be incorporated into an existing water feature by extending the flexible liner out beyond the reaches of the pond. They can also be designed as stand-alone features, completely independent of a pond or water garden. In fact, a bog garden is one of the simplest, cheapest, and most water-efficient ways of creating an environment for plants that demand constantly high soil

BOG GARDEN

moisture. Small boggy areas can be created anywhere in the garden that you would like to add pockets of moisture-loving plants. Simply dig out a depression, line it with polyethylene, fill it with soil, and water by hand as needed. A less laborious option is shown here. The plants are grouped together in an area that has a specially designed irrigation system, so that the entire garden can be watered easily and quickly.

CREATING A BOG GARDEN

CONSTRUCTION GUIDE
To create a round bog garden approximately 8ft (2.4m) across, you will need:
TOOLS
• Spade, rake, garden fork
• Knife or scissors
• Hacksaw, drill
MATERIALS
• Sand or string for marking out
• Heavy-duty polyethylene sheet: 11ft x 11ft (3.5m x 3.5m)
• Bricks or stones to hold liner down temporarily
• Pea gravel: ½cu yd (0.5cu m)
• Rigid plastic pipe: 7ft (2m) long, 1in (2.5cm) in diameter
• 2 elbow joints
• Short length of hose, hose clamp, and hose connector with male/female lock

1 MARK OUT THE REQUIRED SHAPE with string or sand. Dig a hole approximately 2ft (60cm) deep, with sloping sides to minimize the crumbling of light soil. Keep the topsoil nearby on a polyethylene sheet for replacement. Rake the area and remove any large or sharp stones.

LINING AND DRAINING
The lining used in a bog garden that is independent is covered with soil and need not be completely watertight. In fact, since it will have holes pierced in it never use expensive pool liner; polyethylene sheeting will serve the purpose just as well. The holes are necessary to allow water in the soil to drain away, albeit very slowly, otherwise it will become stagnant and anaerobic (allowing harmful bacterial activity). Drainage is vital for the growth of many moisture-loving plants that will not survive in saturated soil. Drainage is aided by the layer of pea gravel, which also prevents the holes in the irrigation pipe becoming blocked.

CONSTRUCTION OF A BOG GARDEN

A bog garden should contain free-draining but moisture-retentive soil; topsoil can be improved by the addition of organic matter (see pp. 150–151) to increase its water-retentiveness. To prevent the bog from drying out too quickly, aim for a minimum depth of 18in (45cm), and plant densely.

PRIMULA JAPONICA

RHEUM PALMATUM

CALTHA PALUSTRIS

MATTEUCCIA STRUTHIOPTERIS

DISGUISING HOSE
Use a large plant to conceal the hose connection.

HOSE CLAMP

HOSE CONNECTOR
Use a short length of hose with a connector to attach garden hose to the pipe.

PLANTING SOIL
Topsoil from the excavation, improved if necessary, is used to refill the hole.

PEA GRAVEL
Layer of gravel protects pipe and aids drainage.

ELBOW JOINT

PERFORATED RIGID PIPE
The perforations allow water to seep slowly and evenly into the soil.

POLYETHYLENE SHEET
Hide the polyethylene liner approximately 3in (6cm) beneath the soil.

BLOCKED END
Block off one end of the rigid pipe to prevent water from saturating the soil.

PERFORATIONS
To assist drainage, pierce the liner at intervals.

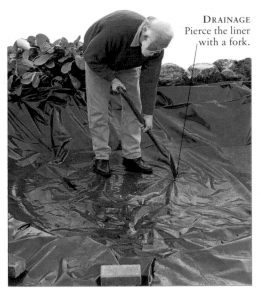

DRAINAGE
Pierce the liner with a fork.

PERFORATED RIGID PIPE
Lay the perforated rigid pipe between two layers of pea gravel before filling the hole with topsoil.

2 **DRAPE THE LINING** material over the excavation and press it into the contours. Put bricks or stones around the edges of the sheet to keep it in place while you walk on it. To make holes for drainage, pierce the liner at 3ft (1m) intervals with a garden fork.

3 **SPREAD A 2IN (5CM) LAYER** of pea gravel over the sheet. Then cut a 2ft (60cm) length off the rigid pipe. Drill holes along the longer section at 6in (15cm) intervals, then lay it across the base.

Block one end and, at the other, use an elbow joint to join on the short pipe so that it extends vertically above ground level. Spread another 2in (5cm) layer of gravel over the pipe.

REPLACING TOPSOIL
Rake the top layer of pea gravel level, then replace the topsoil.

4 **SHOVEL IN THE SOIL** and firm it. Before the soil reaches the top of the excavation, trim off any surplus liner and hide the edges under a 3in (7cm) layer of soil. Remove the bricks and any excess soil. Attach the second elbow joint to the protruding pipe, creating a right-angle turn. Fit the short length of hose onto it with the hose clamp, and attach the garden hose connector.

PLANTED BOG GARDEN
Fill up the bog garden whenever the soil surface is dry (this could be weekly in hot spells), adding water until the soil surface floods, to keep plants growing well. One of the advantages of a separate bog is that garden fertilizer can be used without the danger of it seeping into the water of a pond and affecting its chemistry.

FURTHER INFORMATION
- Wildlife Pond with Bog Garden – pp. 40–43
- Simple Ponds with Flexible Liners – pp. 76–79
- Soils and Containers – pp. 150–151

RIGID POOL UNITS

PREFORMED RIGID POOL units are easy to install, and can be a good choice for a small water feature. Rigid units are particularly well suited to formal gardens, especially if the surrounding area is to be paved, since it is easier to disguise the smooth, often shiny edges of the unit with paving stones *(see p. 127)* rather than with plants. Many commercially available rigid units incorporate shelves designed to

RIGID UNIT IN POSITION

accommodate planting crates that fit into the contours of the unit. Units come in many sizes, styles, and colors; their smooth surfaces make them easy to clean. Although not difficult to install, the units do become very heavy when filled with water. If the site has not been properly prepared *(see also pp. 64–65)*, the build-up of water pressure can cause the unit to fracture as the earth settles under the weight of the water.

INSTALLING A RIGID POOL UNIT

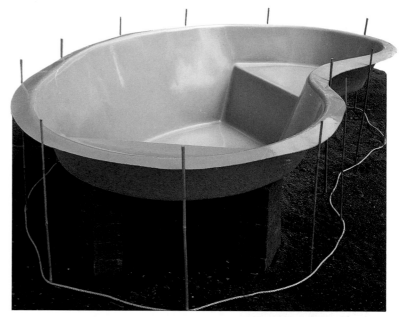

CONSTRUCTION GUIDE

To install a rigid pool unit with marginal shelves, you will need:

TOOLS
- Stakes, string
- Spade, rake
- Straightedge, carpenter's level
- Tamping tool
- Tape measure
- Hose

MATERIALS
- Rigid pool unit
- Bricks to support the unit temporarily
- Soft sand or sifted soil, enough to line the floor of the excavation to a depth of 2in (5cm)

1 IF THE UNIT CHOSEN is completely symmetrical it can simply be turned upside down and its outline marked directly on to the ground. For irregular shapes, supporting the unit in exactly the right position, so that it can be marked around accurately, can be an awkward job and is easier with a helper. You can temporarily support the unit on bricks *(see right)*. Once satisfied with the position of the unit, check that it is level with a carpenter's level, then mark out its shape by pushing stakes into the ground around the perimeter. Lay a length of string around these stakes to indicate the area to be excavated.

CONSTRUCTION TIPS

- Preformed units come in a wide range of sizes and shapes, so shop around for one that matches your requirements.
- Preformed pool units always look smaller after they have been installed and edged, so overestimate the size of unit that you require.
- If you want the pond to be a lasting feature, invest in a good-quality fiberglass unit; these are also easier to repair.
- If intending to stock with fish, check that the unit is of an adequate size and depth. Choose fish species that will be happy in a relatively small pond.
- Check that any marginal shelves are wide enough to accommodate planting baskets securely.
- A non-abrasive bathroom cleaner applied with a soft cloth is ideal for cleaning pool units, but all traces of the cleaner must be rinsed away thoroughly before installing fish and plants.

2 MEASURE THE DEPTH of the unit from the lip to the marginal shelves, and dig a hole to this depth, 4in (10cm) wider than the unit all around. Place the unit (right side up) in the hole and press down gently. The mark left by the deep zone will act as a guide for further digging.

3 EXCAVATE THE DEEP area, checking depths by measuring down from the straightedge *(as above)*. Make the hole 2in (5cm) deeper than the deep zone, and add a 2in (5cm) layer of leveled soft sand or sifted soil. Smooth and firm the sides and shelf areas of the hole, removing all stones.

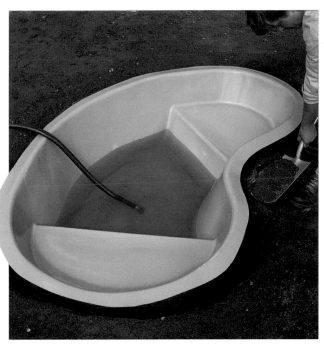

5 To increase the stability of the pool, fill it with water to a depth of 4in (10cm), then start to backfill around the pool with soft sand or sifted soil (see p. 65). Using the straightedge and the carpenter's level, check regularly that the unit is absolutely level, then tamp down the backfill of soft sand or sifted soil at intervals. Continue to add 4in (10cm) of water at a time and to backfill and tamp around the unit. Once the unit is filled to within 2in (5cm) of its final depth, prepare the surrounding area for whichever edging material has been chosen (see pp. 126–129). If paving stones are to overlap the rim of the pool, it is important to make sure that their weight is supported. You will need to add a foundation of crushed stone topped with a thick layer of sand under the lip of the unit.

4 Lower the unit into place and press it down gently so that the deep zone fits snugly into its hole and the unit is completely level. You may need to remove the unit and make adjustments several times until the unit is fully supported by the contours of the excavation.

DISGUISING A RIGID POOL UNIT

This kidney-shaped pool is cleverly disguised, with paving that overlaps the water around the perimeter of the pond. Both the choice and positioning of plants growing outside the surrounding pavement, such as the bearded iris in the foreground, enhance the informal aspects of the pond. However, plants such as these must be able to grow in normal dry soil, as no moisture will escape from the pool. If the pool has built-in marginal shelves, the plants growing in the planting baskets standing on the shelves will also help to disguise the rim of the unit.

FURTHER INFORMATION

- Measuring Areas and Volumes – pp. 60–61
- Semi-raised Rigid Pool Units – pp. 88–89
- Rigid Stream Units – pp. 104–105
- Edging Materials – pp. 126–129
- Decking – pp. 130–131

RAISED POOLS WITH FLEXIBLE LINERS

DECORATIVE BRICKS

RAISED AND SEMI-RAISED pools make excellent focal points in formal or courtyard gardens, especially where their low surrounding walls can be used as casual seats from which to observe water plants and aquatic life at close quarters. Because of freezing winter temperatures, raised pools are best for zones 7 and south. In the North, reinforced high-strength concrete would be more suitable. Raised pools need little

excavation, are less likely to become cluttered with debris and, because their walls can be built to varying heights, they offer a fine design solution on sloping sites. On the other hand, they are more costly than the sunken variety and take more time to build. A raised pool is often set within a paved area. In many cases, the shape of the pavers will suggest the shape of the pool, as with the hexagonal slabs below.

BUILDING A RAISED HEXAGONAL POOL

CONSTRUCTION GUIDE

To build this pool, 2ft (60cm) high, and 9ft 3in (2.8m) between opposite corners, you will need:

TOOLS
- String, stakes, spade, shovel, plank, carpenter's level, straightedge, bricklayer's trowel

MATERIALS
- Concrete mix: ½in (20mm) ballast: ½cu yd (0.5cu m), two 50lb (22kg) bags of cement
- 60 concrete blocks: 12in x 8in x 3in (30cm x 21cm x 8cm); 30 wall ties
- Ready-mix mortar: 10 x 80lb (36kg) bags
- Liner and underlay: 14ft sq (4.2m sq)
- Rigid overflow pipe: 11in (28cm) long, ¾in (2cm) in diameter
- 380 decorative bricks: 12in x 3in x 2½in (30cm x 8cm x 6cm); 18 coping stones: 24in x 10½in x 2in (60cm x 25cm x 5cm)

REINFORCED WATERPROOF CABLE CONDUIT

1 MARK THE PERIMETER OF THE POOL with stakes and string, and install the paving (see p. 127). Dig a trench 18in (45cm) wide and 8in (20cm) deep inside the perimeter. Insert stakes to establish a horizontal level about 1in (2.5cm) below ground or paving level, then pour in concrete, and tamp and level it with a straight plank.

CONSTRUCTION TIPS

Because of the pressure exerted by water, raised pools over 18in (45cm) high should be built with double walls. The foundation trench of this pool's walls is 18in (45cm) wide – twice the width of the 9in (22cm) double wall. The trench is filled with a concrete mix consisting of ballast (a mixture of sand and small stones) and cement, which should be allowed to dry for at least 48 hours before work on the walls begins. Ready-mixed mortar can be used for both walls. Wall ties, set 3ft (1m) apart, will consolidate the strength of the walls. Pavers and coping stones are often available in pre-cut halves. For advice on how to cut stone, see pp. 68–69.

2 WHEN THE CONCRETE IS DRY, build twin walls 2in (5cm) apart. Use two courses of concrete blocks for the inner wall, and the decorative bricks for the outer wall. Work in from each corner; use a line and a carpenter's level regularly to check that the walls are level and vertical. Reinforce with wall ties 3ft (1m) apart (see inset).

3 BUILD THE OUTER WALL to a height of 2ft (60cm), 6in (15cm) higher than the inner wall. Allow 24 hours for the mortar to dry. Drape the underlay and liner in the pool and up and over both walls, and smooth into position (see pp. 76–77). Temporarily secure the overlap of liner on the inner and outer wall with bricks.

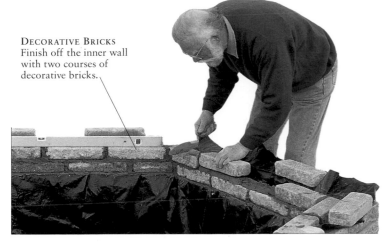

DECORATIVE BRICKS
Finish off the inner wall with two courses of decorative bricks.

CUTTING BRICKS AND STONES
For advice on how to cut bricks, walling stones, and coping stones, see pp. 68–69.

4 TO MAKE THE WALLS LEVEL, mortar two courses of decorative bricks onto the liner overlapping the top of the inner wall. The coping stones will sit across the two walls, so it is important to keep checking levels along the wall *and* across the gap.

5 MORTAR THE COPING STONES onto the inner wall and the overlapping liner on the outer wall. Below one of them, mortar in the plastic tube as an overflow pipe (*see below*). Mortar in another one through which to thread electric cable, if desired. Check that the coping stones are level.

IDEAL HEIGHT
The ideal height for a raised pool is 24–30in (60–75cm).

COPING STONES
Overhanging coping stones provide shade and shelter for fish.

OVERFLOW PIPE
An overflow pipe hidden beneath coping stones will prevent water from flooding over the sides of a pool after prolonged or heavy rainfall.

SECTION THROUGH DOUBLE WALL
This section of a raised pool wall shows how the liner and underlay are hidden by mortaring them beneath the two final courses of decorative bricks on the inner wall.

ORNAMENTAL FINISH
For an attractive finish, use decorative bricks for the outer wall.

INSTALLING ELECTRICITY IN A RAISED POOL

If planning to include electrical features such as lighting (*see pp. 124–125*) or a fountain (*see pp. 108–109*), install the wiring as the pool is being built. When installing electric cables for pumps, fountains, or lighting, safety precautions should be paramount (*see p. 72*). Use only equipment specifically designed for outdoor or underwater use. All cabling attached to electrical equipment used in water comes ready-sealed. As a further precaution, when the cable is to be embedded in the foundation, mortared between courses of bricks, or under a coping stone, run the cable through a length of reinforced waterproof hose – as shown in step one (*facing page*).

COPING STONE

ELECTRIC CABLE

WATERPROOF CONNECTOR

LINER AND UNDERLAY

REINFORCED WATERPROOF CONDUIT

CONCRETE FOUNDATION

FINISHED POOL WITH PLANTING
Although formal pools are not generally as densely planted as informal ponds, floating-leaved plants, irises, and tall grasses are often introduced. The floating leaves of water lilies (Nymphaea) provide shade and shelter for fish, as well as checking the growth of algae by partly blocking out sunlight.

FURTHER INFORMATION

- Choosing a Water Feature – pp. 52–53
- Siting Water Features – pp. 56–57
- Construction Tools and Materials – pp. 62–63
- Construction Techniques – pp. 64–69

SEMI-RAISED RIGID POOL UNITS

Although preformed rigid pool units are most commonly sunk in the ground *(see pp. 84–85)*, they can also be used as semi-raised pools provided the sides are given strong support. Although raised pools installed at ground level can make attractive features, they will freeze during the winter. This is less of a problem if the unit is partially buried in a shallow excavation, so that its deep zones are insulated

FORMAL RAISED POOL

by the surrounding earth. Use a pond heater to completely prevent freezing in winter. Materials such as log-roll edging, large rocks, decorative coping stones, or bricks are ideal for surrounding a pool. In addition to concealing the outer surfaces of the raised unit, they can provide support for topsoil packed between the outer wall and the rigid mold; spreading plants grown here will soon cover the lip of the pool.

INSTALLING A SEMI-RAISED RIGID POOL UNIT

CONSTRUCTION GUIDE

To install a 6ft (2m) long, 18in (45cm) deep, 3ft (1m) wide rigid pool unit and log-roll edging, you will need:

TOOLS
- Rake, spade
- Carpenter's level, straightedge
- Tamping tool
- Hammer, wirecutters

MATERIALS
- Soft sand or sifted soil: enough to line the floor of the excavation and for backfilling
- 9 treated, pointed wood stakes: 18in x 1½in (45cm x 4cm)
- Log-roll edging: 20ft x 9in (6m x 22cm)
- Twenty-four 2in (5cm) galvanized nails

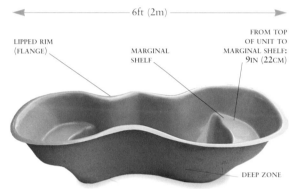

6ft (2m)

LIPPED RIM (FLANGE)

MARGINAL SHELF

FROM TOP OF UNIT TO MARGINAL SHELF: 9IN (22CM)

DEEP ZONE

RIGID POOL UNIT
This preformed pool unit is of average size: 6ft (2m) long, 18in (45cm) deep, and 3ft (1m) at its widest point. It has two marginal shelves and is made of fiberglass, which has a life expectancy of at least 20 years. The pool's shiny surface makes it easy to clean.

1 WHEN A SITE has been chosen, clear the area of stones and organic debris and rake the surface of the area. To make a clearly visible imprint of the base of the unit, place it on the raked area and press down firmly. The impression left on the soil will show you where to dig.

CROSS-SECTION OF RIGID UNIT IN PLACE

The pool will look more pleasing if the unit is buried to the height of its marginal shelf, leaving only 9in (22cm) of the mold above the ground. Partial burying is also a fairly simple way to install preformed units on a sloping site, as only the upper part of the slope will need to be excavated to ensure that the unit is level.

LOG ROLL

MARGINAL SHELF

ALPINE PLANTS

POINTED WOODEN STAKE

EXCAVATION FOR DEEP ZONE

TOPSOIL

2 DIG A HOLE with slightly sloping sides, 2in (5cm) wider than the imprint left by the unit's base, and 2in (5cm) deeper than the deep zone of the unit. The extra depth allows for a layer of soft sand or sifted soil, the extra width for backfilling to support the unit sides.

3 PLACE THE UNIT in the hole and use the straightedge and carpenter's level to check that it is level. If adjustments are necessary, remove the unit and add or remove sand beneath it. Begin backfilling around the sides *(see p. 64)* with soft sand or sifted soil.

4 **FILL THE UNIT WITH WATER** to a depth of approximately 3–4in (7–10cm). This will stabilize the pool while the backfill is being tamped. Use a hammer to drive stakes into the ground around the perimeter of the unit at 3ft (1m) intervals. To ensure that the stakes firmly support the log-roll edging at least as much of the stake should be below as above ground. The top of the stakes should be level with the lip of the unit and with the top of the log roll when it is in place. The height of the edging should equal the depth of the unit from the lip to the marginal shelf (here 9in/22cm).

5 **UNROLL THE STRIP OF LOG EDGING** and place it in position around the stakes. The logs are attached to each other with wire, so the roll is fairly flexible and should fit easily around the contours of the pool. If at any point the top of the log roll is found to be slightly higher than the rim of the unit and the top of the stakes, dig a narrow trench and partially bury the base of the log roll. Since log rolls are sold in fixed lengths, you will need extra wire to join on another section if the edging comes up short. Use wirecutters to cut the connecting wires if there is surplus log roll.

ADDING PLANTS

Small plants in the free-draining topsoil between the log roll and the rigid unit will soon disguise and soften the shiny rim of the unit. Alpines such as Sempervivum *(houseleek),* Cyclamen, *and* Saxifraga *are ideal. Topdress the soil with grit to conserve moisture and prevent soil dispersal.*

6 **ONCE THE LOG ROLL** has been wrapped around and cut to length, join the two ends with wire. Then use 2in (5cm) nails to fix the log rolls to the wooden stakes already in place. For extra strength, use two nails, one at the top and one at the bottom of each stake. Keep the level in place to be sure that the sides of the pool are not squeezed inward as the log roll is nailed in place.

7 **WITH THE LOG ROLL** securely fixed, backfill the area between the logs and the unit with topsoil. Tamp the soil down firmly with a thin piece of wood. When compressed, the soil should be level with the rim of the unit. If soil spills into the unit, bale or siphon out the water, clean the unit's surface with a wet sponge, then refill to the correct depth.

FURTHER INFORMATION

- Siting Water Features – pp. 56–57
- Construction Tools and Materials – pp. 62–63
- Construction Techniques – pp. 64–69
- Rigid Pool Units – pp. 84–85
- Edging Materials – pp. 126–127

SUNKEN CONCRETE POOLS

CONCRETE IS A strong and long-lasting material for formally shaped pools, made either with solid poured concrete or concrete blocks with a cement rendering (as below). Pools made entirely with poured concrete can deteriorate in time, being prone to cracking in severe weather or if the surrounding earth moves. The thin layer of special, fiber-reinforced cement skimming used below dramatically reduces the risk of

SUNKEN CONCRETE POOL

fracturing when the soil swells or shrinks. However, this method is best used only in zones 8 and South. Concrete pools in areas where the ground freezes for considerable periods, must be poured using forms (see facing page). They can also be constructed using gunnite or shotcreting, a technique that involves spraying layers of concrete over a reinforced wire mesh from from a truck equipped with a pump.

CONSTRUCTING A SUNKEN CONCRETE POOL

CONSTRUCTION GUIDE

To build a 13ft x 10ft x 2ft (4m x 3m x 60cm) pool, you will need:

TOOLS
- Stakes, string, spade, shovel, tamping block, rake, length of timber for leveling concrete, plasterer's trowel, carpenter's level, straightedge, paintbrush

MATERIALS
- Soft sand or sifted soil: 1cu yd (1cu m)
- Concrete mix – ballast: 1cu yd (1cu m); cement: two 50lb (22kg) bag
- Mortar – soft sand: 0.5cu m (½cu yd); cement: two 80lb (36kg) bag
- Cement rendering – sharp sand: 1cu yd (1cu m); cement: 3 x 50lb (22kg) bags; 50lb (225kg) reinforced fibers:
- 64 concrete blocks: 18in x 9in x 4in (45cm x 22cm x 10cm); 128 house bricks; 128 brick-shaped pavers
- Waterproof sealant for water gardens

1 **MARK OUT AND EXCAVATE** a straight-sided hole 4in (10cm) deeper and 8in (20cm) wider all round than the intended size of the pool. Dig a trench 8in (20cm) wide around the inside of the excavation for poured concrete wall foundations. Presoak the trench; pour in, tamp, and level the wet concrete mix; then leave to dry.

2 **RAKE THE POOL'S BASE** and remove any stones, then spread, rake level, and firm a 2in (5cm) layer of soft sand or sifted soil level with the foundations. To make a firm, flexible base, use a plasterer's trowel to skim the sand with a ½in (1cm) layer of fiber-reinforced cement, overlapping the concrete of the foundations by 2in (5cm).

CROSS-SECTION, SUNKEN CONCRETE POOL

The walls of this pool are built on a concrete-filled trench, and consist of two courses of concrete blocks and two courses of bricks topped with coping stones. The entire inner surface of the pool is lined with a ½in (1cm) layer of fiber-reinforced cement. Below the floor is a base layer of the cement mix on a firm layer of sand.

BRICKS
FIBER-REINFORCED CEMENT LINING
COPING STONE
CONCRETE INFILL
DECORATIVE BLOCKS
SOFT SAND OR SIFTED SOIL
MORTAR
FIBER-REINFORCED CEMENT BASE
CONCRETE WALL FOUNDATIONS

3 **ALLOW AT LEAST 24 HOURS** for the cement to dry, then mortar two courses of concrete blocks onto the foundations in the trench. As you go along, fill up the holes in the blocks with a stiffish concrete mix to give them additional strength. When the mortar has set, fill the space between the block wall and the surrounding soil with the same concrete mix (see inset).

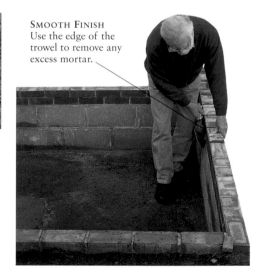

SMOOTH FINISH
Use the edge of the trowel to remove any excess mortar.

4 **MORTAR TWO COURSES** of house bricks onto the concrete blocks (see p. 69). Use a carpenter's level to check that each course is level, both vertically and horizontally. As you tap the bricks down with the trowel handle, scoop up the mortar that oozes out with the edge of the trowel. If this mortar is allowed to harden, you will be unable to achieve a smooth finish.

5 ALLOW 48 HOURS for the structure to harden, then, dampening each surface as you proceed, cover the floor and the insides of the walls with a ½in (1cm) layer of fiber-reinforced cement. To give the corners additional strength, build up a furrow where the base and side walls meet.

6 MORTAR THE COPING STONES onto the side walls so that there is a 2in (5cm) overlap on the inside of the pool; this will stop fish from leaping out and provide them with shade and shelter. The coping stones used here are brick-sized concrete paving blocks, laid sideways.

7 HAVING ALLOWED 48 HOURS for drying, brush the inner surfaces of the pool to remove any fine debris. Then paint the whole inside with a waterproof sealant for water gardens. This will prevent any impurities seeping from the cement rendering into the water (*see pp. 136–137*).

TRADITIONAL CONCRETE-LINED POOL USING FORMS

Without the use of a fiber-reinforced coating, the construction of a concrete pool is a skilled, labor-intensive task, involving the construction of wooden forms that create a mold into which concrete is poured to create the side walls. The base of the pool is formed by concrete poured over crushed stone; flexible wire mesh, sandwiched between two layers of wet concrete, provides extra strength. The wooden forms, erected inside the excavation and braced with wood, are sprayed with water to stop the concrete from sticking to the wood. Once wire mesh has been placed between the forms and the sides of the excavation, layers of concrete are poured in – and firmly tamped – until the walls reach the required height. When the concrete is dry the forms are removed.

WOODEN BRACING

STABILIZING THE MESH
Fold the top of the mesh at right angles and flatten it into the area around the pool.

WOOD FORMS

WALL TIES
Right-angled metal rods embedded in the floor and walls reinforce corners.

CROSS-SECTION OF POOL

COPING STONE

MORTAR

SIDE WALK-TYPE WIRE MESH

CONCRETE

CRUSHED STONE BASE

REBAR

CONCRETE

CRUSHED STONE

WIRE MESH
Wire mesh reinforces both the base and the side walls of the pond.

CONCRETE RESERVOIR POOL
This concrete pool serves as a reservoir for the water flowing down a shallow canal (see pp. 106–107). The water, circulated by a pump housed in a chamber alongside the pool (see p. 73), passes through a surface filter installed at the top end of the canal .

FURTHER INFORMATION

- Large Formal Pond – pp. 24–25
- Construction Tools and Materials – pp. 62–63
- Construction Techniques – pp. 64–69
- Raised Pools with Flexible Liners – pp. 86–87
- Concrete Canals – pp. 106–107

CLAY-LINED PONDS

IT IS RARE TO BE able to construct a truly natural pond, but lining an informal pond with gently sloping sides with a layer of compacted clay gives a near-natural effect. If the existing soil is unsuitable, clay may be bought in. Local clay is usually available at a very modest price; importing clay from a distance, however, is expensive. An excellent alternative is sodium bentonite, a powdered clay available from specialists,

NATURAL CLAY POND

which swells into a water-resistant gel when mixed with water. Bentonite also comes in the much more convenient form of a mat – bentomat – that can be laid in much the same way as flexible pond liner. All types of clay linings should always be completely covered with soil, which will both protect the clay and prevent it from drying out; the soil layer also forms a bed in which plants may spread informally.

USING NATURAL CLAY

If the existing soil is suitable *(see right)*, then, once the hole is excavated, its surface must be very well compacted to make it watertight. This can be done with booted feet, with a heavy wooden post, or rented machinery. If the water table is high, a temporary sump *(see p. 59)* may be needed to drain away water as you dig and compact soil.

Constructing a clay pond simply involves lining a hole with a thick, well-compacted layer of clay. It is best to build up several thin layers, to at least 6in (10cm) thick on lighter soils. Excavate as for a pond with a flexible liner *(see pp. 76–77)*. Remove all sharp stones or roots, and fork in a layer of bentonite; this deters tunneling animals. Either plaster the clay on by hand or with a flat piece of wood, compacting it thoroughly. For large ponds, it is worth hiring a mechanical roller to do the job. While lining the pond, you must keep the clay wet. Dip your hands in water regularly as you work. As areas are covered, either keep them moist with a sprinkler or cover temporarily with wet burlap. Then, add a 4in (10cm) layer of topsoil and fill the pond with water from a slowly trickling hose.

ASSESSING CLAY CONTENT IN SOIL

A site with soil that is sticky and pliable *(as below)* may be suitable for lining a pond. To test its suitability more accurately, place a small, sifted sample in a jar, adding water and a teaspoon of dishwasher detergent. Screw the lid on firmly and shake vigorously. Leave the jar undisturbed for at least two days (occasionally, it can take longer to obtain a satisfactory result), until the water has cleared and the soil particles have separated into individual layers of sand and clay. The sand will form the bottom layer, followed by a layer of clay, with organic matter floating on the surface. A suitable soil should have a clay content of approximately two-thirds.

TESTING SOIL CONSISTENCY
Roll and mold some dampened soil in your hand. If it is smooth, pliable, and sticky – holding together well (as above) *– it has a high clay content.*

PROBLEM SOILS

HARDPAN
This is a virtually impermeable layer of compacted soil. Since clay ponds are generally large, it is advisable to rent a mechanical digger if a hardpan is present.

BLUE MOTTLING
Blue mottling on the soil surface indicates waterlogged soil. It is a good soil for a clay pond, but plan for temporary drainage while work proceeds (see p. 59).

CLAY-LINED POND
All clay-lined ponds must be kept well filled with water at all times. Otherwise the clay will dry out and crack. Deep-rooted and vigorous plants are best kept in containers, or they will penetrate the clay lining, making holes and causing problems if they need to be lifted and thinned. Do not plant trees or shrubs at the water's edge; their roots can penetrate the clay and cause water loss.

DRYING HEAT
Cracks will develop in the clay if the water level drops and the sun dries out the soil.

SHALLOW-ROOTING PLANTS
Plants such as *Myosotis* or *Caltha* (right) can be planted directly in the layer of soil.

SOIL

CLAY

TREE ROOTS
Tree roots can penetrate the clay and cause the pond to leak.

TUNNELING ANIMALS
A layer of bentonite under the clay usually repels moles and worms.

WATER LILY
Vigorous plants can be container-grown to restrict spread.

WATERPROOFING WITH BENTONITE

Bentonite is a clay derived from fossilized volcanic ash and is sold in powdered crystal form or in the form of matting – bentomat – which, although heavy, is as easy to lay as flexible pond liner. In addition, unlike a clay lining, bentomat is not vulnerable to tunneling animals and most plant roots, as the geotextile that forms the base layer is thick and impenetrable.

LAYING BENTOMAT

On very light soils, or where several pieces of matting will overlap, additional waterproofing is advisable (see below). Spread loose bentonite over the surface of the excavation, till into the soil, and compact. Unroll the bentomat evenly over the excavation, as if laying a flexible liner. There should be as few wrinkles or creases as possible; if necessary, either make large, loose pleats or cut and overlap (see right) the matting. Cover the surface with a 12in (30cm) layer of topsoil. Slowly fill the pond with water – the moisture will soon penetrate the bentonite, causing it to swell and form an impermeable layer.

PLANTING A BENTOMAT-LINED POND

The sides of the excavation should not be steep; bentomat will sit more happily on a gentle slope, allowing plenty of informal marginal planting. You may wish to keep vigorous marginals and deep-water plants in containers to make regular maintenance, lifting, and division easier. Tiles prevent the crates from sinking into the soil and the roots escaping.

BENTONITE MATTING

Bentomat consists of bentonite granules sandwiched between two layers of geotextile. Bentomat is easy to handle and environmentally sound. It is ideal for lining large informal ponds, as pieces can be overlapped (see below) to cover an extensive area. Bentomat has a "right" and "wrong" side; always lay the non-woven side downward.

WOVEN GEOTEXTILE
NON-WOVEN GEOTEXTILE
GRANULES

JOINING BENTOMAT

To attach one piece of bentomat to another, spread a layer of bentonite granules onto the edge of the matting. Place the edge of the second piece over the granules, and press firmly. The granules will swell when wet, forming a watertight seal.

CAREX
CANDELABRA PRIMULA

ALISMA PLANTAGO-AQUATICA
Most non-invasive marginal plants need not be kept in containers.

CALTHA PALUSTRIS

EXTRA PRECAUTION
Fork or till loose bentonite into the soil below for extra waterproofing; the granules will swell and form an extra impermeable layer.

LAGAROSIPHON MAJOR

TUNNEL-RESISTANT
Moles are unable to burrow through bentomat.

BENTONITE GRANULES   BENTOMAT   SOIL

CONTAINERIZED DEEP-WATER PLANT
Vigorous plants in deep zones, such as large water lilies, are easier to lift and divide if kept in containers.

HARD-WEARING
Tree roots cannot penetrate bentomat.

CONTAINERIZED MARGINAL
Typha, *Glyceria*, and certain other marginals with sharp roots should be confined in crates.

LAYING BENTOMAT

Make sure that the hole is deep enough to accommodate both the required depth of water and the layer of topsoil that will cover the bentomat. Spread the bentomat over the base of the pond, extend it up the sides, and tamp down with boots or, over large areas, a roller. Finally, cover with a layer of topsoil.

FURTHER INFORMATION

- Excavation and Drainage – pp. 58–59
- Construction Tools and Materials – pp. 62–63
- Construction Techniques – pp. 64–69
- Simple Ponds with Flexible Liners – pp. 76–77

WATER GARDENS IN CONTAINERS

SUNKEN BARREL

ALTHOUGH LIMITED IN SIZE, containers make water gardening possible in very small gardens and on patios, verandas, and terraces. Even the most modest container, once planted, will quickly become a focal point, especially if it houses a small fountain. The addition of a couple of small fish transforms it into a fascinating feature for children. The only drawback container water gardens have is their susceptibility to rapid fluctuations in temperature; in summer the water can become extremely hot, and in winter, container gardens will freeze solid. Sink the container into the ground so that only 4–6in (10–15cm) remains visible above ground to insulate the water somewhat. In winter north of zone 9, move hardy plants and fish to a larger outdoor pool or overwinter them indoors.

CHOICE OF CONTAINER

Almost any container, from barrels and decorative urns to sinks and homemade hypertufa troughs *(see facing page)*, can be used, as long as they are watertight. Earthenware pots should be glazed, and wooden barrels and tubs should be sealed; older, leaky barrels may also need a waterproof lining *(see p. 78)*. A plastic dishpan makes an ideal, inexpensive miniature water garden that can be sunk into the ground, or surrounded by other containers, to disguise its unattractive exterior. A group of container water gardens makes a striking arrangement, particularly if one of the larger containers is used to house a small pump and fountain. The humidifying effect of the circulating water will benefit surrounding plants and keep the water fresh and sparkling; in containers without a fountain, submerged plants must always be included to keep the water clear. With the exception of this one essential, planting can be as varied as space permits.

WATERPROOFING A BARREL
Always clean tubs and barrels thoroughly. New ones will be watertight, but older ones may leak and require lining (see p. 79). In order to protect the wood and make sure any residues in the wood do not seep into the water, paint the insides of wooden containers with a commercial sealant safe for fish.

PLANTED BARREL
The plants in this barrel are in planting baskets, to prevent their roots from mingling. Marginal plants are placed on bricks or on empty upturned baskets to bring them up to the correct planting depth.

CONTAINER SHAPES
The most popular containers for miniature water gardens are barrels and glazed earthenware pots. To achieve the best effects, select containers with a wide neck, no narrower than 18–24in (45–60cm) across. The depth of the container need be no more than 15–18in (38–45cm).

GLAZED POT

CERAMIC POT

BARREL

EQUISETUM HYEMALE

ISOLEPIS CERNUA

ACORUS GRAMINEUS 'VARIEGATUS'

EICHHORNIA CRASSIPES

MYRIOPHYLLUM AQUATICUM

PISTIA STRATIOTES

VERONICA BECCABUNGA

MAKING A HYPERTUFA TROUGH

CONSTRUCTION GUIDE

To complete this step-by-step sequence, you will need:

TOOLS
- Paintbrush, spade, tamping tool, hammer, wide mason's chisel, wire brush

MATERIALS
- 2 wooden boxes made with inexpensive timber, one box 2–3in (5–7cm) bigger than the other
- Linseed oil
- Hypertufa mix: 2 parts peat substitute, 1 part coarse sand or grit, and 1 part cement made into a stiff mixture with water
- Wire netting: ¾in (2cm) mesh
- Plastic sheet, bricks or stones
- Commercial liquid manure

1 COAT THE INSIDE of the larger wooden box and the outside of the small box with linseed oil *(see inset)* to stop the hypertufa from sticking. Line the base of the larger box with 1in (2.5cm) of hypertufa mix. Put reinforcing wire netting over this layer and around the sides of the box.

COVERING A GLAZED SINK

Thoroughly score the outside and rim with a tile- or glass cutter, then coat with a bonding agent. Working from the bottom up, press hypertufa mix on to the sticky surface. To seal the drainhole, use a drain-plug and cover with waterproof sealant.

2 ADD ANOTHER LAYER of hypertufa to the base, then put the smaller box on top of the base. Make sure that the netting between the sides of the boxes is vertical, then pour hypertufa mix in the cavity between the boxes. To prevent air pockets from forming, keep tamping the mixture.

3 PROTECT THE TROUGH from sunlight, rain, and frost while the hypertufa sets. Do this by covering the top with plastic sheeting, securing it in place with bricks and stones. The hypertufa mix will form a strong shell if it is allowed to dry out slowly; a week or so should be sufficient.

4 WHEN THE MIX has set, use a wide mason's chisel to gently pry the outer, then the inner box free of the hypertufa. For a more natural look, roughen the outside of the trough with a wire brush, then paint it with commercial liquid manure to encourage moss and algae to grow.

PLANTED HYPERTUFA TROUGH

Even in this small trough, a good mix of marginal plants suited to the shallow water level can be included. Always choose some, like the Isolepis *here, that will spill and trail down the sides of the trough, otherwise the plants will tend to look as if they are sharing a bath. On the trough's surface, algae and mosses will grow, encouraged by the peat in the hypertufa mix and a coating of liquid manure.*

JUNCUS EFFUSUS 'SPIRALIS'

ZANTEDESCHIA AETHIOPICA 'CROWBOROUGH'

EQUISETUM HYEMALE

VERONICA BECCABUNGA

ISOLEPIS CERNUA

ACORUS GRAMINEUS 'VARIEGATUS'

FURTHER INFORMATION
- Container Gardens – pp. 26–27
- Construction Techniques – pp. 64–69
- Routine Plant Care – pp. 158–159

FEATURES WITH MOVING WATER

THE VISUAL EXCITEMENT and refreshing sound of moving water can enhance the smallest garden. Moving water is also beneficial to submerged life in creating additional oxygenation of the water. The range of pumps that is now available enables fountains, reservoir features, streams, and watercourses to be introduced in a wide variety of styles and sizes.

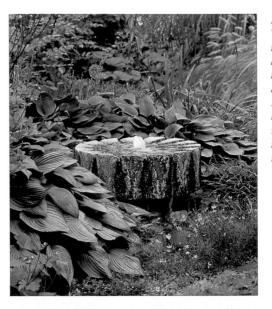

A MILLSTONE
This reservoir feature makes an attractive and compact fountain that is simple to install and easy to maintain. A small pump is housed in the reservoir, which is hidden underneath the fountain.

PLANNING AND INSTALLATION

Unless your garden encompasses a natural spring or stream, it will be necessary to create a feature where the water is mechanically recirculated. While gravity will carry water down a watercourse and over falls and cascades, you will need a pump in order to drive the water back to its supposed "source." Distance, gradient, and volume of water will influence the strength of pump that you require *(see pp. 70–73)*.

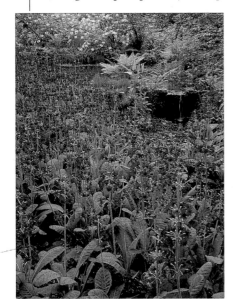

SIMPLE SPILL STONE
Water trickles over moss-covered stones and then through boggy areas to give the impression of a woodland spring falling into a rocky hollow.

INFORMAL WATERCOURSE
This gentle slope with a cascading stream is enhanced by the use of flat-topped rocks along the sides. The areas immediately surrounding the rock stream are unplanted, allowing access to and over the water and creating the illusion of the stream having weathered the rocks through the years. The water itself is clear and inviting.

TIERED SPRAY

A fountain adds light, sound, and hypnotic movement to a water feature, especially when the sun is shining. Fountains originated in hot climates, where they provided refreshment from the heat. Illuminating a fountain with artificial lighting can be spectacular, especially where the light source highlights fine droplets.

Only the largest features need a pump that cannot be hidden underwater. Today's submersible pumps are small and silent, making them unobtrusive. The delivery pipe can be buried until it reaches the source or header pool. This can then be styled to disguise the water outlet *(see pp. 102–103)*.

INFORMAL STREAMS AND WATERFALLS

A simple stream is created by digging a shallow trench, which may be lined either with flexible liner *(see pp. 98–99)* or rigid units *(see pp. 104–105)*. With more ambitious designs, a stream may meander into a series of pools and waterfalls *(see pp. 100–101)*. In informal settings, make the watercourse as natural as possible by disguising the edges with plants or rocks. The speed of flow and appearance of cascades and falls can be adjusted by narrowing or widening the watercourse or by altering the pump's flow adjuster *(see pp. 70–73)*.

FORMAL CANALS AND FOUNTAINS

A formal watercourse consists of symmetrical lines and straight channels. Materials such as pavers are used for the edging *(see pp. 126–131)*. Canals *(see pp. 106–107)* may be installed in formal gardens, providing a refreshing focal point in hot, sunny situations. Fountains *(see pp. 108–111)* are good focal points and come in a multitude of styles and sizes. There is a wide variety of sprays to choose from, including tiered and plume sprays, and geysers; a geyser is ideal for hot or windy climates.

SMALL MOVING WATER FEATURES

Small water features *(see pp. 112–117)* can be accommodated in very little space. No pool is necessary to install a reservoir feature such as a river rock fountain or a wall feature, where water falls from an ornamental spout into a basin below.

RECIRCULATING WATER SYSTEMS

The standard terms used below to describe the elements of a feature with recirculating water will help in the choice and purchase of materials.

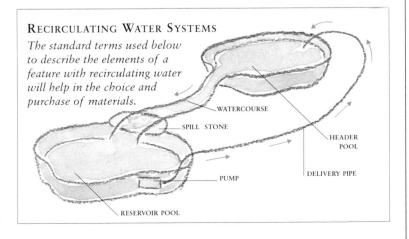

WATERCOURSE

SPILL STONE

HEADER POOL

DELIVERY PIPE

PUMP

RESERVOIR POOL

SIMPLE STREAMS WITH WATERFALLS

ANY GARDEN CAN incorporate a stream with waterfalls, provided there is a slight change of level between the upper and lower pools. Even where the terrain has no natural incline, it is reasonably simple to create an artificial slope. In the example below, a rigid pool unit with a marginal shelf was already installed *(see pp. 84–85)*. A simple stream made with flexible liner was added to enhance the existing

THE ORIGINAL SITE

feature, using the rigid unit as a reservoir pool. The versatility of flexible liner makes it an obvious choice for the construction of informal streams. Light-weight liners made of butyl rubber, EPDM, or PVC are ideal for novices, because most mistakes can be rectified with some judicious tugging, packing, and filling. Rocks, pebbles, and plantings will disguise the liner and protect it from the damaging effects of sunlight.

CONSTRUCTING A STREAM

CONSTRUCTION GUIDE

To build this header pool and stream with waterfall into an existing pond, you will need:

TOOLS
- Stakes and string for marking, spade, shovel, rake, trowel, watering can or hose, carpenter's level
- Submersible pump

MATERIALS
- Flexible liner and underlay: 13ft x 6ft (4m x 2m)
- 40 large rocks (including spill stones, foundation stones, and retaining wall stones) weighing approximately 55–110lb (20–50kg) each
- Ready-mixed mortar: 8 bags, each weighing 80lb (36kg)
- 7 x 50lb (23kg) bags of smaller rocks

1 MARK OUT THE PROPOSED course of the stream, and the outline of the header pool *(see p. 64)*. Working up from the existing pool, dig out a long trench plus a backward-sloping header pool *(see illustration on facing page)*. Rake the areas to remove large or sharp stones.

2 PARTLY UNROLL THE flexible liner and drape one end over the edge of the pool. Make sure that the liner – although only partly unrolled – is correctly positioned over the excavation, and that there will be enough to overlap the sides of the stream once it has been pressed into the contours *(see pp. 76–79)*.

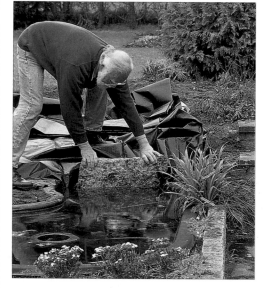

3 PLACE THE FOUNDATION stone on the marginal shelf in the pool; the stone should be hard up against the liner draped over the edge of the pool. If the foundation stone is not flat-bottomed, the pond will have to be drained and the stone mortared onto the base or marginal shelf.

4 PACK STIFF MORTAR between the foundation stone and the overlapping liner, then roll up the liner again until it is lying over the foundation stone *(see above)*. To further increase the stability of the foundation stone, pack stiff mortar between the liner and the earth bank.

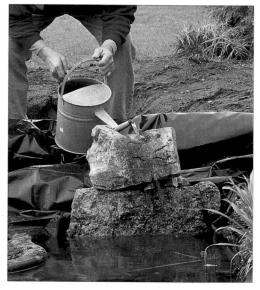

5 PARTLY UNROLL THE liner again. To make an unbroken fall of water into the pool below, place the spill stone on top of, and slightly overlapping, the foundation stone *(see pp. 102–103)*. Check the flow pattern with a watering can or a hose, then mortar the spill stone in position.

A Stream in Profile

A stream is essentially a series of elongated sections excavated on sloping ground and linked by waterfalls. The higher retaining rocks on either side of the spill stones ensure that water is funneled over the fall.

WATERFALL
To prevent spillage, the flanking rocks should be higher than the spill stone.

SPILL STONE

FIRM FOUNDATION
For added stability, the liner is mortared behind the foundation stone, with stiff mortar between the liner and the earth bank (*see Steps 3 and 4*).

MINI-WATERFALL
Create mini-waterfalls by pleating and mortaring the liner between two rocks.

FLEXIBLE LINER AND UNDERLAY

DELIVERY PIPE
Lay the delivery pipe in a trench alongside the stream and cover with soil.

OUT OF SIGHT
Use a large, flat stone to hide the entry of the delivery pipe into the header pool.

HEADER POOL
A backward-sloping header pool will not run dry in the event of pump failure.

SOFT SAND

RIGID POOL UNIT

SUBMERSIBLE PUMP

6 WHEN BUILDING UP the side walls, mortar the first layer of retaining rocks securely onto the liner before mortaring the others in place. To create a central channel for the flow of water over the waterfall, make sure that the rocks flanking the spill stone are higher than the spill stone itself.

7 CHECK THE water flow again with a watering can or a hose. To prevent the seepage of water, pull the liner level with the top of the spill stone, then pleat and mortar it behind the stone. Next, wedge and mortar another stone behind the pleated liner to keep it in place.

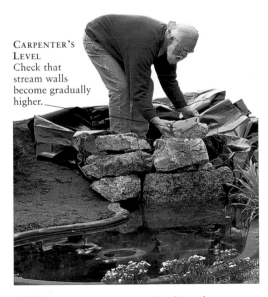

CARPENTER'S LEVEL
Check that stream walls become gradually higher.

8 UNROLL THE LINER completely, and arrange large rocks along the outer edges of the stream and around the header pool. Check regularly to be sure the edges are level with a carpenter's level. Mortar down another spill stone at the header pool's outlet (*see pp. 102–103*).

9 LOWER A SUBMERSIBLE pump (*see pp. 70–73*) into the reservoir pool and bury the delivery pipe, which will take the water up to the header pool, along the side of the stream. Use a large, flat stone to conceal the delivery pipe where it enters the header pool.

10 FOR ADDED AUTHENTICITY – and to hide the liner – place smaller rocks of mixed sizes and shapes on the floor of the stream. Fill soil pockets between the rocks with plants to soften the edging and emphasize the natural, informal design of the watercourse.

MORE IDEAS FOR STREAM CONSTRUCTION

ALTHOUGH THE BASIC PRINCIPLES of stream construction are quite straightforward, several factors should be considered if the stream is to be a complete success. For example, if you plan to create planting pockets, it is vital to make sure that the pump has sufficient output to maintain an adequate flow rate *(see pp. 70–73)*, and that the reservoir pool is big enough to supply both the header pool and the boggy soil. If the reservoir pool is too small, there will be a dramatic fall in the level of water as it circulates around the system. This will both endanger plants and water life and mar the visual appeal of the feature. For best results, the surface area of the reservoir pool should be approximately equal to or more than the total surface area *(see pp. 60–61)* of the rest of the water feature.

WORKING WITH THE SITE CONTOURS
When determining the course of any informal stream, try to work with the natural contours of the site, especially when deciding the best place for any change of direction or drop in height. A gently meandering stream *(see below)* can be created by using a single broad strip of liner; curved channels can be created for the water by mortaring rocks onto the liner. The outer areas can then be filled with soil to give the appearance of natural banks.

A STAIRCASE OF STONE
Although the principles of stream construction are always the same, the steeper the site of the stream, the more dramatic the effect. Using attractive spill stones for the falls will give the feature added charm.

CREATING AREAS FOR STREAMSIDE PLANTING
In a wide, liner-covered trench, create a stream by mortaring two rows of retaining rocks onto the liner, which will act as a channel for the water. Fill bordering areas with soil for streamside planting.

DELIVERY PIPE Conceal the pipe in a trench alongside the stream.

RETAINING WALL Create the course of a stream by mortaring rocks onto the liner.

STREAMSIDE PLANTING Line this area with rocks for drainage, then fill with topsoil.

LINER INSTALLATION Smooth the liner into place, leaving a generous flap at the edges; these edges can later be hidden under soil.

EXCAVATION The streamside planting areas should be roughly the same depth as the stream: 6–12in (15–30cm).

RESERVOIR POOL The reservoir pool should have enough capacity to supply the header pool and the streamside pockets.

SUBMERSIBLE PUMP Make sure that the pump has sufficient output to keep up an adequate flow rate *(see pp. 70–73).*

CROSS-SECTION, STREAMSIDE BEDS

Much of the attraction of a stream lies in the plantings along its edges. Areas of boggy soil can be incorporated at the stream edges by creating elongated planting pockets that follow the contours of the watercourse. Once filled with soil, these pockets can be filled plants such as *Parnassia palustris*, *Iris ensata*, and *Eriophorum angustifolium*, which thrive in saturated earth. Any plant that might be invasive should be confined to sunken, close-weave planting baskets. The retaining walls at the edges of the stream will help to prevent the planting soil from silting up the stream.

CARING FOR PLANTS Never use ordinary garden fertilizer on marginal plants; this will leak into the water.

PEBBLE FLOOR To disguise the liner, place pebbles on the base.

SOIL

RETAINING ROCKS

EXTREME CHANGES OF DIRECTION

When constructing a stream of any kind, always work upward from the reservoir pool. If a meandering watercourse is made with one piece of liner, the liner will have to be folded to incorporate changes of direction (*see pp. 66–67*). If the stream is to include waterfalls and extreme changes of direction, however, separate pieces of liner may have to be used (*see below*). Once the overall route has been marked out, you need to decide where the waterfalls are to be sited, since the watercourse should narrow considerably at these points. Where these narrow sections do occur, full use of the width of the liner can be made by incorporating adjacent planting beds.

In measuring for each length of liner, make allowances for an overlap at the end of each section. Measure the length between each waterfall, and the depth of the stream behind the waterfall at the downstream end where the liner will have to overlap another piece of liner (*see below*). The liner should be long enough to extend above the waterline at the upstream end, where it will be overlapped by the next piece of liner. Once the liner is in position, the rocks that make up the retaining walls of the stream can be mortared onto it. The top of each waterfall spill stone should be high enough to retain at least 4–6in (10–15cm) of water in the stream behind it; this will prevent underwater creatures from being stranded when the pump is switched off. The edges of the stream can then be built up. The edges should be fairly level and at least 2in (5cm) higher than the top of the spill stone; this will ensure that the recirculating water is contained within the system rather than flooding over the sides.

COPING WITH SEASONAL EVAPORATION

Even the most carefully constructed water feature may need filling up, particularly in warm months when evaporation from water surfaces, rocks, and boggy soil takes place. This loss can be replaced with water from a water addition float valve or with tap water trickling from a garden hose (*see pp. 138–139*). Replace water regularly, rather than leave it until the level is low enough to avoid harming fish and plants.

USING SEVERAL PIECES OF LINER

If a water feature has sharp changes of direction, it can be awkward as well as unnecessarily expensive to use a single piece of liner. Using several overlapping pieces of liner of different lengths and widths will eliminate the problem of difficult folds and will frequently reduce the amount of wasted liner.

DIRECTION OF WATER FLOW

DELIVERY PIPE
Conceal the pipe in a trench alongside the stream.

OVERLAPPING LINER
Each section of liner should overlap the one directly downstream from it.

WATER LEVEL
In hot weather, keep the water level in the reservoir pool filled up.

STREAMSIDE PLANTING
Make full use of the width of the liner by incorporating streamside planting.

SPILL STONE

FINISHING TOUCHES
Do not permanently secure the edging until the pond is full and the weight of the water has allowed the liner to settle naturally.

FURTHER INFORMATION

- Measuring Areas and Volumes – pp. 60–61
- Pumps and Filters – pp. 70–73
- Simple Streams with Waterfalls – pp. 98–99

HEADER POOLS AND SPILLWAYS

BOTH FORMAL AND INFORMAL watercourses usually terminate in a pond. The pump, which is either in or next to the reservoir pool, draws water from it, sending it up to the head of the feature. At this point the delivery pipe fills a smaller reservoir of water, known as the "header pool," which brims over into the watercourse. This gives a much better effect than if the pipe simply discharges into the start of a channel. The header pool may be concealed, with water spilling out of a culvert, or styled to match the rest of the feature. The header pool, and any intermediate pools along a watercourse, should always be deep enough to retain water when the pump is off.

POSITIONING THE DELIVERY PIPE

Make sure that the end of the delivery pipe is above the water level of the header pool so that it does not siphon water back as soon as the pump is turned off. If it is necessary to keep the end of the pipe under water, a non-return valve should be fitted at a convenient point in the delivery pipe to prevent siphon action (*see* Preventing backflow, *p. 73*).

INFORMAL STYLING

Informal header pools and streams are generally flanked by rocks of different sizes and shapes in order to retain surrounding soil and to direct the water along the watercourse. Use more rocks than are necessary; additional stones placed around the

INFORMAL STREAM WITH CHANGES OF LEVEL
The delivery pipe in the header pool is disguised with a pile of large stones and smaller pebbles to fill the gaps (see inset), and the flow adjusted so that water ripples out over the rocks. Flat-topped stones are placed in the stream to create shallow spills of water that are no more than 3–4in (7–10cm) high and achieve a natural effect.

CASCADING WATERFALL

INTERRUPTED FLOW
By using an uneven spill stone that is wider at the bottom than it is at the top, it is possible to create a cascading waterfall, rather than an unbroken curtain of water. It is also possible to create a cascade by using several rocks, each set back slightly from the one below, so that the water spills downward in an uneven way.

WATER · MORTAR

SPILLWAY

SPILL STONE

UNDERLAY · LINER

BACK SUPPORT
Direct water over the spill stone with a small rock behind it.

INTERRUPTED FLOW
Fall of water is broken up by the sloping, uneven rock surface.

CURTAIN OF WATER

UNBROKEN FLOW
Here, the spill stone projects outward over the fall to produce an unbroken curtain of water. A wide stone set just below the water level to produce a broad film of brimming water is most attractive. Few natural stones jut out this way, so a foundation stone is usually used, with a flat stone mortared on top of and overhanging it.

WATER · LINER FOLD

SPILLWAY

SPILL STONE

MORTAR

UNDERLAY · LINER · FOUNDATION STONE

WATERTIGHT STONEWORK
Mortar is packed between the stone and liner to avoid seepage, and the liner is pinched up behind the spill stone and secured with a stone.

sides and upstream of the source will create a more natural effect, which planting will enhance. The shape and arrangement of stones at spill points will determine whether the water descends in a free-falling curtain or cascading rivulets. For the latter, use a garden hose to judge the effect, and reposition stones as necessary before finally mortaring them down.

FORMAL SPILLWAYS

The simplest way of constructing a formal fall of water from a reservoir pool into a canal or another pool is to use a flat paver or tile as an overlapping spill stone: this method is ideal for a split-level pool *(see pp. 106–107)*, where water falls from one level to another over a common dividing wall. In order to construct the spillway, a gap is left in the last course of stone to take the flat spill stone. Any overlapping liner can be tucked under the spill stone. The stone must be precisely horizontal for the effect to be achieved: use a carpenter's level across both axes of the stone. The wall can be built up and around and over the spillway to form a formal culvert *(see below)*.

LARGE-SCALE FEATURE
Even when not in use, formal culverts can add a note of classical grandeur. Here, they have been integrated into a double stairway leading down to a broad pool. Remember that for water lilies to thrive in the vicinity of waterfalls, the flow must be little more than a gentle trickle.

FORMAL CULVERT

CONSTRUCTING A CULVERT IN A WALL
Culverts allow water to flow out from concealed header pools that are ideal housings for filter boxes (see p. 73). In order to construct a culvert, a wooden template is shaped to the internal measurements of the opening and laid onto the tile mortared on the course of bricks that will support the spillway. Bricks can then be cut and laid to form the arched shape within the next two courses. After about two days, when the mortar is completely hard, the template can be tapped out.

FORMAL HEADER POOL
Even if concealed, a header pool provides a more convincing flow of water than simply positioning the delivery pipe to discharge through a hole in a wall. Careful adjustment of the flow is necessary to be sure that water just brims over the spill stone. The pool's delivery pipe is set at a higher level than the spillway to prevent siphoning back when the pump is turned off.

RECIRCULATING FEATURE

FORMAL SPILLWAYS
In this formal feature, water falls from a raised reservoir through gaps in the top course of bricks. To interrupt the flow and create a splashing cascade rather than a smooth fall, the wall has been built with bricks protruding at intervals. Rounded bricks provide gentle, smooth spillways in this series of coordinated shallow drops. The same type of brick has been used for all the surfaces — edging, spillways, and the base of the canal. Warm-toned terra-cotta, with plants softening the edges, prevents a severe effect.

CONCEALED PLUMBING
The reservoir pool can be concealed beneath a path, suggesting an ongoing system of canals rather than a small recirculating feature.

RIGID STREAM UNITS

Most preformed rigid stream units provide a relatively easy way to create a stream and a series of waterfalls. Installing fiberglass rigid units is simpler, for example, than making a stream with flexible liner (*see pp. 98–101*). Once units are purchased, hardly any other materials are necessary, although some extra rocks can help blend the feature into its surroundings. Rigid units come in different sizes,

STREAM UNITS IN PLACE

materials, and finishes, including textured rock. Most units are made of fiberglass, which gives them resistance to damaging ultraviolet light. In addition to the bolted type (*see facing page*), units also come in PVC and vacuum-formed plastic molds, which are cheaper but have a limited life. A combination of units can include "connecting" units that link header pools, waterfalls, and miniature rock pools.

INSTALLING FIBERGLASS RIGID STREAM UNITS

CONSTRUCTION GUIDE

To install these rigid stream units (*dimensions given below*) above an existing pond with a submersible pump, you will need:

TOOLS
- String and stakes
- Spade, shovel
- Carpenter's level, straightedge
- Tamping block

MATERIALS
- Soft sand or sifted soil: ½cu yd (0.5cu m)
- 15ft (5m) delivery pipe with flow adjuster
- Topsoil, rocks, and plants

1 AFTER MARKING OUT THE SITE, work from the bottom up and dig a shallow trench with a slight backward slope. Set the first unit on soft sand or sifted soil, its lip slightly overlapping the edge of the pond.

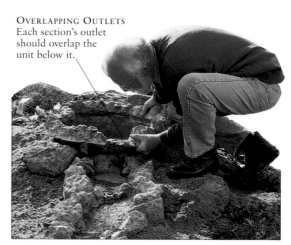

OVERLAPPING OUTLETS
Each section's outlet should overlap the unit below it.

2 REPEAT THE PROCESS up to and including the header pool. The lip of each unit, including that of the header pool, should overhang the unit below it. Hide the delivery pipe in a 6in (15cm) trench alongside the stream.

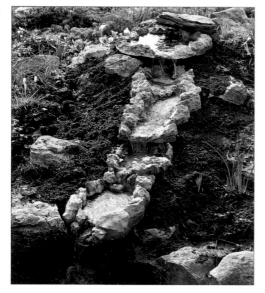

3 FIRM IN THE UNITS with tamped soft sand or sifted soil, then add a layer of topsoil and some surrounding rocks. Use a flat rock to hide the delivery pipe entering the header pool, then turn on the pump to check the flow of water. Use the flow adjuster to achieve the desired effect.

WATERCOURSE CONSTRUCTED WITH RIGID STREAM UNITS

The addition of randomly placed rocks and plants is the key to making preformed units blend in with their surroundings. The layer of soft sand or sifted soil and the free drainage afforded by the slope make the site ideal for many alpine plants, which look good among rocks.

SINGLE UNIT:
3FT X 18IN
(1M X 45CM)

PERFECT BLEND
Choose rocks that are the same color as the units' finish.

TRICKLING STREAM
These small features look best with a very gentle flow of water.

RAISED PUMP
A base under the pump will help to prevent it from filling up with debris.

RESERVOIR POOL

INSTALLING BOLTED RIGID UNITS

Bolted rigid units in regular shapes are available in Great Britain, but not yet in Canada and the United States. They are particularly suited to more formal gardens and can be used to construct interlocking pools at different heights. Cladding with a variety of finishes is available to disguise the connecting plates. Once installed, the units make a more permanent feature than smaller and lighter preformed units, so be sure to create level and stable foundations for them. When excavating, always allow extra depth for a 2in (5cm) layer of sand.

DURABILITY AND PERMANENCE

Strong interlocking and bolted rigid units are not only extremely stable, they are also much less prone to being damaged by soil settling. They are, however, a great deal heavier and sturdier than preformed fiberglass or plastic units and are subsequently more difficult to install. It is advisable, therefore, to enlist the help of at least one other person when lifting, positioning, and backfilling around the units.

Because of their size and bulk, more skill will be required in disguising the hard edges of the units. Since they completely contain the water, no moisture will seep into the surrounding ground. A combination of quick-growing carpeting alpines and small shrubs that tolerate the dry, well-drained soil along the perimeter of the stream will help to integrate the feature into its surroundings. Alternatively, you may use flexible liner to make independent boggy areas *(see pp. 82–83)*.

HEADER POOL: 3FT (1M) IN DIAMETER

DOUBLE UNIT: 4FT X 18IN (1.2M X 45CM)

NATURAL DISGUISE A flat rock hides the delivery pipe as it enters the header pool.

CREATIVE EDGING Careful planting and rock placement disguises the edges of the units.

DELIVERY PIPE Bury the pipe in a 6in (15cm) trench alongside the stream.

CROSS-SECTION OF A WATERCOURSE

Provided that the units have been carefully positioned, the slight backward slope of each unit will ensure that the pools retain water if the pump fails. As long as the pump has sufficient output *(see pp. 70–73)*, more units may be incorporated.

RESERVOIR POOL UNIT — SINGLE UNIT — DOUBLE UNIT — HEADER POOL UNIT — SUBMERSIBLE PUMP — DELIVERY PIPE

MAKING A WATERCOURSE WITH BOLTED RIGID UNITS

1 **AT THE EDGE OF** the pond, here made with flexible liner *(see pp. 76–79)*, dig out a platform for the first unit. Spread 2in (5cm) of soft sand or sifted soil over the base and check that it is level.

2 **REMOVE THE UNIT**, bolt it to the plate forming the fall, and seal the joins with silicone sealant. Install the unit, making sure it is level. Backfill behind the plate when excavating the header pool.

3 **LINE THE BASE** of the header pool with soft sand or sifted soil. Bolt its unit to the top of the vertical plate and seal the joins. Check that the unit is level, then backfill around it.

4 **INSTALL A SUBMERSIBLE PUMP** in the reservoir pool. Connect one end of a delivery pipe to the pump, and bring it up to the header pool, burying it alongside the watercourse.

5 **SNAP INTO PLACE** the textured cladding, then disguise the edges of the units by placing stones along the edges. Stones placed beneath the lip of the lowest unit will effectively camouflage the flexible liner used in the reservoir pool. Two large, flat stones will also disguise the entry and exit points of the delivery pipe.

FURTHER INFORMATION

- Pumps and Filters – pp. 70–73
- Simple Ponds with Flexible Liners – pp. 76–79
- Simple Streams with Waterfalls – pp. 98–99
- Edging Materials – pp. 126–129

CONCRETE CANALS

STRAIGHT, SHALLOW CANALS of moving water, whether sunken, semi-raised, or completely raised, are ideally suited to flat terrain in formal settings *(see pp. 56–57)*. Canals can be of practical use – forming the boundary of a garden, or linking a formal garden to the more "natural" landscape around it – or they can be purely ornamental. The formal impact of a canal can be heightened by flanking it with symmetrical

FORMAL CANAL

plantings – perhaps of columnar evergreens or trained standards of bushes and trees. The canals themselves are best left free of plants. Bear in mind that the longer a concrete canal, the greater the risk of cracking caused by earth movements. The method shown here uses a skimming of strong but flexible reinforced cement to line the canal, greatly reducing the risk of such damage.

CANAL LINKED TO RESERVOIR POOL

This feature is enhanced by its clear water and by the fact that its workings are concealed. A filter is housed in the upper brick chamber with culvert (see p. 73), while a surface pump sits in a ventilated chamber (see pp. 102–103) to the left of the lower cascade.

REMOVABLE COVER

OVERFLOW PIPE

SURFACE FILTER
Biological filter and UV clarifier housed inside brick structure.

CULVERT

DELIVERY PIPE
Bury the delivery pipe in a trench under the paving.

CONCRETE SKIMMING
Concrete mixed with reinforcing fibers makes a flexible lining for the canal.

PUMP CHAMBER
Ventilated brick chamber with removable cover contains the surface pump.

SURFACE PUMP ON WOODEN BASE

BRICK PAVING

WATERFALL
An overhanging spill stone will accentuate the drop of the water.

DECORATIVE PAVERS
Matching paving unites the edges of the reservoir pool and the canal.

CROSS-SECTION OF A FORMAL CANAL

The decorative pavers used as edging for this canal stand above the surrounding brick-paved area, giving the feature a semi-raised effect. Skimming the floor and walls with a ½in (1cm) layer of cement mixed with coarse sand and reinforcing fibers creates a crack-resistant waterproof lining. Drain concrete canals for winter in northern areas where they will be damaged by freezing weather.

DECORATIVE PAVERS

MORTAR

HOUSE BRICKS

CONCRETE

POLYETHYLENE SHEET

SOFT SAND OR SIFTED SOIL

SOIL

FIBER-REINFORCED CEMENT

MAKING A CONCRETE CANAL

CONSTRUCTION GUIDE

To build the 8ft (2.5m) x 16in (40cm) concrete canal illustrated *(facing page)* you will need:

TOOLS

- Marking stakes, string, spade, straightedge, level, thin straight plank, pointed trowel, plasterer's trowel

MATERIALS

- Soft sand: ½cu yd (0.5cu m)
- Heavy-duty polyethylene sheet: 8ft (2.5m) x 24in (60cm)
- Concrete: 80lb (36kg) cement; ⅔cu yd (⅔cu m) sand; 330lb (150kg) aggregate
- Mortar: 50lb (23kg) cement; ⅙cu yd (⅙cu m) sand
- Cement rendering: one 18oz (0.5kg) bag reinforcing fibers; 55lb (25kg) cement; ⅙cu yd (0.5cu m) sand
- 44 house bricks; 48 decorative pavers
- Commercial water sealant

HEAVY-DUTY
POLYETHYLENE SHEET

1 MARK OUT THE LENGTH AND WIDTH of the proposed canal. Excavate the area to a depth of 8in (20cm), which includes 2in (5cm) for a lining of soft sand. Rake the sand and check that the site is absolutely level, then line the floor and walls with the polyethylene sheet.

CIRCULATING WATER IN CANALS

Canals rely on pumps to push water along their length, and not on slope; they must be built on level ground, or they will empty too rapidly. The delivery pipe from the pump can discharge into either a header pool or, as shown on the facing page, a concealed brick chamber from which the water emerges via a formal conduit *(see pp. 102–103)*. An enclosed chamber can also be used to house a filter box *(see p. 73)*. It is important to make sure that the pump has sufficient output to maintain an unbroken fall into a reservoir pool *(see pp. 70–73)*.

2 LAY THE FOUNDATION by pouring a 2in (5cm) layer of concrete on to the polyethylene sheet, then firming and leveling it. Use a straightedge and a carpenter's level to check that the sides of the excavation are at exactly the same height. Consolidate the foundation by tamping it down and leveling it with a straight plank.

LEVEL FOUNDATION
Level the concrete with a thin straight plank.

3 ALLOW TWO DAYS for the concrete to harden. Then construct the sidewalls by first mortaring a course of house bricks *(see p. 69)* onto the foundation. Check regularly to ensure that the bricks are level. Mortar the decorative pavers at right angles on top of the bricks. Move the string guide to help lay the pavers overlapping the inside edge of the canal by 2in (5cm).

4 ONCE THE MORTAR HAS SET, use a plasterer's trowel to skim the floor and walls of the canal with the cement rendering mix containing the reinforcing fibers. This forms the canal's watertight lining, so ensure that coverage is complete, particularly up under the decorative pavers. When the skimming is completely dry, paint on a coat of sealant for a water garden to prevent harmful chemicals from seeping from the cement mix into the water and having an adverse effect on fish and plant life.

CANALS LINKING RESERVOIR FEATURES

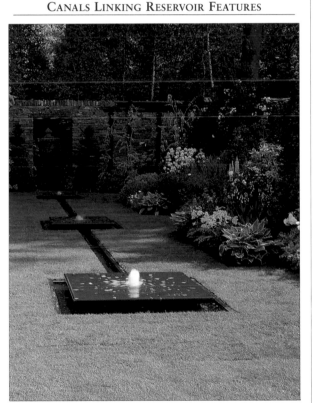

CANAL IN A GARDEN SETTING

Formal canals need not be associated with paving to have impact. This arrangement of narrow, turf-edged canals linking three sunken reservoir pools, each with its own fountain, culminates in a recessed urn flanked by pergolas.

FURTHER INFORMATION

- Siting Water Features – pp. 56–57
- Construction Tools and Materials – pp. 62–63
- Construction Techniques – pp. 64–69
- Pumps and Filters – pp. 70–73
- Concrete-lined Pools – pp. 90–91

FOUNTAINS

FOUNTAINS DATE BACK to antiquity, and their design can range from elaborate displays of hydraulic technology and ornamental stonework to a simple spray of water playing on the surface of a pool. In today's climate of eclectic and individualistic design, fountains can be installed in order to embellish all types of water garden, providing movement, sound, and refreshment in a range of styles. Fountains all work

FOUNTAIN IN POSITION

in the same way; the fountain head is connected to an electric pump, which drives water through the head, creating a spray. There are a range of fountain nozzles that will produce different spray patterns; the height of spray will depend on the power of the pump. In addition to their ornamental attraction, fountains also have practical value – in creating water movement they produce oxygen, beneficial to pond life.

INSTALLING FOUNTAINS

The simplest fountains discharge water from a vertical rigid pipe leading off a submersible pump, which sits on a base at the bottom of the pond. The pump may be disguised within an ornamental housing. For larger pools, it may be more convenient to site the pump close to the poolside *(right)*, using a delivery hose to connect it to the fountain.

SIMPLE PUMP INSTALLATION
The easiest method of installing a fountain is to place a pump on a base in the center of the pond, using a vertical discharge pipe with a fountain jet. Do not place certain plants too close – water lilies and free-floaters are disturbed by water movement.

<table>
<tr><td>REMOTE PUMP INSTALLATION</td></tr>
</table>

If you wish the pump to be within easy reach for maintenance, install it at the edge of the pond. The pump can be concealed by extending the pond edging to include an overhanging paving stone.

FOUNTAIN JET
The pump need not be directly beneath the nozzle.

INSTALLING A PUMP IN A SMALL FOUNTAIN ORNAMENT

SAFETY PRECAUTIONS

A fountain may be connected to the main electrical supply with a waterproof switch box at the poolside. Or, a waterproof cable connector can be used, which in turn is connected to a standard switchbox inside. Except where the system is extra low-voltage, it should be protected by a circuit breaker and ground fault interrupter (GFI).

WATERPROOF SWITCHES
You must use equipment designed for outdoor use.

1 TO INSTALL A SUBMERSIBLE pump inside the base of an ornamental fountain, first remove the top section, place the pump inside, and thread the cable through one of the several openings. Then attach a short length of hose to the pump's outlet and secure with a hose clip.

2 INSIDE THE ORNAMENTAL fountain there will be an integrated, rigid pipe. Using another hose clip, join this to the hose from the pump outlet. Then set the top half of the ornament securely onto the base and test the flow rate, altering it by using the flow adjuster if necessary.

SPRAY PATTERNS

A standard fountain kit consists of a pump, a rigid pipe, and a nozzle. The spray pattern is affected by the size and placing of holes in the nozzle. Standard nozzles may be connected directly to the pipe; use adaptors to connect more complicated nozzles. The flow adjuster controls the height and width of spray. For spray heights of up to 4ft (1.2m) a small submersible pump; to 7ft (2.2m), a larger submersible pump; over 7ft (2.2m), a high-head exterior pump may be required.

SINGLE SPRAY
A single spray pattern can be accommodated in a small pool and can be achieved with a standard nozzle. The narrower the delivery pipe, the higher the spray will lift.

HOW A FOUNTAIN WORKS
The pump sucks water through an inlet pipe and pushes it out through the fountain's rigid pipe to a fitted jet, or to a remote jet via a delivery pipe (see p. 108).

BELL-JET NOZZLE

FOUNTAIN JET The nozzle should be removed regularly and cleaned with vinegar.

RIGID PIPE The fountain pipe is usually made of plastic or PVC.

SINGLE SPRAY NOZZLE

T-PIECE This enables water to be directed sideways if desired.

FLOW ADJUSTER This controls the water flow to the fountain.

TWO-TIERED SPRAY NOZZLE

SUBMERSIBLE PUMP The height and width of fountain spray depends on the power of the pump.

BELL JET
A specially designed nozzle produces a thin, hemispherical film of water that causes little water-surface disturbance.

TWO-TIERED SPRAY
By altering the design arrangement and size of the holes in the nozzle of a single spray fountain, it is possible to produce a tiered effect.

DIFFERENT TYPES OF FOUNTAIN SPRAY PATTERNS

SIMPLE SPRAY
This is the simplest and cheapest of all fountain sprays and suits simple ponds better than the more elaborate types of spray such as a tiffany jet.

ROTATING NOZZLE
To create a whirling effect, pressure from the pump forces the arms of the fountain jet to rotate in a way similar to that of a water sprinkler.

TIERED EFFECT
By arranging the position and size of the holes in the nozzle of a basic surface jet (see left), the spray will reach different heights and tiers.

DOUBLE DOMES
This combines the design of the bell jet fountain and a surface tiered jet to create the effect of a fountain within a fountain.

COLUMN OF WATER
This is a popular fountain for exposed, windy sites, where the dense foaming plume is less likely to be broken up by wind than fine-spray fountains.

SURFACE JET

WHIRLING SPRAY

THREE-TIERED SPRAY

TIFFANY JET

GEYSER FOUNTAIN

CHOOSING FOUNTAIN STYLES

Perhaps more than any other feature, fountains can be used not only for their refreshing effects and inherent beauty but also to influence the style and mood of water in the garden.

STYLES OF FOUNTAIN IN ISLAM

In Islamic gardens attention was focused on the appreciation of water itself. The early technology of fountain design aimed to make minimal disturbance of the natural environment, making the garden a place of contemplation. Elsewhere, simple arching sprays used over long canals drew the eye toward beautiful examples of architecture without ornamental distraction.

FOUNTAINS IN MOGUL INDIA

Innovative fountain technology was taken a stage further in the gardens of Mogul India, where gardens were often associated with places of worship. Many of these gardens used fountain jets in retaining walls, forming chutes of sparkling water flowing into long formal pools beneath. Water pressure was harnessed from reservoirs in surrounding hills: the ample supply enabled water to animate every aspect of these exceptional gardens.

FOUNTAINS TO THE PRESENT

In the more formal approach to gardens in the Renaissance, fountains were sculptural, surrounded by symmetrical pools. As the naturalistic design movement gathered momentum during the 19th century, fountains became less widely used.

FINE, SINGLE SPRAY

An element of formality accents an otherwise informal garden, where the circular outline of the pool lends itself to the fine single spray of a tall fountain. Its height is about equal to the pool's width. In exposed sites, height should not exceed half the pool's diameter.

SIMPLE SPOUT

This type of single fountain spout works in both formal and informal settings. It is best suited to a formal design, as here, where a circular pool is surrounded by clear grass and tightly clipped, specimen yews. The spout is formed by a single jet that is wide enough to release a substantial column of water. This type of fountain must be absolutely vertical; any slight variation would ruin its effect.

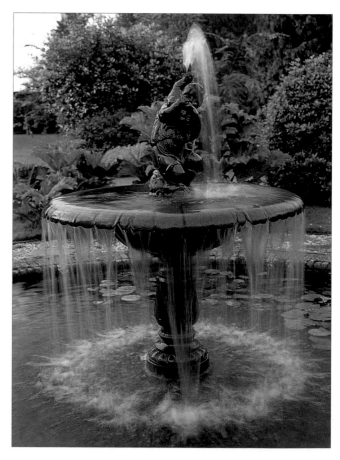

FOUNTAIN ORNAMENT

This traditional fountain ornament is perfectly proportioned for this formal pool, edged with decorative half-bricks. The pool is sufficiently large for the turbulence created by the fountain to be limited to the central area, allowing water lilies to thrive nearer the edge. The piping from the pump is hidden inside the base column and statue. The rate of flow is perfectly adjusted so that the water neither drifts away from the pool nor breaks up into small rivulets.

Moving water was more commonly featured in stream, grotto, and waterfall arrangements that convincingly mirrored nature, often with awesome arrangements of boulders.

In the present day, however, good garden design and water features are no longer the preserve of the wealthier classes and are less dominated by prevailing fashions and trends. As a result, there is an enormous range of fountain equipment in "antique," international, and modern styles to complement any garden, be it large or small.

SPRAY FOUNTAINS

These fountains have their source close to or at water level, thus sending the water upward, rather than falling from a receptacle, ornament, or orifice. Spray fountains are ideal for plant-oriented gardens where elaborate fountain ornaments would be lost in the surrounding plantings.

ORNAMENTAL FOUNTAINS

There is a plethora of fountains manufactured in reconstituted stone or concrete, incuding small copies of the huge classical fountains found worldwide. For something more contemporary in style, modern fountains are available, and it is worth seeking out examples from young, innovative designers working in this field. Good design and manufacture will allow ornamental fountains to be assembled with relative ease, requiring only a simple pump, since the piping is built into the framework of the fountain. The main priority in their installation is making sure that they are perfectly level and have a good foundation.

CIRCULAR RING FOUNTAIN

HOW IT WORKS
The pump is powerful enough to drive both the ring and a rose spray. The T-piece on the delivery pipe feeds the jets by a short piece of flexible tubing connected to an inlet spur on the underside of the ring. It is important to have individual control of both central spray and the ring by separate flow adjusters (see p. 72).

INSTALLING A RING FOUNTAIN

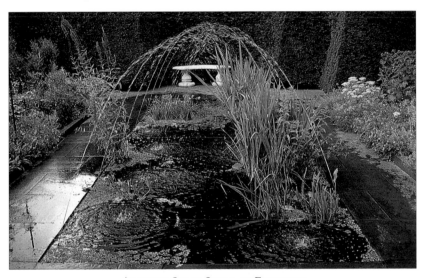

ARCHING SPRAY STYLE OF FOUNTAIN

HOW IT WORKS
Piping for the spray is fixed at the water surface along each side of the pool. The jets are placed just above water level and angled so that the spout of water forms an arch. To achieve the correct angle for the spouts, the pipe is fixed loosely and turned until the correct position is reached, when the pipe is tightened to the holding clamps. This rule can be applied with the jets turned downward to form a cascade (see right).

PRODUCING AN ARCHED SPRAY

CREATING A CASCADING EFFECT

RESERVOIR FEATURES

Fountains that use the reservoir principle are among the most simple and inexpensive ways to introduce the sound and sparkle of water into a garden. A reservoir fountain using rounded stones, called river rocks, is an ideal first-time construction project. It requires only a small pump and minimal maintenance, is very safe for family gardens, and can easily be integrated into both formal and informal settings. The

MILLSTONE FOUNTAIN

surrounding area can be planted and styled to make the feature's size appropriate to the scale of the site. Changing the positioning of loose rocks or stones close to, or overlapping, the nozzle of the fountain's delivery pipe provides ongoing opportunities to alter and refine the flow of water. An amber spotlight trained on the moving water *(see pp. 124–125)* will create the same relaxing effect as the flickering of a fire.

MAKING A RIVER ROCK FOUNTAIN

CONSTRUCTION GUIDE

To complete this step-by-step sequence, you will need:

TOOLS
- Tape measure, shovel, straightedge, carpenter's level, rake, scissors, wire cutters, tamping tool

MATERIALS
- Large plastic tub or garbage can
- Heavy-duty polyethylene sheet: 6ft x 6ft (2m x 2m)
- Submersible pump with filter *(see pp. 70–73)*
- Delivery pipe with flow adjuster
- Brick base for pump
- Square of galvanized metal mesh, at least 4in (10cm) larger than the diameter of the tub
- Rigid plastic pipe to protect pump cable
- River rocks

1 MEASURE THE DEPTH AND DIAMETER – including the handles – of the tub. Then dig a hole that is slightly wider and deeper than it is. Place the tub or garbage can – which will act as a reservoir pool – in the hole and use a straightedge and a carpenter's level to make sure that it is level, with the rim flush with the ground.

2 ONCE THE TUB IS IN PLACE, backfill the gap around its sides, tamping the soil down firmly. Rake the surrounding area to remove stones, then rake the soil up slightly away from the edges of the sunken tub to create a saucer-shaped depression with the tub at its center. Remove any soil that has fallen into the tub.

3 LAY THE POLYETHYLENE SHEET over the prepared area and cut out a circle 2in (5cm) smaller in diameter than the plastic tub. The purpose of the sheet is to collect the water being pumped out of the fountain and allow it to drain back down the slight slope into the reservoir.

4 CONNECT THE DELIVERY PIPE – complete with flow adjuster – to the pump outlet *(see pp. 70–73)*. Do not trim back the delivery pipe yet *(see Step 6)*. Lower the pump on to a brick base at the bottom of the tub; the base helps to prevent any debris from clogging up the pump.

5 CENTER THE GALVANIZED mesh over the hole in the polyethylene, then use wire cutters to cut a small hole in the middle, wide enough for the delivery pipe. The cable that links the pump to the electrical outlet should be fed through rigid pipe; this will be hidden under the stones.

6 TEST THE FLOW by filling the tub with enough water to cover the pump. Working from the edges inward, start to arrange stones over the mesh. If using a flexible delivery pipe, wedge it upright with stones. Trim the pipe to length. Arrange just enough stones around the feature to assess what the effect will be, then turn on the pump. If the flow needs to be adjusted, the stones and the mesh will have to be removed. Once satisfied with the flow rate, fill the tub with water to a level approximately 2–3in (5–8cm) from the top.

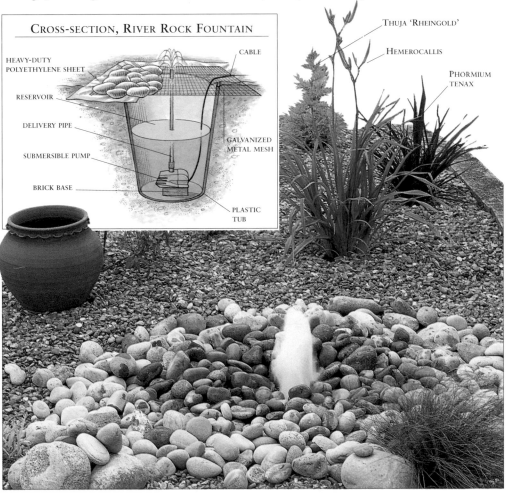

CROSS-SECTION, RIVER ROCK FOUNTAIN

HEAVY-DUTY POLYETHYLENE SHEET
CABLE
RESERVOIR
DELIVERY PIPE
SUBMERSIBLE PUMP
GALVANIZED METAL MESH
BRICK BASE
PLASTIC TUB

THUJA 'RHEINGOLD'
HEMEROCALLIS
PHORMIUM TENAX

7 ARRANGE MORE STONES around the pipe until the desired effect is achieved. Once the area onto which water falls is established, trim surplus polyethylene and bury the edges under soil – or, to allow future enlargement of the feature, fold or roll up the polyethylene before burying it.

STYLING THE FEATURE

This fountain is the centerpiece of a minimalist, low-maintenance design. A landscape fabric, which allows water through but prevents weeds from growing, has been laid over the surrounding soil. Cut small crosses in this material and fold back each corner in order to make planting holes. Once the plants are in place, spread gravel evenly over the surface of the fabric.

OTHER RESERVOIR FEATURES

THE SIMPLE PRINCIPLE of recirculating water demonstrated by the river rock fountain *(see pp. 112–113)* can be exploited with a variety of decorative outlets, including urns, bamboo cane, and old cast-iron water pumps. The sound and movement of the water can be controlled and enhanced by increasing or decreasing the flow from the pump.

All the following features have the advantage of minimal maintenance. The growth of algae in most reservoir features is reduced because sunlight makes little contact with the water surface *(see pp. 136–137)*. Any open reservoirs may be covered with fine mesh to prevent debris from falling into the water. If mesh is used, it is important to make sure that it is strong enough to support any ornament. To compensate for the loss of water by evaporation, fill up reservoirs regularly in hot weather.

BUBBLING URNS

The psychological effect of the sound of gentle running water has a major impact upon how a garden is perceived. One of the most calming sights and sounds is of a brimming urn that softly overflows, with the water sparkling in the sunshine and highlighting the rich colors of a terra-cotta or ceramic pot. Urns can either be supported on timbers over a sunken reservoir or raised above ground on supporting bases. Raised urns will be less dominated by surrounding plants and foliage.

MILLSTONES AND HAND PUMPS

A millstone with water rippling over its surface into a reservoir below makes another restful water feature. The hole in the middle of the mill-stone may have to be widened to accommodate a small delivery pipe from a pump housed in a reservoir below the stone. Genuine millstones can be difficult to obtain and are very heavy. You can, however, buy fiberglass millstones that have coarse sand dusted over and glued to the surface, giving a natural finish. They may be sold complete with a pump as an easy-to-build fountain kit.

MILLSTONE FOUNTAIN
The simplicity of a millstone fountain overflowing into a stone or river rock area is enhanced by a planting of iris, trollius, and bugleweed.

Cast-iron hand pumps make a feature that produces louder splashing sounds than those of urns and millstones. The hand pump can be free-standing over a sunken reservoir or set in or next to a barrel filled with water, in which case it will not require a sunken reservoir. As with all features requiring electricity, it is important to protect the cable leading from the pump to the outlet. As a safety precaution, always use a circuit-breaker and ground-fault interupter (GFI) *(see p. 72)*.

CAST-IRON ORNAMENTS
Cast-iron hand pumps make delightful reservoir features. Here, the spout releasing water is almost hidden by an abundance of flowers and foliage. The pump is not above, but next to, its reservoir pool. Whether raised or sunken, it is advisable to cover reservoirs with fine wire mesh to prevent debris from falling in. If possible, submersible pumps should be placed on a base at the bottom of the reservoir pool; this helps to stop the pump from becoming clogged up. With most ornaments, it is possible to hide the delivery pipe inside the feature.

THE JAPANESE TSUKUBAI

Recirculating water is also used to create many of the symbolic or functional features frequently seen in Japanese gardens. The Japanese use a variety of containers, such as troughs or hollowed-out rocks, to collect water to honor their tea ceremonies and to support other rituals of purification. One of the most popular of these is the *tsukubai*, a low stone basin that is continually refilled with water. This was traditionally used for handwashing before entering the teahouse. In order to make the visitor stoop in humility to use the vessel, it was also traditional for its height to be no more than 8–12in (20–30cm).

Water reaches the stone basin through a bamboo cane spout that conceals, or is attached to, the delivery pipe from the pump housed in the reservoir below. Having been filled with water, the basin gently overflows from one point only. The overflowing water trickles over stones and falls into the reservoir, which is protected from encroaching debris by wire mesh covered with stones. The mesh must be strong enough to support the weight of the stones. Polyethylene sheeting surrounding the feature ensures that any water seepage will be directed back into the reservoir. To complete the feature, appropriate plants such as evergreen grasses and ferns can be added.

THE SHISHI ODOSHI

Another feature using bamboo cane as a water outlet is known as the *shishi odoshi* ("deer scarer"). This was developed by Japanese farmers to ward off wild animals with an intermittent clicking noise, caused when a hinged length of bamboo cane strikes a stone. The *shishi odoshi* works on the same principle as the *tsukubai*. Water from a sunken reservoir is pumped up through a delivery pipe that is concealed within a vertical "post" of hollowed-out bamboo. The delivery pipe is connected to a thinner, hollowed-out bamboo spout set near the top of the post, through which the water runs out.

Approximately halfway up the fixed post a hole is cut, into which another length of bamboo is set to pivot on an axle (*see below*). This piece of bamboo is hollowed out only as far as its first node or joint, so that the opposite, and heavier, end falls under its own weight to strike a stone positioned beneath it. The hollow, lighter end lies beneath the spout to receive water pouring from it. The weight of the water accumulating in the hollowed section of the pipe eventually overbalances the pipe, the water runs out, the pipe swings back up, and the far end strikes the stone as it falls.

STYLING JAPANESE WATER FEATURES

Water, foliage, and stone are the main elements in Oriental-style gardens. To achieve a subtle balance between the existing landscape and the newly planned elements, water features like the *tsukubai* and *shishi odoshi* should be integrated with great care. With the exception of evergreen azaleas, flowering plants do not play a major role in the overall design of a Japanese garden; plants such as bamboos and Japanese maples are chosen for their ornamental stems and leaf interest.

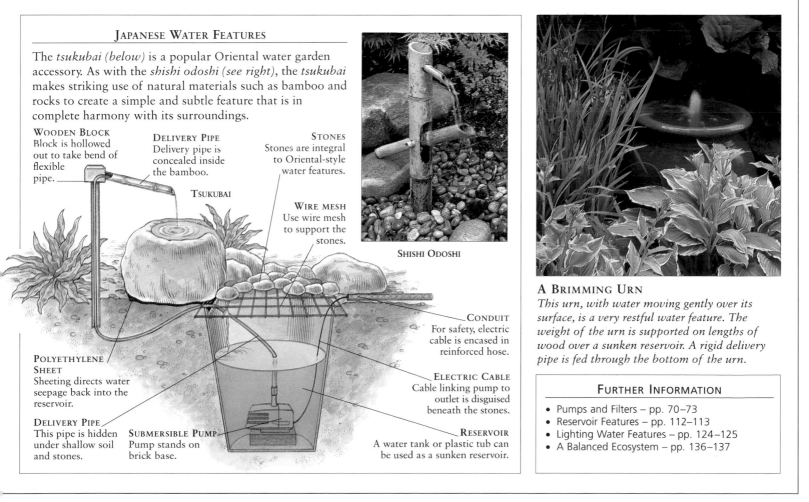

JAPANESE WATER FEATURES

The *tsukubai (below)* is a popular Oriental water garden accessory. As with the *shishi odoshi (see right)*, the *tsukubai* makes striking use of natural materials such as bamboo and rocks to create a simple and subtle feature that is in complete harmony with its surroundings.

WOODEN BLOCK
Block is hollowed out to take bend of flexible pipe.

DELIVERY PIPE
Delivery pipe is concealed inside the bamboo.

STONES
Stones are integral to Oriental-style water features.

TSUKUBAI

WIRE MESH
Use wire mesh to support the stones.

POLYETHYLENE SHEET
Sheeting directs water seepage back into the reservoir.

DELIVERY PIPE
This pipe is hidden under shallow soil and stones.

SUBMERSIBLE PUMP
Pump stands on brick base.

CONDUIT
For safety, electric cable is encased in reinforced hose.

ELECTRIC CABLE
Cable linking pump to outlet is disguised beneath the stones.

RESERVOIR
A water tank or plastic tub can be used as a sunken reservoir.

SHISHI ODOSHI

A BRIMMING URN

This urn, with water moving gently over its surface, is a very restful water feature. The weight of the urn is supported on lengths of wood over a sunken reservoir. A rigid delivery pipe is fed through the bottom of the urn.

FURTHER INFORMATION

- Pumps and Filters – pp. 70–73
- Reservoir Features – pp. 112–113
- Lighting Water Features – pp. 124–125
- A Balanced Ecosystem – pp. 136–137

WALL FOUNTAINS

WALL FOUNTAINS BRING water to patios, courtyards, conservatories, and small, enclosed gardens – anywhere, in fact, where there is insufficient room for a full-scale pool. Stone masks and other decorative forms are popular as outlets. Antique stone features are expensive, but new terra-cotta and convincingly textured plastic and fiberglass versions are not, and since they are lighter, do not need such a strong

ORNAMENTAL MASK

supporting wall. The water falls into a reservoir pool, which may take various forms: a small brick tank, an old sink or cistern disguised with plants, or a decorative stone bowl. The pump may be submerged in the pool, or in a chamber to the side of it; a small, extra low-voltage pump is easily powerful enough for most wall features. Also available are preformed, easy-to-install kits, with built-in pump and reservoir pool.

INSTALLING A MASK FOUNTAIN OUTLET

CONSTRUCTION GUIDE

To install a mask on a brick wall approx. 4ft (1.2m) above a reservoir pool, you will need:

TOOLS
- Electric drill with ¾in (2cm) masonry bit
- Mortaring trowel
- Screwdriver
- Hacksaw

MATERIALS
- Small submersible pump
- 4ft (1.2m) length of ¾in (2cm) copper piping
- Two ¾in (2cm) elbow joints
- Three ¾in (2cm) hose clips
- 6ft (2m) length of ¾in (2cm) flexible plastic delivery pipe
- Small quantity of mortar mix

1 AT THE HEIGHT that the mouth will be, drill a hole between bricks. Outlets usually look best just below eye level. Drill a second hole about 4ft (1.2m) below it where the pipe will come back through the wall to enter the reservoir pool.

2 CUT LENGTHS of copper pipe for the two holes, the lower one 2in (5cm) longer than the width of the wall, the upper one 2in (5cm) longer than the width of the wall and the mask; angle the end of this pipe and smooth its edges with a file.

3 THREAD THE PIPES through the holes in the wall. The burred end of the pipe at the front of the wall should fit into the mouth of the mask. The protruding end of the pipe at the back of the wall will be attached to the delivery pipe.

4 WHERE THE COPPER pipes appear behind the wall, attach an elbow joint (the upper one turning down and the lower one up) and another 8in (20cm) length of copper pipe. Clip flexible delivery pipe between them.

5 MIX THE MORTAR into a stiffish paste. Wet the back of the mask so that the mortar will stick more effectively to its surface. When spreading the mortar, do not cover the area around the mouth opening. Also leave the edges of the mask clear, so that mortar will not escape when the mask is pressed against the wall.

6 SLIDE THE MASK over the copper pipe, and press it firmly against the wall. Wipe up spilled mortar. While waiting for the mortar to dry (this can take up to 36 hours), install and connect the pump, using flexible delivery pipe to run from the pump's outlet to the lower protruding end of copper pipe, securing with a hose clip.

4ft (1.2m)

WATER FLOW

The flow of water issuing from the mouth of the mask should be strong enough to allow the water to spout into the center of the reservoir pool without splashing over the sides. If the force of the water is too strong, turn down the flow adjuster on the outlet of the pump (see pp. 72). Depending on the distance between the spout and the reservoir pool, there will inevitably be a degree of splashing against the brickwork. This will encourage the growth of mosses and algae that will, in time, make the feature look attractively weathered.

TIERED FOUNTAIN

The delivery pipe, which feeds into the back of the upper triangle of this tiered wall fountain, is hidden behind the trellis supporting a variety of climbing plants. This feature works with the merest trickle of water; short lengths of chain have been added to create links of water between the tiers.

WALL FOUNTAIN WITH SPILL BASIN

TWO-COURSE BRICK WALL
If the wall feature is made from stone, it must be mounted on a wall strong enough to support its weight and the weight of the water in the spill basin.

CIRCULATING WATER
The pump pushes the water from the reservoir pool up through the delivery pipe and through the mouth of the mask.

DELIVERY PIPE

SPILL BASIN

FLOW ADJUSTER

WEATHERPROOF CONNECTOR   BASE   SUBMERSIBLE PUMP

RESERVOIR POOL

PREFORMED WALL FOUNTAIN

To consolidate the visual appeal of this type of wall feature, it is important to disguise the pipes used in its installation. One way is to fit and mortar the pipe into a channel chiseled into the wall. Another way is to camouflage the pipe with climbing plants, such as ivy and Virginia creeper, which will complement the bricks and stonework.

SPILL BASIN WITH INTEGRAL T-BLOCK

T-BLOCK

ORNATE "SHELL" SPILL BASIN

SPILL BASIN MORTARED TO BASE

WALL PLUG

BASE

This spill basin, which is made from reconstituted stone, is so heavy that it requires a T-block fitted into the wall to support it. The base is fixed to the wall with wall plugs. The basin is mortared to the base.

FURTHER INFORMATION

- Pumps and Filters – pp. 70–73
- Fountains – pp. 108–111
- Reservoir Features – pp. 112–115

FINISHING TOUCHES

EXTRA FEATURES THAT enhance the look of a pond can also be functional: bridges and stepping stones, for example, add interest and provide access across a pond. Lighting brings a magical quality to a garden and allows one to see at night. Edging materials such as paving and wooden decking not only strengthen pond edges but add enormously to their aesthetic appeal.

STEPPING STONES AND BRIDGES

Stepping stones are popular additions to informal ponds and streams but can also be incorporated in a formal pool. Use the same, or complementary, materials as the edging for a unified effect. Stepping stones require a firm foundation and, if necessary, should be set on stone or brick piers *(see p. 122)*. They should be considered carefully in sites where children play regularly – a large, flat boulder at the poolside may be more appropriate. Avoid crumbly or porous stone, even if well out of the water, as it encourages the growth of algae and moss.

STONE STATUETTE
The focal point of this feature is the stone statuette positioned in the center of the pond. A stone table toward the back of the garden continues the use of ornament, and informal planting complements the figure's naturalistic pose. Planting in the pond is restrained, leaving clear areas of water so that the figure's reflection can be seen.

INFORMAL STEPPING STONES
The ornamental use of rocks and stones is an important element in Oriental-style gardens. Beyond the huge boulder in the foreground, lily pads echo the natural placement of stepping stones.

FORMAL STEPPING STONES
Squares of wood decking on piers form a pathway over a large pond, their clean lines flattered by the neat definition of Pontederia foliage. The wood is in good condition, having been regularly scoured with a wire brush to make sure that it is free of slippery mosses and algae.

LIGHTING A WATER GARDEN
Here, powerful lighting brings boulders, stones, and leaf shapes into focus, contrasting with the darkness of the water. The pond can also be approached in safety.

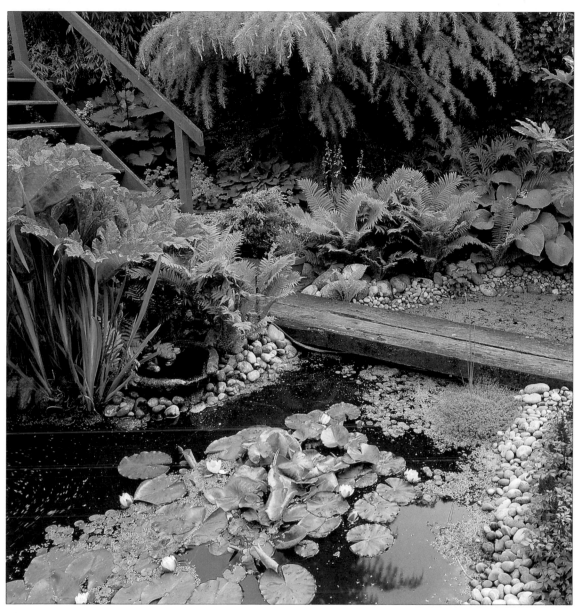

INFORMAL WOODEN BRIDGE
This simple bridge is made from two parallel thick wood planks. Bridges can be used to divide as well as cross the water. Here, young fish, tadpoles, and any other small creatures are separated from the main pool by a submerged barrier of fine mesh underneath the bridge, retaining them in the smaller pool area behind and protecting them from predators.

A bridge *(see pp. 122–123)* may serve a functional purpose, allowing access from one side of a pond or stream to the other, as well as adding visual interest to a water garden. In order to make sure that a bridge is completely safe, the construction must be sturdy and its surface nonslip; if necessary, firm handrails should be installed. There are a number of building materials from which a bridge can be constructed, including traditional stone, thick wood planks, concrete, steel, and iron. To a certain extent, the material used will be determined by both the style of garden and the available budget. If the sides of the bank are soft, foundations will be necessary to stabilize the bridge.

EXTERNAL AND SUBMERSIBLE LIGHTING
Carefully positioned lighting *(see pp. 124–125)* can transform a feature; illuminating a water garden also enables people to use the area at night. A water garden can be lit with both surface and underwater lights. Surface lighting accentuates pool surroundings; underwater lighting is ideal for fountains or waterfalls. All lighting should be well concealed so that the source is not visible. It is essential that lighting is installed correctly, since the combination of electricity and water can be extremely dangerous. Installing an efficient lighting system requires expert advice – if you have any doubts it is advisable to employ a qualified electrician to set up the system. A dedicated circuit may be necessary for powerful lighting; a wide range of extra low-voltage lighting is also available and requires a transformer to step down the voltage.

EDGING MATERIALS
Edging *(see pp. 126–131)* provides a means of blending a water feature with its surroundings; in many cases it also has a practical function, consolidating a feature and keeping soil out of the pond. Decoration is provided by choice of materials – even cement can be enlivened by mosaic tiles or shells. Edging materials for formal ponds include bricks, tiles, and slabs, and these surfaces need regular cleaning and maintenance to remain nonslip *(see pp. 140–141)*. Formal edging may either echo or contrast with the surroundings in both color and texture. Informal edging should provide as natural a finish as possible – materials include gravel, pebbles, sod, and wood.

STEPPING STONES

STEPPING STONES LEAD the eye from one part of the garden to another, and offer an irresistible invitation to cross water. Keep this fact in mind in gardens used by small children. They also make it possible to tend plants in the center of a pond. Consider carefully both the size and placing of stepping stones at the design stage; to install them later may entail draining the water feature. Each stone should be at least 18in

FORMAL STEPPING STONES

(45cm) square, and the gaps between stones no wider than 15–18in (38–45cm). If in doubt as to how many stones to use, it is better to err on the side of too many. The crisp outlines of paving slabs particularly suit formal ponds; they will, however, need strong supporting piers, installed as the pool is being built. Large, rounded or flat-topped boulders, irregularly placed, suit more informal ponds.

BUILDING FORMAL STEPPING STONES

CONSTRUCTION GUIDE

To build each of these stepping stones with pier, you will need:

TOOLS
- Carpenter's level
- Shovel
- Pointing trowel and mortar board
- Wire brush to clean up mortar droppings

MATERIALS
- 32 water-resistant bricks
- Ready-mix mortar: 44lb (20kg)
- One 2ft x 2ft (60cm x 60cm) paving stone

1 IN THIS CONCRETE-LINED POOL, the piers can built directly onto the pool floor *(for flexible-liner ponds, see box, below right).* For a small slab, 2ft (60cm) square, in water no deeper than 2ft (60cm), make a slender pier using courses of four bricks butted at right angles to each other; this will eliminate the need to cut bricks and allow the slab to conceal the pier by overhanging it slightly. Lay the first course of bricks onto a mortar base ½in (1cm) thick. Press the bricks down firmly until a little mortar is squeezed out. Use a carpenter's level to make sure that this first course of bricks is absolutely level.

FORMAL MATERIALS

For safety, when building stepping stones on piers, make the piers tall enough to allow the stepping stone to sit at least 2in (5cm) above the water surface, to keep it dry. If using concrete slabs, choose those with a nonslip, textured surface. Square paving stones are used mainly in formal designs that have square or rectangular outlines. Round pavers are particularly attractive in water gardens, echoing the shape of water-lily leaves. Irregularly-shaped concrete paving stones are manufactured in pleasant colors for use in more informal gardens. Make sure that each stone is big enough to stand on comfortably.

2 LAY THE REMAINING bricks in seven more courses, alternating the direction in which the bricks run. Use a carpenter's level to check that each course is level. Retain enough mortar for a ½in (1cm) layer on top of the pier, and pile any surplus into the center for extra strength.

3 SPREAD THE REMAINING mortar over the top course of bricks, and position the paving stone squarely over the bricks. Tap it down evenly onto the soft mortar *(see p. 69),* checking that it is absolutely level. Let it dry for at least two days before filling the pool.

FORMAL PIER WITH FOUNDATION

Piers installed in pools or bog gardens that have a flexible liner will need a solid base to make them stable. Pour concrete into an excavation lined with crushed stone. Make sure that the surface of the concrete is absolutely level. When the concrete is dry, lay the liner and underlay, then mortar the first course of bricks onto the liner.

BRICKS MORTARED TO LINER — PAVING STONE

FLEXIBLE LINER AND UNDERLAY — CRUSHED STONE AND CONCRETE FOUNDATION

INFORMAL STEPPING STONES

Flat stones and sections of wood make perfect stepping stones in shallow water, and are by far the safest option in family gardens. Rounded boulders suit the Oriental style, and look particularly good in slightly deeper water in which they can be partially submerged. The top of a waterfall is an excellent point at which to introduce a few stepping stones that will give a view of the clear, still water of the header pool as well as the more turbulent water falling over the spill stone.

It is important to select hard-wearing, nonporous stone such as granite. Softer stones, in particular limestone and certain sandstones, will crumble in time and are notorious for attracting slippery algae. While softwood will eventually rot, sections of round, hardwood tree trunks are likely to last for several years. Treat wooden rounds with a fish- and plant-friendly wood preservative at least once a year.

SAFETY PRECAUTIONS

It is imperative that informal stepping stones do not slide or wobble underfoot. In shallow water, flat stones or wooden rounds can be mortared directly to pool bases. Irregular boulders must be either sunken well into the floor of a natural or clay-lined pond, or, in flexible-liner or concrete ponds, mortared onto a concrete base (see below right). Staple chicken wire over wooden rounds to give a more secure footing, and clean all stepping stones regularly with a stiff brush to remove slime and algae.

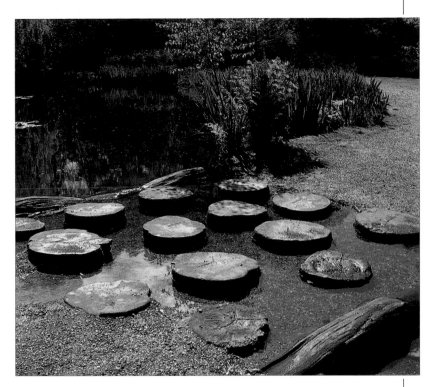

WOODEN STEPPING STONES
Irregularly placed rounds of hardwood can be used to make an attractive and unusual ford over shallow water. These sections, about 6in (15cm) thick and 20–24in (50–60cm) in diameter, have been mortared directly onto flexible liner, which is hidden under a layer of pea gravel.

FORMING A LINK
Large, flat or gently rounded boulders make "natural" stepping stones which can provide a link between different parts of a pond or stream, or make a shortcut across the corner of a pond, as above, where the mass of the boulder also provides continuity between the broad wooden deck and the stones at the poolside. Clean algae off stones regularly with a stiff brush.

STABILIZING BOULDERS

Unless the size, shape, or weight of a boulder precludes movement, it will need a foundation to make it stable and safe to step on. Make a concrete "nest" that approximates the contours of the bottom of the boulder. Allow the concrete to dry for a day, then mortar the boulder onto it. Extra layers of underlay can be used under the concrete to protect the liner.

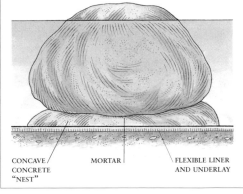

CONCAVE CONCRETE "NEST"   MORTAR   FLEXIBLE LINER AND UNDERLAY

FURTHER INFORMATION

- Courtyard Pool – pp. 32–33
- Siting Water Features – pp. 56–57
- Construction Tools and Materials – pp. 62–63
- Construction Techniques – pp. 64–69

BRIDGES

Bridges, like ponds and streams, can be as simple or as ornamental as the setting suggests. Although ready-made bridges are available in a range of materials, such as iron and steel, they can be expensive: a simple wooden bridge *(see below)* is both easy and economical to build, and can be up to 8ft (2.5m) wide without requiring a central pier or support. A bridge should be functional as well as decorative; bridges

BRIDGE IN POSITION

installed solely for visual effect can look contrived and may actually spoil the feature they are meant to enhance. If possible, design and build a bridge at the same time as you install a pond or a watercourse. The pond or stream can be "waisted" to create a narrower width to span with the bridge: if its ends are surrounded with plants, the bridge will make the water appear wider than it really is.

SIMPLE TIMBER BRIDGE

CONSTRUCTION GUIDE

To build this 8ft x 2ft (2.5m x 60cm) bridge, you will need:

TOOLS
- Spade, shovel, straightedge, level, screwdriver, drill

MATERIALS
- 8 rough boards: 4in x 2in (10cm x 5cm); four 2ft (60cm) long, four 4ft (1.2m) long
- Ready-mixed concrete: three 80lb (36kg) bags
- 2 treated wooden joists: 8ft x 6in x 2in (2.4m x 15cm x 5cm)
- Four 5in (12cm) galvanized brackets with 8 galvanized 2in (5cm) bolts and nuts
- 15 cross-planks: 2ft x 6in x 1in (60cm x 15cm x 2.5cm)
- 68 countersunk 2in (5cm) 8-gauge screws

1 TO MAKE FORMS for semi-raised concrete block foundations at the bridge's ends, dig two holes 6ft (2m) apart on either side of the water, 4ft (1.2m) x 8in (20cm) x 4in (10cm) deep. Surround the holes with the rough boards to make two rectangular forms *(right)*, and hold them in place with bricks and shovel in concrete. Use a carpenter's level and a long straightedge to make sure the two foundation blocks are level with each other.

FIRM FOUNDATIONS Foundations should be built at least 9in (22cm) from the water's edge so that sloping poolsides do not affect their stability.

2 BEFORE THE CONCRETE DRIES, set the two joists 20in (45cm) apart, hold the brackets against them and mark through the holes to show where to put the bolts. Embed bolts in the concrete, screw end protruding by 1in (2.5cm). Bolt the brackets onto the concrete when dry.

3 REMOVE THE FOUNDATION forms, and screw the joists to the brackets. Pull up and secure any liner under the bridge. Lay treated cross-planks over the joists, ½in (1cm) apart to allow expansion when wet. Fix each end plank first, and stretch string between them as a position guide for the rest.

CONSTRUCTION OF A TIMBER BRIDGE

This simple bridge is easy-to-make even for an amateur. A well-made bridge of thick, good-quality wood (consider using rot-resistant wood such as cedar) with firm foundations at each end, will be solid and durable. For safety, make any steps leading up to bridge ends firm and conspicuous, or build earth or wooden ramps.

JOIST

CONCRETE BLOCK FOUNDATION

UNDER THE BRIDGE
Before screwing on the final planks, mortar stones on each side and just under the bridge to disguise pool liner.

SERVING A PURPOSE

To make them practical and safe, bridges should be at least 2ft (60cm) wide; wider, if it is necessary to cross them with garden equipment such as lawn mowers or wheelbarrows. Always make sure that paths and paving are absolutely flush with the ends of the bridge to avoid tripping. In addition to providing a path across water, bridges offer excellent viewpoints from which to watch fish, or simply enjoy the reflection of light and color on the surface of the water; adding a handrail will make pausing on the bridge more inviting and comfortable.

HANDRAILS

Like the bridge itself, rails should blend as naturally as possible into the surroundings. Thin, overly ornate handrails usually tend to clutter an otherwise restful scene. In addition, they may be unsafe: handrails should always be strong enough to bear the weight of an adult leaning against them. A height of at least 3ft (1m) is essential if a bridge is very narrow or crosses particularly deep water. If the bridge is to be used by young children, it is a good idea to cover the space between the rails with wire netting.

Try to merge the ends of the rails into plantings, rather than coming to an abrupt, vertical stop. The vertical uprights of a bridge can be extended upward and joined over the top to form a frame, so that the bridge resembles a tunnel. The impact can be dramatically increased by festooning the uprights and top rails with climbing plants such as wisteria and clematis.

SAFETY

For safety reasons, the maximum span of an unsupported bridge should be 8ft (2.5m). Wider bridges need additional supporting piers or posts (minimum size 4in x 4in/10cm x 10cm). Either build brick piers like those used to support stepping stones (see p. 120), or drive supporting posts deep into the floor of the pond – this will involve renting a pile driver.

Any materials used for walking on should have a textured rather than a varnished or glazed finish. To ensure a safe, non-slip surface on a wooden bridge, firmly nail in place a covering of fine wire mesh (see p. 140), and prevent the growth of moss or algae by regularly scrubbing with water to remove dirt.

WOODEN BRIDGE

This zigzag wooden bridge over shallow water is not used to cross the pond, but to tend the plants in the center with ease. A brick pier supports the central section where the timbers meet. The plants softening the sides of the bridge give added emphasis to the rustic simplicity of the wood.

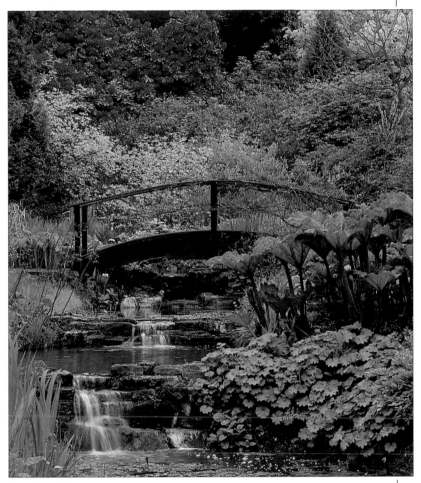

ARCHED BRIDGES

Arched bridges built from scratch demand very skilled construction techniques. They can, however, be bought ready-made. Choose one with a gentle gradient; a handrail is also recommended. Ask for installation advice: a good supplier will tell you what type of foundation is necessary.

Although they are the simplest and often the most successful, bridges made from wood have a shorter lifespan (10–15 years), and require more maintenance than those made from concrete, stone, or metal; eventually rotting wood will become weak and slippery. Treat lumber with a wood preservative at least once a year, and scrub all exposed areas with a wire brush at least twice a year to prevent the buildup of slippery algae. Be sure to check that the wood preservative will not affect plants and fish.

Finally, remember that the temptation to not only cross but also dangle feet and hands from a bridge is often more than young children can resist. A flat bridge set low over shallow water is the safest, nevertheless, it is advisable to supervise children as they play.

FURTHER INFORMATION
• Construction Tools and Materials – pp. 62–63
• Construction Techniques – pp. 64–69
• Stepping Stones – pp. 120–121
• Decking – pp. 130–131

LIGHTING WATER FEATURES

LIGHTING NOT ONLY extends the hours of viewing pleasure, it also brings a new dimension to the appeal of a water garden. When darkness falls, textures and contrasts dulled by sunlight are newly defined, greatly enhancing the appearance of plants and ornaments. Surface lighting will sharpen any image, and can be more effective when it does not shine directly on the water. Underwater lighting, though, produces the

UNDERLIT FOUNTAIN

most atmospheric results, illuminating fish, plants, and features such as fountains. For safety, durability, and strength of illumination, use good-quality equipment made for this purpose. If a pump *(see pp. 70–73)* is already in place, the main work and expense of bringing electricity to the feature will already have been incurred, but even if you are adding lighting to an existing system, professional advice is advisable.

TYPES OF INSTALLATION

Lighting a large area or feature usually demands standard-voltage lighting. (Do not light up the entire pond, as this might disturb the fish). Only a qualified electrician should install these systems *(see p. 72)*. A circuit breaker is essential, as well as a ground fault interrupter (GFI). The in-ground cable also must be protected *(see box, below right)*. However, an inexpensive extra low-voltage system, which reduces the current through a transformer, is powerful enough to light a group of plants or a small pool with a small fountain. Extra low-voltage systems come in simple kit form *(see facing page)*, often sold complete with pump and attachments. For any system, it is preferable to site switches indoors; switches outside must be encased in a safety-approved waterproof switch box *(see p. 108)*.

GAUGING THE EFFECT

Restraint and subtle placing are the keys to successful lighting. Experiment with underlighting by using a powerful flashlight or a spotlight on a long cord *(never place it in water)*. Do not let lights shine directly on water; indirect lighting turns the surface into a dark mirror, reflecting plants and ornaments.

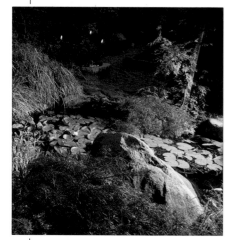

TRANSFORMING A FEATURE
A low spotlight creates a sense of drama and mystery, throwing shadows over the water, foliage, and rocks in this pond. Subdued lights that point down in the background illuminate pathways beyond the pond.

UNDERLIGHTING A FOUNTAIN
Use a high-intensity submersible light to illuminate water gushing from a fountain. Make sure that the beam is pointing upward into the spray – this will create the illusion that the light is "moving" with the water.

SAFETY PRECAUTIONS

For high-intensity lighting, use only equipment specifically designed for outdoor or underwater use. Have a qualified electrician install the system. Always include a circuit breaker and a ground fault interrupter (GFI); these cut off power immediately if a problem occurrs. Never use any lights or electrical equipment designed for indoor use outdoors. The sealed cable leading from the light must be connected to the main supply cable with a waterproof connector located near the pool – most ready-to-use systems come complete with connectors. The cable between the connector and the main socket must be suitable for outdoor use as well. Bury this cable at least 18in (45cm) underground. For extra safety, place roofing tiles over the cable or run in steel conduits. Put bright warning tapes on the tiles before filling the trench *(see also* Pumps and Filters, *pp. 70–73)*. There is little danger of serious electric shock from an extra low-voltage system, provided that it is properly installed.

CABLE

CHOOSING AND POSITIONING LIGHTING EQUIPMENT

Choose subdued colors for bulbs, lenses, and the casings of the lights; shiny stainless steel or bright white casings can be obtrusive in daylight. If possible, conceal equipment and casings behind rocks or plants. External or underwater spotlights trained on a specific area are the simplest forms of lighting. A spotlight behind a waterfall or cascade can be dramatic; underlighting a fountain *(see facing page)* is also very effective. Make sure that the beam is pointing upward into the spray to create the illusion that the light is traveling in the same direction as the spurting water. Floating lights *(right)* add an informal note of unpredictability, they may also be submerged to reveal the underwater world usually hidden by the glare of day.

FLOATING SPOTLIGHT
Most of the lights sold in kit form can be detached from the pump to be used as either floating or submerged illumination. To submerge, place a heavy object on the power cable to anchor the light in position.

TRANSFORMER

A transformer greatly reduces the voltage of an alternating current, making it safe in case equipment beyond it is damaged. Transformers should be weatherproof or installed indoors so that only extra low-voltage cable is used in the garden.

EXTRA LOW-VOLTAGE CABLE

FULL-VOLTAGE CABLE

PUSH-CONNECTOR FOR EXTRA LOW-VOLTAGE LEAD

TRANSFORMER IN SEALED CASING

PUMP AND LIGHTS IN KIT FORM
This lights on this kit need not be attached to the pump. Extra low-voltage cables from the pump and each light are joined in a waterproof connector box outside the water, from which one cable runs to a transformer.

FOUNTAIN NOZZLE

BEZEL

MOUNTING BRACKET

LIGHTS MOUNTED ON SUBMERSIBLE PUMP

LENS

SUBMERSIBLE PUMP

LIGHTING CABLES LEADING TO TRANSFORMER

PUMP CABLE LEADING TO TRANSFORMER

KIT ILLUMINATING FOUNTAIN
The three evenly spaced lights around the fountain nozzle provide even uplighting for the spray. For a more diffuse effect, the lamps can be detached to float around the fountain.

LIT STONE FOUNTAIN
Small, bubbling fountains can be illuminated by an angled spotlight at ground level. With suitable connectors lights can use the same extra low-voltage power source as the small pump. Choose a lens color that will complement the color of the stones. Use plants to disguise the casing or hide it in rounded stones.

BULBS AND LENSES

Tungsten bulbs, such as those used indoors, are the most popular extra low-voltage bulbs for lighting water gardens. If a more intense light is required, halogen bulbs are ideal, as they provide more light for the same wattage. As technology evolves, new techniques involving laser lighting and fiber optics will become more common. Although lenses are available in a variety of colors, white is the most popular and is usually the most effective. Avoid using too many different-colored lights.

COLORED LENSES

WROUGHT IRON CANDLE HOLDER

HANDLE

GLASS CASING

PORTABLE CANDLE HOLDER
The simplest way to light small areas is with candles in windproof casings; this holder has a tall ground spike so that it can be moved around. Citronella-scented candles will also discourage gnats and mosquitos, which congregate by water.

FURTHER INFORMATION
- Siting Water Features – pp. 56–57
- Construction Techniques – pp. 64–69
- Pumps and Filters – pp. 70–73

EDGING MATERIALS

Edging is vital to the durability of water features, consolidating poolsides to give a firm footing and also disguising pond linings. It also contributes greatly to the visual impact of the feature. Always consider the edging you will use from the earliest planning stages, so that it will suit the style both of the water feature and of existing garden materials. The more adventurous range of colors and textures now available means that even the most traditional or inexpensive materials can, with imaginative use, give a completely fresh look.

EDGING WITH NATURAL STONES AND ROCKS

INFORMAL STONE
Sandstone of varying sizes creates a natural-looking edge to this pond, echoed by a stepping stone path to the beach.

Informal ponds and streams can be enhanced by the placing of natural rocks or stones around the edges. Large retailers supply a wide range of stone types. Local stone is generally the least expensive and will blend most effectively with its surroundings. The two most common types of stone available are limestone and sandstone, both of which come in a variety of colors.

Rocks and stones should be placed as naturally as possible around an informal pond; where stones have clearly defined strata lines, aligning these *(see below and facing page)* will create the illusion that the rocks are naturally outcropping the water. Use loose, small pieces of stone to fill any gaps. To create extra cushioning and protect the liner, place extra pieces of underlay on top of the liner.

Rounded pebbles, river rocks, and cobblestones make good informal edging. River rocks are especially effective when wet, as the water brings out their natural colors. Where they are likely to slip, press them into a layer of mortar. Gravel and stone beaches *(see pp. 80–81)* also complement informal ponds, and provide an excellent textural contrast to the water.

INFORMAL STONE EDGING
Rocks, pebbles, and gravel create an informal transition from dry ground to water. The materials are easy to place and come in a variety of colors and sizes, making it possible to choose an edging material that will match existing materials. If used to disguise a liner, place pieces of underlay on top of the liner in order to prevent it from tearing.

RED GRAVEL

GRAVEL

GRAY GRAVEL

SLATE CHIPS

PEBBLES AND STONES

GRANITE

LAYING ROCKS AND STONES

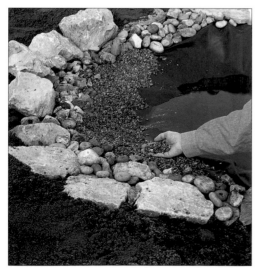

AN INFORMALLY LAID BEACH
The rocks and stones that edge this pond gradually decrease in size as they get closer to the water, creating a natural effect. Rocks and stones have been placed at the edge of the liner to secure and disguise it. The gradual slope provides both an informal finish and invites wildlife to approach the water.

MORTARED ABSORBENT ROCK
Position absorbent rocks so that the strata lines run along the sides, and are invisible from above (as left). A gently overlapping diagonal arrangement enhances the weathered appearance.

MORTARED NON-ABSORBENT ROCK
Most nonabsorbent rocks, such as granite, have cleavage planes rather than strata lines; try and make these appear broadly parallel. They look better angled more acutely than softer stones.

USING ROCKS WITH STRATA LINES ON SLOPES

When positioning rocks with strata lines down a slope or along the edge of a stream, make sure the strata lines are visible from the side, as in nature, not from above. After positioning the first rock, make sure that the strata lines of each successive rock are parallel. Again, the angle at which each rock is set must be the same. This may involve burying some of the stone or fitting small pieces of rock among larger stones to set them at the proper angle.

STRATA LINE

SLATE SLABS
Dark, wet slate is a good foil for cascading water. Position it so that any natural veining runs parallel with the water flow.

INFORMAL ROCK WALLS

Where rock walls are built up as internal edges to hide liner, use flattish stones mortared together for stability. Disguise the mortar at the front with small pebbles wedged in to create a "dry stone" effect.

BALLAST BACKFILL

EXTRA CUSHIONING UNDERLAY

FORMAL EDGING AND PAVING

FORMAL PAVING
Bricks and paving slabs have been combined to produce an effective edge to this formal stream; the bricks also echo the wall and arch.

Bricks, slabs, setts, and pavers are available in many different materials, colors, and textures. Large paving slabs are easier to lay regularly, but their sheer weight makes them difficult to handle. Concrete is the most cost-effective material to use and is also extremely hard-wearing, although not particularly decorative. Concrete pavers are simple to lay; just place them side by side and spread dry mortar over the surface. Alternatives to costly natural stone slabs are granite or clay setts, clay pavers, or terra-cotta tiles. Always lay bricks, slabs, setts, or tiles on a leveled crushed-stone base *(see p. 68)* with mortar on top for a firm finish; if necessary, fill the joints with bedding mortar. Note that sedimentary rock as well as concrete bricks around a pond will raise pH, thus harming fish. Test and adjust pH regularly.

TYPES OF BRICK
Be sure to use weatherproof bricks as edging, such as those shown below. Different colors are available that can be used singly or together. When using bricks with "frogs" – hollows – lay the the brick with the frog facing downward.

ENGINEERING BRICK

COMMON HOUSE BRICK

"FROG"

TERRA-COTTA HOUSE BRICK

PATTERNS IN BRICK

Brick edging can be extended to form a broad surrounding or terrace, which will be enhanced by laying the bricks in patterns *(see below)*. A simple theme is often more effective than an over-ornate one – a complicated design may lessen the overall impact of the feature. Do not let the cut edges of bricks show at the water's edge, as they do not make an attractive finish.

"BASKETWEAVE"

"INTERLOCKING BOXES"

"INTERLOCKING BOXES"

"HERRINGBONE"

LAYING BRICKS AS A POOL EDGING

1 EXCAVATE AROUND THE pool, allowing for a 4in (10cm) layer of crushed stone and 1in (2.5cm) of mortar. Lay the perimeter bricks first, using string and stakes to make sure that they are level.

2 AFTER MORTARING the perimeter bricks, bed the remaining bricks onto a layer of mortar, spacing them evenly. Using a carpenter's level and straightedge, tap down until the bricks are level.

3 SPREAD A LAYER of dry mortar over the surface and brush it between the joints. Use a watering can to sprinkle the bricks with water in order to set the mortar. Brush over the surface thoroughly.

LAYING CRAZY PAVING

CRAZY PAVING MATERIALS
Sandstone is particularly suitable for crazy paving, since it breaks up easily into flat, thin pieces. More random shapes must be carefully positioned for a level surface.

1 USE STAKES AND string to establish a level, horizontal surface. Spread a layer of crushed stone and compact firmly. Lay the edging pieces first, with their straight edges facing outward.

2 FILL IN THE rest of the area with large slabs infilled with smaller ones. Check that all the stones are level. To adjust the height, tap with a mallet over a wood block.

3 FILL THE JOINTS with almost dry mortar or brush in sand. To achieve a good finish, use a trowel to bevel mortar so that any surface water will drain away.

CUT SLABS

NATURAL FINISH
The range of reconstituted stone slabs now available provides far more convincing substitutes for natural stone than previously. Even cement slabs are now textured and colored to be more compatible with the existing landscape.

GRANITE SLABS

LAYING SQUARE SLABS

WATERTIGHT EDGE
In order to disguise the liner, lay it under two widths of granite blocks and wedge the edges upright with a paving slab. Trim the liner level with the top of the paving slabs and infill with mortar between the slabs and the blocks.

RECONSTITUTED STONE

TEXTURED RED CEMENT

BLEND OF MATERIALS
Concrete setts form the edge of this pool, and are surrounded by larger, traditional paving stones that have a rough, non-slip finish. The dark color of the concrete contrasts with the light paving slabs; both blend well with the water.

MAKING CURVED EDGES FOR FORMAL PONDS

PAVING BLOCKS

CONCRETE BLOCKS
In addition to being inexpensive, formed concrete blocks are versatile, coming in a wide range of shapes and sizes. These blocks are convincingly textured and have been produced in a "keyed" shape that makes them ideal for curved pond edges.

USING SMALL BLOCKS
The smaller the blocks, the easier it is to fit them closely around curving edges, filling the gaps with mortar (see p. 126).

SOFT AND HARD TEXTURES
Square slabs arranged in a circular pattern inevitably leave key-shaped gaps. These can be turned to advantage as planting spaces.

FORMAL EDGING
To avoid the labor and expense of hand-cut "keyed" slabs, buy pavers that are produced specially shaped for circular pond edges.

USING WOOD TO EDGE A POND

Wood edging is a popular choice for both formal and informal water features and combines particularly well with turf. Hardwood or treated softwood planks may be arranged horizontally; strips of log roll, vertically *(see pp. 88–89)*. Wooden edging can also be extended to create a deck for seating or a patio *(see pp. 130–131)*. Railroad ties make very durable edges, but are usually too heavy to use on top of the walls of raised pools. When exposed to water, wood tends to warp and rot, and should be treated with a preservative. To make sure that harmful chemicals do not seep into the water, a commercial sealant should always be applied. Make sure that all wood is held firmly in place, whether nailed to a wood support or fixed to a wall or a concrete foundation *(see below)*.

WOODEN EDGING
Treated railroad ties create completely watertight edging for this spillway. Wood also creates a discreet finish.

DECKING SQUARES

WOOD EDGINGS
Due to its versatility and natural look, wood has become very popular as an edging material. Decking squares and planks that overlap the edge of the water can hide unsightly liner and provide partial shade and shelter for fish. Log rolls, easy to install, can enhance the simplest pond. Planks and railroad ties are hard-wearing but heavy to handle – do not attempt to install them single-handed.

LOG ROLL

WOOD PLANK

DECKING SQUARES
Here, decking squares make attractive and serviceable edging for a concrete pool. Diagonally grooved tiles laid at right angles to each other make the surface less slippery.

DECKING SQUARES

TREATED WOOD
Preservative prevents the wood from rotting.

COUNTERSUNK SCREWS

WALL SCREWS

FASCIA BOARD

LOG ROLLS
Because they are flexible, log rolls are easy to install around irregularly shaped ponds. They can be attached to wooden stakes driven into the ground outside the pool (see pp. 88–89) or embedded in concrete, as shown here.

GRAVEL   SOD   LOG ROLL

FLEXIBLE LINER

UNDERLAY

CONCRETE

SECURING THE EDGING
Galvanized, countersunk screws secure edging to vertical support posts.

RAILROAD TIE   WOOD PLANK   COUNTERSUNK SCREW

WOOD PLANK

CONCRETE FOUNDATION

CRUSHED STONE

UNDERLAY

CONCRETE BASE

FLEXIBLE LINER

CRUSHED STONE

FASCIA BOARD

WOOD PLANKS
These treated wood planks border a regularly shaped pool constructed with flexible liner. Use countersunk screws to attach the plank to vertical support posts, which are set into concrete at 2in (6cm) intervals. Use thin wooden planks as fascia boards to disguise the supports.

RAILROAD TIES
To stabilize a railroad tie, install it on a concrete foundation. Use countersunk screws to fix planks over the ties in order to make an even surface for walking on.

WOOD POST   LINER   UNDERLAY

FURTHER INFORMATION
- Construction Tools and Materials – pp. 62–63
- Construction Techniques – pp. 64–69
- Raised Pools with Rigid Units – pp. 80–81
- Decking – pp. 130–131

DECKING

ONE OF THE many advantages of using wooden decking as edging is that it is easier to overlap the edge of the water with wood – thus providing a platform to view and feed fish from – than with paving or other hard-edged material. Decking not only makes an ideal edging, it can also be designed to form a seating area at the waterside or a jetty extending well over the edge of the water. Wooden decking squares with

WATERSIDE DECKING

a diagonal pattern are particularly attractive when laid at right angles to each other. If possible, use rot-resistant wood, but if cheaper wood is used, make sure that it is pressure-treated with a preservative that will not adversely affect plants, fish, or wildlife. As with bridges and stepping stones (*see pp. 120–123*), carefully consider the safety aspects of wooden decking, especially if young children are likely to play on it.

LAYING DECKING AT THE WATERSIDE

CONSTRUCTION GUIDE

To build a 10ft x 6ft (3m x 2m) deck with jetty, you will need:

TOOLS
- Spade, straightedge, level, tape measure, saw, screwdriver, hammer

MATERIALS
- 10 pressure-treated wood posts: 3in sq (8cm sq); 10 steel supports; 40 wall bolts 2in (5cm); galvanized nails: 1lb (½ kilo) 3in (75mm); 250 2in (5cm) 8-gauge screws; battens, fascia boards
- Ready-mixed concrete: 6 bags 80lb (36kg); crushed stone: 1cu yd (1cu m); sand: 1cu yd (1cu m); 10 house bricks
- 4in x 2in (10cm x 5cm) beams: two at 10ft (3m) long, two at 6ft (2m) long
- 4in x 2in (10cm x 5cm) joists: five at 10ft (3m) long, two at 6ft (2m) long, five at 3ft (1m) long; 28 decking squares: 20in sq (50cm sq)

1 WOOD POSTS IN steel supports bolted onto concrete foundations provide the firmest underpinning for a framework of beams and joists. Lay foundations – consisting of 4in (10cm) of concrete above the same depth of crushed stone – in holes 1ft x 1ft (30cm x 30cm) at the ends of each bearer, at 4ft (1.2m) intervals. Let the concrete harden, then place the steel supports on the concrete, and mark the four bolt positions. Drill four corresponding holes and insert and tighten four 2in (5cm) commercial wall bolts into the foundations. Use a straightedge and a carpenter's level to make sure that the uprights are completely level, then nail the beams, wider side down, on the uprights.

ALTERNATIVE FOUNDATION

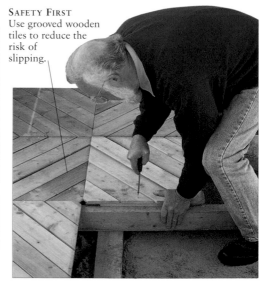

Bed the beams on firm soil in excavated channels containing crushed stone covered with a 2in (5cm) layer of sand. If necessary, use bricks to adjust the height of the beams.

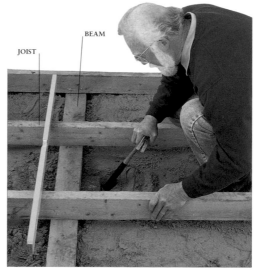

JOIST

BEAM

SAFETY FIRST
Use grooved wooden tiles to reduce the risk of slipping.

2 NAIL THE THREE middle joists diagonally – 18in (45cm) apart – to the beams. If joists have to be joined, make a 2in (5cm) horizontal cut and a 4in (10cm) vertical cut at one end of each joist, and half-lap them at the point where they cross the beam. Then nail the two end joists in place.

3 FOR ADDITIONAL SUPPORT, wedge bricks underneath beams where they are crossed by joists. Check levels along and across joists as you do so, so that you can make adjustments to height where necessary by varying the depth of the depressions you scrape out for the bricks.

4 USE EIGHT 2in (5cm) screws to fasten each grooved, nonslip decking square to the joists. To achieve a checkerboard effect, as well as to further reduce the chance of slipping, position the tiles so that the diagonal treads are at right angles to each other.

5 IF USING FLEXIBLE liner and underlay, pull these materials up over the top of the joists, and secure them well above the waterline with wood battens nailed horizonally behind the joist *(see also illustration below, left)*. This step should be completed before screwing the decking squares that overlap the edges of the structure in place.

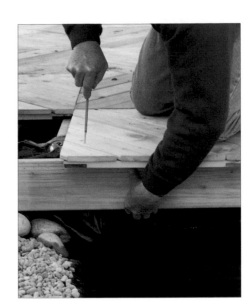

6 ONCE THE OVERLAPPING wooden tiles are in place, screw on a wood fascia board to hide the liner and the rough wood of the beams from side view. If desired, the fascia board can be wide enough to extend down to the waterline. Where the edge of the pond meets the decking, mortar a row of rounded rocks onto it well below the waterline. Then add smaller river rocks.

CONSTRUCTION OF DECKING WITH JETTY

To incorporate this small jetty over water, two of the beams should be 3ft (1m) longer than the others. To support the ends of the beams, bolt steel supports with wooden posts (see Step 1) onto brick piers (see pp. 120–121). The positioning of three 34in (85cm) joists will ensure a firm base on which to screw the last four decking squares: nail the first joist where the jetty joins the main structure, the next 18in (45cm) away and, to provide for a 2in (5cm) tile overhang at the end of the jetty, position the last joist 16in (40cm) away. Then nail in place the two 3ft (1m) long end joists on eitherside of the jetty (see illustration, right).

SECURING THE LINER

Decking that forms a right angle over the water creates the illusion that water laps up to and beneath the decking. Where the liner has to fit around a sharp corner, it should be carefully pulled and pleated *(see pp. 78–79)* before being secured with battens, and hidden from side view by wood fascia boards.

BEAM

DECKING SQUARE

JOIST

FASCIA BOARD

SMOOTHING THE LINER
Before battening down the liner where joist and end joist cross, smooth and flatten the liner as much as possible.

FLEXIBLE LINER AND UNDERLAY

PLANNED OVERHANG
Positioning this last joist just 16in (40cm) from the middle joist will ensure that the squares overhang the edge of the jetty.

BEAM

END JOIST

JETTY FOUNDATIONS
To raise the wooden posts above water, build brick piers *(see pp. 120–121)* and bolt on the steel supports.

WATER LEVEL
To prevent the wood from rotting, make sure that the level of water does not reach the wooden posts.

FASCIA BOARD

SUNKEN FOUNDATIONS
For firm underpinning, line the excavation with crushed stone before filling with concrete.

SUBSOIL

FURTHER INFORMATION

- Construction Techniques – pp. 64–69
- Simple Ponds with Flexible Liners – pp. 76–79
- Lighting Water Features – pp. 124–125

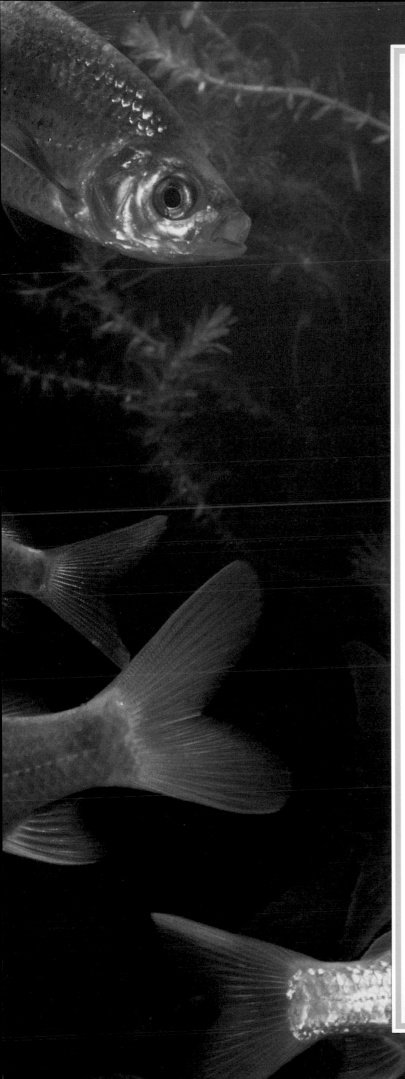

STOCKING &
MAINTENANCE

ORNAMENTAL FISH (*LEFT*)
*Goldfish are among the most popular fish for ponds and have been
kept in captivity longer than any other fish. They are hardy and
easily cared for and come in a wide variety of decorative types.*

MAINTAINING A HEALTHY POND

PROVIDED THAT A POND has been well sited, designed, and built, and that care is taken to ensure a healthy balance when stocking with plants *(see pp. 152–153)* and fish *(see pp. 170–171)*, it should not be difficult to tend. Major emptying and cleaning of a water feature *(see pp. 142–144)* is really not necessary or advisable, in the majority of cases, for at least two or three years.

CREATING A HEALTHY POND

The planning, construction, and stocking of a pond is crucial to the ecological balance or ecosystem *(see pp. 136–137)* that exists within it. The well-being of plant and animal life depends upon many factors, including light levels, water temperature, and the proportions of the various gases dissolved in the pond's water. Appropriate functional planting *(see pp. 152–153)* will help initially to achieve a natural balance and clear water.

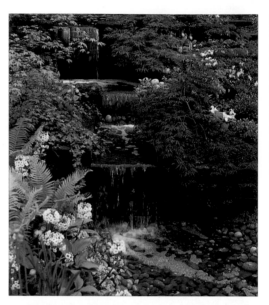

CLEAR WATER
The condition of this cascading waterfall is very satisfactory; the water is extremely clear, with no sign of algal growth allowing the decorative pebbles to be seen. The bubbles show how the splashing is increasing the oxygen content of the water.

THE POND IN WINTER
In cold climates precautions must be taken to make sure that ice does not completely cover the water surface. Not only does a solid sheet of ice exert pressure on the pond edges, it also traps waste gases that may build up in the water and harm fish and other animal life.

SUMMER REFRESHMENT
A well-kept feature needs little attention in the summer months, allowing time for relaxation and enjoyment of the water. In prolonged hot weather, be aware of the need for frequent filling, particularly if a fountain is increasing the rate of evaporation.

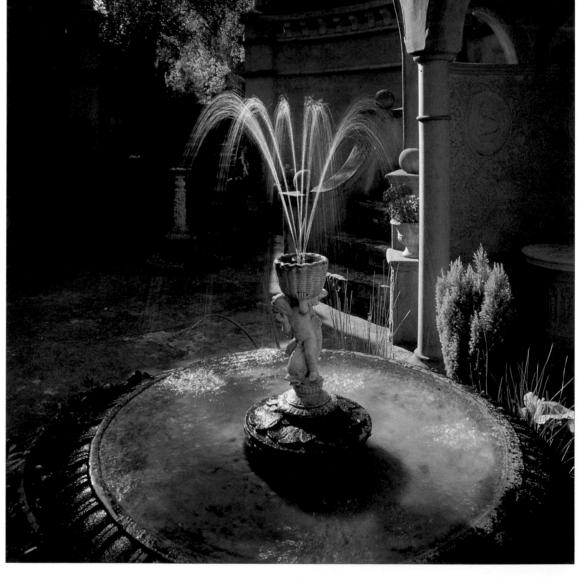

GREEN WATER
Small, free-floating plants such as duckweed multiply extremely rapidly and may soon choke a pond. Although useful additions to a new pond, providing temporary shade and shelter, they should be rigorously controlled as the pond becomes established. Over-hanging trees and shrubs should be avoided when siting a pond, or they will, as here, shed leaves into the water. These will eventually sink and decompose if they are not removed.

Routine maintenance *(see pp. 140–141)* is necessary to make sure that the water remains healthy – in particular, the regular thinning of plants so that the pond does not become blocked up. While all water features benefit from a major clean-up from time to time, it is vital not to do this too often. Each time a pond is emptied and refilled, it can take up to two years for a balanced ecosystem to reestablish itself.

WATER FEATURES THROUGH THE YEAR

The structure of a water feature and the surrounding area should be inspected regularly throughout the year to make sure that leaks have not appeared. Other tasks are appropriate only in various seasons. In winter, fish become dormant at the bottom of the pool. Water plants are largely herbaceous, dying back in winter and remaining dormant until regrowth begins in the spring. Therefore, pond life is best left undisturbed in winter. Before cold winter weather arrives, take steps to protect the pond and its residents from freezing. A stock tank deicer, which floats on the water's surface, will keep temperatures just above freezing, thus protecting fish and other pond life.

When the pond warms up again in spring, plants and fish should be checked for health, and any restocking done so that the feature looks its best for summer. Prolonged spells of hot

weather can damage pond life – the pond should be filled up regularly *(see p. 138)* to combat water loss caused by evaporation. Remember that over the years, debris accumulating at the bottom of a pond will gradually make it more shallow, leaving fish with no cool, deep water where they can escape the heat. The removal of this layer of sludge is one of the principal reasons for emptying and cleaning a pond. Pumps, filter, and other equipment need regular maintenance to function well. Check them regularly in summer and clean off debris, especially from the pump intake.

STRUCTURAL REPAIRS

Pond repairs may become urgently necessary if a large leak develops, but more often small underwater punctures and cracks go unnoticed until a pond is drained for cleaning. Most of the materials used to line ponds can be repaired quite satisfactorily *(see p. 145)*. However, year-round attention must also always be paid to the condition of any structures above water, such as wooden edging, bridges, or stepping stones. If not kept in good condition, they are a threat to safety. Keep wooden surfaces clean and free of moss and algae; otherwise they can be extremely slippery. Also check stepping stones for stability and joints on wooden structures to make sure they do not wobble.

A BALANCED ECOSYSTEM

THE ECOSYSTEM OF A POND involves the interaction of many factors – water, gases, minerals, sunshine, plants, and animals. In every pond, a balance must be found between clinically clean water that offers no hospitality to submerged and amphibious creatures, and a murky, crowded environment that begins to stifle life. The health of a pond is affected by its size and shape, the surface area exposed to the air and to the sun, the acidity or alkalinity (pH level) of the water, the type of plants used, and the presence of pond life. If the ecological balance is disrupted, green algae will spread, and the water quality will deteriorate rapidly.

LIFE IN THE WATER

Most ponds must initially be filled with tapwater, which is generally alkaline and may contain additives. It is advisable to treat the water for chlorine and other additives, then let the pond settle for a week or so and become more hospitable to life before stocking with plants or fish. Wherever possible, use rainwater for filling up the pond, although it can be acidic.

The larger the pond, the more likely it is that a balanced ecosystem, in which many varied life forms interact, will develop naturally. The deeper the water, the less likely it is that water temperatures will fluctuate and disturb the ecosystem.

EXCHANGE OF GASES

Healthy water contains enough oxygen to support life. Fish and other aquatic creatures consume oxygen and produce carbon dioxide. In sunlight, submerged plants absorb carbon dioxide and release oxygen back into the water in a process called photosynthesis. The action of sunlight on mineral salts also causes algae to spread; these microscopic plants can rapidly deplete the water of oxygen, harming wildlife. As the water becomes murky with algal growth, plants starved of light will also begin to decay. Dead and decomposing plant and animal matter release poisonous methane into the water, further endangering life. It is essential, therefore, to partially shade a pond with floating-leaved plants to prevent too much sunlight from reaching the water, and that submerged plants (see pp. 148–149), which compete with algae for nutrients, are present.

A HEALTHY POND
Water quality is a good indicator of pond health. This pond's clear bright water and healthy plantings indicate that it has been well tended. The water is free of algae – due in part to the shade provided by both water lilies and marginal plants, and in part to submerged plants that have absorbed the nutrients on which algae thrive.

GUIDELINES FOR A BALANCED ECOLOGY

The following tips will help to create and maintain a healthy ecosystem:
- Site pond in the optimum position (see pp. 56–57)
- Make sure that part of the pond has a minimum water depth of 18in (45cm)
- Use floating plants and water lilies to shade about half the pond (see p. 152)
- Add submerged plants (see p. 152)
- Do not overcrowd with plants or fish
- Do not overfeed fish (see pp. 172–173)
- To boost oxygen levels, install a fountain or waterfall (see pp. 108–115)
- Regularly check pH levels (see p. 151)
- Carry out seasonal tasks on time

AN UNHEALTHY POND
The appearance of this pond indicates neglect. Due to the lack of floating or submerged plants, algae has been allowed to spread over much of the water surface. No sunlight is able to reach the water, causing a further fall in the level of oxygen. Evaporation has also occurred – evident in the drastic drop in the water level. A layer of scum suggests that the water is also polluted, which may have been caused by a number of factors (see facing page). Because of these unhealthy conditions, the plants have not been able to survive.

NATURAL POND CYCLE

In a healthy pond, plants and animals coexist within an efficient and interconnected food chain. The process involves the interaction of bacteria, plants, herbivores, and carnivores with inorganic matter. The water level may be affected by the pH level: municipal tapwater tends to be alkaline; rainwater can be acidic. All pond life will suffer if the water quality is poor, so be sure to keep a regular check on the pH level (see p. 151).

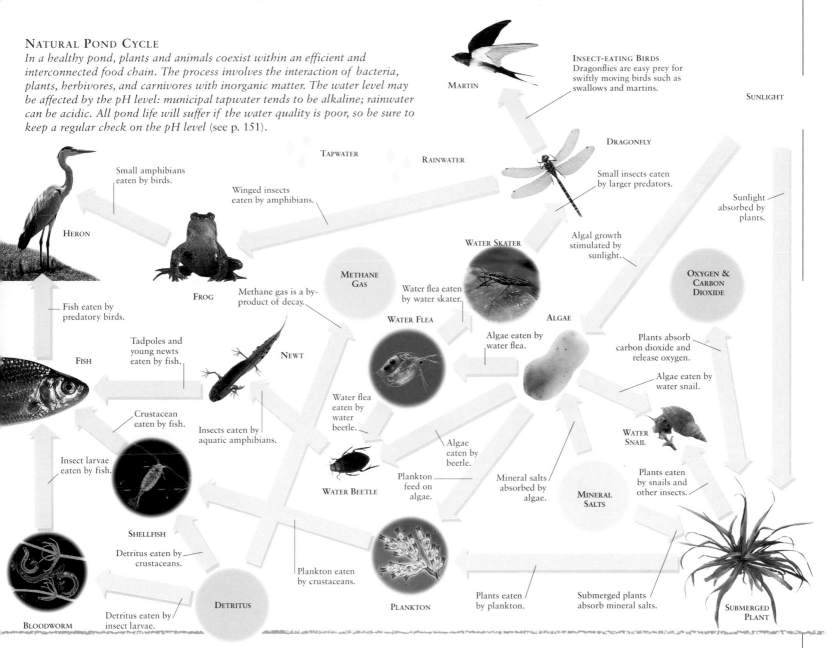

INSECT-EATING BIRDS
Dragonflies are easy prey for swiftly moving birds such as swallows and martins.

MARTIN

SUNLIGHT

TAPWATER

RAINWATER

DRAGONFLY

Small insects eaten by larger predators.

Sunlight absorbed by plants.

Small amphibians eaten by birds.

Winged insects eaten by amphibians.

Algal growth stimulated by sunlight.

HERON

WATER SKATER

METHANE GAS

Water flea eaten by water skater.

OXYGEN & CARBON DIOXIDE

Fish eaten by predatory birds.

FROG

Methane gas is a by-product of decay.

WATER FLEA

ALGAE

Algae eaten by water flea.

Plants absorb carbon dioxide and release oxygen.

Tadpoles and young newts eaten by fish.

NEWT

Water flea eaten by water beetle.

Algae eaten by water snail.

FISH

Crustacean eaten by fish.

Insects eaten by aquatic amphibians.

Algae eaten by beetle.

WATER SNAIL

Insect larvae eaten by fish.

Plankton feed on algae.

Mineral salts absorbed by algae.

Plants eaten by snails and other insects.

WATER BEETLE

MINERAL SALTS

SHELLFISH

Detritus eaten by crustaceans.

Plankton eaten by crustaceans.

Plants eaten by plankton.

Submerged plants absorb mineral salts.

DETRITUS

PLANKTON

SUBMERGED PLANT

BLOODWORM

Detritus eaten by insect larvae.

FEEDING AND WASTE

Most ponds support a complex food chain. Bacteria, snails, and worms feed on organic debris; they are then eaten by water beetles and dragonfly larvae, which in turn are eaten by fish and frogs. In all but large wildlife ponds, fish may need additional feeding. The plants feed on nutrients such as mineral salts dissolved in the water: they will, however, benefit from slow-release plant fertilizers *(see p. 150)* from time to time.

MAINTAINING A BALANCED ECOSYSTEM

Regular maintenance is necessary *(see pp. 140–141)*, but avoid emptying the pond too often. Do not overstock with plants – their dying leaves will create much decomposing matter that releases methane. A surplus of fish will deplete the pond of oxygen; overfeeding will leave surplus food to rot. If the water freezes over, make sure that there is an ice-free area so that waste gases can escape *(see p. 139)*. Avoid using pesticides and do not use ordinary fertilizers on water plants. Finally, test the water pH regularly *(see p. 151)* – an imbalance can harm pond life.

POOR WATER QUALITY

	Symptoms	Possible Causes
PH OUT OF BALANCE	• Fish more prone to disease • Plant growth diminished • Biological filters less effective	• Tapwater, lime seeping from cement or decorative limestone (high alkalinity) • Rainwater, decomposing plants or fish waste, nitrites building up (high acidity)
LOW OXYGEN LEVEL	• Fish gasp for breath at pond surface • Fish start to die with no symptoms of disease • Water blackens or becomes malodorous	• Too many floating plants or fish • Decomposing organic waste • Prolonged hot weather • Excessive algal growth
POLLUTION	• Dead fish • Discoloration of water • Yellowing of plants • Numerous bubbles (particularly noticeable under ice)	• Buildup of methane • Buildup of nitrites and ammonia • Run-off from local farmland using nitrogenous fertilizers • Overfeeding fish

SEASONAL CHANGES

In MILD WEATHER CONDITIONS routine attention and occasional pond cleaning *(see pp. 142–145)* will maintain a healthy and attractive water environment. However, when weather becomes severe – long, hot summers and bitterly cold winters – special care must be taken to ensure that both the structure and the plant and animal inhabitants of a pond are not harmed. In climates or sites that are regularly subject to extreme weather, careful siting and design and appropriate choice of plant and fish species are necessary preventive measures. In temperate climates, there are many practical tips that will protect a pond from fluctuations in temperature.

HOT, DRY WEATHER

Long periods of hot sun with little rain will cause the water level to drop through evaporation. If the pond is not filled up, this will result in warmer water, which will encourage the growth of algae and reduce the level of oxygen *(see pp. 136–137)*. Lack of oxygen may be manifested by distressed fish gulping for air. There may also be structural problems – a severe drop in water depth will expose flexible liner to sunlight, for example, which will eventually cause less expensive brands to crack.

MAINTAINING A POND IN HOT WEATHER
Keep the pond filled throughout summer from a slowly trickling hose. Whenever you need to add more than 20 percent tapwater to a pond, treat it with one of the products that eliminate chlorine, chloramine, and ammonia from the water, which are toxic to fish. If algal growth becomes excessive, you may need to use an algicide. Oxygen levels can be increased by creating water movement: either spray the surface with a garden hose or, better still, install a low-bubble fountain. If necessary, transfer fish to a temporary cool tank and move plants to lower depths, or shade them.

DESIGNS FOR HOT, DRY GARDENS

An informal pond with shallow margins and a large surface area is particularly vulnerable to water loss. In hot, sunny sites, it is worthwhile considering a more formal design, with a deeper pool that has overhanging edges to further minimize water loss through evaporation.

DECORATIVE CANAL
Canals originated in cultures with hot climates, such as those of ancient Egypt, Persia, and Rome. With their small surface area, they conserve water extremely efficiently.

SEVERE HOT-WEATHER PRECAUTIONS
During prolonged spells of hot, dry weather there are a number of ways to protect fish and plants and improve the condition of a pond. Remember when building a fish pond that a deep area of cool water where the fish may retreat is essential.

EMERGENCY MEASURES
To rapidly oxygenate and cool water if fish are in distress, use a hose with a fine spray nozzle.

FLEXIBLE LINER
When the water level drops, the liner is exposed to sunlight, which may in time cause it to crack.

FILLING UP
Fill up the pond with a slowly trickling hose to minimize disruption to the water ecology.

UV CLARIFIER
Where algal spread is a continual problem, consider adding a UV clarifier *(see p. 71)*.

UV-SYSTEM MAGNET

PERMANENT RELIEF
A low-bubble fountain oxygenates water while minimizing evaporation.

WARNING SIGNAL
Turn on a fountain or hose if fish rise to the surface and gulp for air.

OVERWINTERING A POND

Every precaution should be taken to protect the pond and its wildlife before the onset of winter. A sheet of ice puts an enormous strain on a pond's structure and can seriously affect water quality. Check the pond daily, and take every advance measure possible to protect the plants and fish.

WOODEN PLANKS

STRAW

POND HEATER
Before winter sets in, install a heater or stock tank deicer in order to keep a section of the pond from freezing.

POLYETHYLENE SHEETING
Cover a section of the pond with canvas or polyethylene to provide shelter for plants. Add straw for extra insulation.

SHELTERED PLANTS

TERRA-COTTA PIPE
Place terra-cotta pipes at the bottom of the pond to provide fish with shelter from hungry predators.

DORMANT PLANTS
Hardy deep-water plants lie dormant and protected at the bottom of the pond during the winter months.

POISONOUS GASES
An open area in the ice will allow poisonous gases such as methane to escape.

ABSORBING PRESSURE

Floats such as a rubber ball, boat tenders, or pieces of wood will help absorb the pressure of expanding water as it freezes. This method may not be fully effective in severe winter weather.

FLOAT

ICE

DORMANT PLANT

GARDEN HOSE

FREEZING WEATHER

Except in northern zones, it is unlikely that a water feature of adequate depth will freeze solid, but when water surface freezes, the ice expands, placing great pressure on the sides of a pond. Flexible-liner ponds resist this pressure better than concrete, particularly if the sides are slightly sloping. When building with concrete, reinforcing fibers will give flexibility and strength *(see pp. 90–91)*. Where walls are vertical and made of bricks, a polystyrene layer that will compact under pressure *(see right)* is invaluable. Floating objects placed on the water surface before the pond freezes absorb some of the stress, but a stock tank deicer is the most effective protection.

POISONOUS GASES

When ice seals a pond, the exchange of gases is prevented. Removing snow from the surface will allow light to reach the pond, increasing oxygen levels, but methane released by decomposing organic matter is trapped under the ice, and a hole must be created to allow it to escape. Never smash the ice: the vibrations will shock and may even kill the fish. Always melt the ice gently – use a pond heater or stand a pan of boiling water on the ice. Siphoning off a small quantity of water under the ice creates an insulating layer of warmer air beneath the ice that will protect pond life.

INSULATING A POND

Raised ponds are particularly vulnerable to freezing temperatures. Polystyrene, in sheet or granular form, can be used both for its insulating effects and to absorb ice pressure, protecting the pond's structure.

COPING STONE

INSULATING BEADS
Use polystyrene beads to fill the gap between double walls.

BRICKS

MORTAR

POLYSTYRENE CUSHION
Polystyrene between the liner and the bricks will provide insulation and also reduce ice pressure.

HARDCORE

CONCRETE

FLEXIBLE LINER

UNDERLAY

ROUTINE TASKS FOR POND HEALTH

Provided that a pond is well constructed and sensibly stocked, it should not be too difficult to care for and maintain. It is important to ensure that the water is at the correct level at all times; insufficient depth will cause temperature fluctuations, which will affect the water quality and consequently the well-being of plants and fish. Structural damage to the pond may occur and thus necessitate repair work *(see p. 145)*. Lining materials are especially vulnerable in extreme weather conditions *(see pp. 138–139)*. Any surrounding structures such as paving and bridges should be checked regularly; this is especially important for safety reasons.

Maintaining a Water Feature

Pond care involves maintaining every component of a water feature, and this includes both the plants and wildlife within the pond, the quality of the water, and all surrounding surfaces and structures.

REGULAR CLEANING
With a formal feature such as this, any neglect in the maintenance of water clarity, plants, and surroundings will be apparent.

STRUCTURAL CARE
Any structures incorporated by and over the water such as bridges, stepping stones, and decking should be checked regularly for structural damage. A screw missing on the handrail of a bridge, for example, could be potentially dangerous. Make sure that supporting foundations are sound; check also for rusting ironwork, and make sure that brickwork does not need repointing, especially after freezing weather.

Any surfaces should be regularly cleaned. Wood should be treated with preservatives once a year and any wooden or stone surfaces scoured with a wire brush in order to remove moss or algae. A slippery surface could be extremely dangerous – if necessary, cover the surface with fine wire mesh *(see below)*.

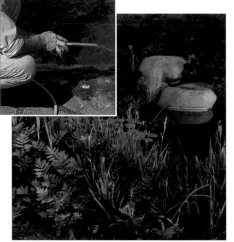

WATER LEVEL
During periods of hot weather when water evaporation is likely to occur, fill up the pond regularly with a slowly trickling hose (see inset). Failure to do this will allow the water level to drop, as is evident here in the water marks on the stepping stones. If the water level remains low for too long a period, pond life will suffer, and flexible liner may crack.

A NATURAL WATER BALANCE
Pond water is host to a community of microscopic organisms that are an important part of the water's ecology *(see pp. 136–137)*. In early spring, as the water begins to warm up and receives higher levels of sunlight, it becomes rich in minerals; phytoplankton (free-floating algae) feed on these minerals, and their presence causes the water to turn green and cloudy. This is only a temporary condition, indicating that the microscopic pond life is starting to reemerge, after having been dormant

SAFETY AND GENERAL CARE

WOODEN DECKING
Wooden decking complements water well. It may be used in any climate, provided that it has been treated with a wood preservative. Bear in mind that all wooden surfaces need regular maintenance, even in hot, dry climates. Check surface areas for any splits or cracks at least once a year, and make sure that no screws or brackets have rusted. Wooden surfaces require regular cleaning with a scrub brush, especially in damp climates. Chicken wire tacked to the decking (see inset) will provide an unobtrusive, nonslip surface.

SECURING AND CLEANING STONES
Any stones used as stepping stones must be completely stable and, if necessary, secured with mortar (see pp. 68–69). Surfaces should also be scrubbed regularly with a wire brush, to make sure that they are free of algae and not slippery.

SEASONAL TASKS FOR POND CARE

Spring	Summer	Autumn	Winter
• Clean out the pond, if necessary (see pp. 142–144).	• Check water chemistry with a commercial test kit (see p. 151).	• Secure a net over the pond to collect falling leaves and debris (see p. 159).	• Install a pond heater or stock tank deicer (see p. 139).
• Carry out any repair work (see p. 145).	• Clean the pump's strainer to make sure that it remains unclogged. Do this once a week (see below).	• Keep the water clear of dying foliage (see pp. 158–159).	• If not being used, remove, clean, and store pumps, filters, and lights.
• Clean off algae from surrounding paving, decking, or stepping stones	• Control algae with algicide, if necessary.	• Cut down foliage of marginal plants (see pp. 158–159).	• If the pump is still operating, add extra bricks to its base to raise it nearer to the surface of the water.
• Remove water heater for storage.	• Remove blanketweed regularly (see below).	• Cut back excess growth of submerged oxygenators (see pp.158–159).	• Remove any dead leaves from water.
• Reinstall pumps, filters, and lights.	• To combat blanketweed add barley straw in nets (the type of bacteria attracted to the straw feed on algae).		• In warmer zones, place a floating object on the water to stop the water from freezing (see p. 139).
• Check the water chemistry with a commercial test kit (see p. 151) and, if necessary, treat water with a pH adjuster.	• Keep the water free from decaying foliage (see pp. 158–159).		• Remove snow from ice sheets, if necessary, to allow light to enter (see p. 139).
• If plants are diseased, treat water with fungicide (see pp. 136–137).	• Check the water level weekly, and fill up if necessary (see p.138).		
	• If herons are preying on fish, fence the pond or cover with netting.		
	• Keep any fountains on all night in sultry weather (see p. 138).		

during the winter months. Algae play an important role in forming the first link in the food chain. As they use up nutrients and other creatures devour them, the algae will slowly diminish, leaving the pond water clear.

MAINTAINING CLEAR WATER

Functional planting (see pp. 152–153) and regular care should maintain clear water, but a long period of hot weather could disrupt the ecological balance, encouraging algal growth (see pp. 136–137), particularly of blanketweed. For quick results, algicides are available, but be sure to follow the instructions carefully. For a long-term solution, a biological pond filter and a UV clarifier with a magnet (see p. 71) is appropriate. To prevent water evaporation in long periods of hot weather (see p. 138), keep the pond filled up with a slowly trickling hose. Decomposing plant tissue will cloud or even blacken the pond,

polluting the water with toxic by-products and creating an unhealthy environment for fish. By regularly thinning and cutting back plants (see pp. 160–161) – especially in late summer when plants are beginning to die back – this potential problem may be averted. During autumn, place a net over the pond to catch the accumulation of fallen leaves before they enter the water (see p. 159). Before turning off the pump and installing a heater or stock tank deicer for winter, clear away any dead leaves in the water.

REMOVING EXCESS PLANT GROWTH

BLANKETWEED
Blanketweed, a mat of filamentous algae, should be removed regularly. To do this, rest a long stick on the water surface, turn gently, and pull out the strands of blanketweed that wrap around the stick.

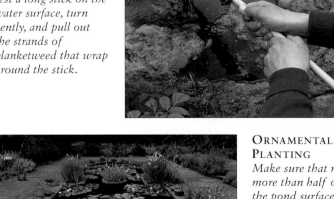

CLEANING ACCESSORIES

PUMP MAINTENANCE
Clean the pump and strainer as recommended by the manufacturer; this may be as often as once a week during summer. Pumps should also be stripped and serviced once a year.

NOZZLE

FOUNTAIN ADJUSTMENT

MOTOR

PRE-FILTER

STRAINER

OPEN-CELL FOAM

FILTER FOAM
Filter foam will clog rapidly if water becomes dirty and should be cleaned twice a month.

ORNAMENTAL PLANTING
Make sure that no more than half of the pond surface is covered with floating-leaved plants. If the plants become invasive, thin them in order to to allow sunlight to enter.

CLEANING OUT A POND

EVERY POND NEEDS periodic emptying and cleaning, the frequency depending on its size. Small ponds require attention every two to three years, while large ponds may need cleaning less frequently. The process involves emptying the pond of water and its inhabitants in order to remove the layer of decomposing debris lying on the bottom of the pond. The debris mainly consists of rotting leaves; but there may also be dead creatures. The clean-out also provides an opportunity for dividing established clumps of deep-water plants, such as water lilies, which may have become overgrown. While the pond is empty, examine its structure for cracks or punctures. Late spring is the best time to clean out a pond, allowing time for plants and wildlife to recover and reestablish over the summer. If you have large or expensive fish, it is worthwhile seeking advice from a specialist supplier on temporary holding facilities that will keep them safe and stress-free.

HOW TO EMPTY YOUR POND

YOU WILL NEED

TOOLS
- Pump or length of flexible tubing to siphon water
- Garden hose
- Several plastic buckets
- Dustpan
- Soft broom or brush

MATERIALS
- Rubber boots or waders, with cleated rather than studded soles
- Old newspapers
- For fish, a wading pool or large holding container, e.g., plastic garbage can
- Large, soft fish net
- Net or towel for covering fish
- Water treatment product for chlorine, chloramine, and ammonia

AN UNTENDED POND
When a pond becomes overgrown, it is advisable to carry out a major clean-up. This will provide the opportunity to control the plants' growth by dividing or thinning where necessary.

1 IF THE POND HAS a submersible pump, you can drain the pond by disconnecting the delivery pipe and connecting a hose in its place: otherwise, start to siphon away the water. If the pond contains fish, remove just enough water at first to make it easier to catch them. Fill a holding container for fish with pond water.

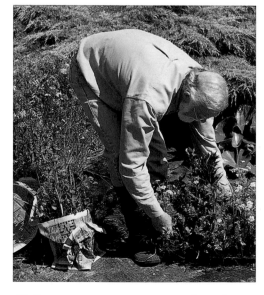

2 REMOVE CONTAINERIZED PLANTS from the margins of the pond; integral planting beds need not be disturbed, unless plants need dividing. Wrap planting crates in wet newspaper and place in a shady area. Water the plants and wet the newspaper every few hours.

CONTAINERIZED PLANTS
Remove any aquatic plants that are in containers.

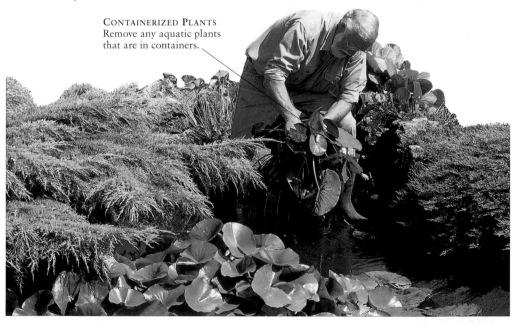

3 CATCH AS MANY FISH as are visible with a net and bowl (*see facing page*) and place them in the holding container in the shade. Remove containerized deep-water plants and water lilies, wrap the containers in wet newspaper, and place them with the marginals. Remove floating plants and submerged plants, retaining a few bunches of each in a bucket of water.

4 REMOVE ANY DECAYING plant matter that may be concealing more fish. Trawl the net through the water to catch any remaining fish. Place them in the holding container *(see inset)* and cover with a net or wet towel. Switch off the pump and remove it.

5 USE A PLASTIC BUCKET to remove the remaining water. Check the bucket for any beneficial creatures, such as frogs or tadpoles, and place them in the holding container. The water may be used on adjacent borders – do not pour it down a drain – it will clog the silt traps.

6 SCOOP UP THE MUD with a dustpan. Take care not to score the surface of any lining material. Reserve a small amount of mud and water in a bucket to help reacclimatize the fish when releasing them into the clean pond. The remaining mud can be added to compost.

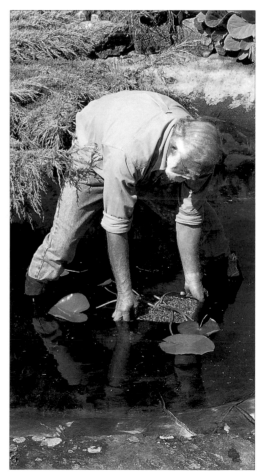

7 WITH THE POND now empty of fish, plants, and most of the mud, add a little water and brush away any remaining algae, mud, or plant debris. Then bail or siphon out the dirty water. Inspect the surface of the lining for damage and carry out repairs, if necessary *(see p. 145)*.

8 PARTIALLY REFILL THE POND to a depth that will allow you to stand in the water in rubber boots or waders. Unwrap the water lilies and other deep-water plants. Divide them *(see pp. 160–161)* and trim them in order to remove any damaged stems and foliage.

9 SUBMERGE THE WATER PLANTS in the deeper areas of the pond. Any new, small plants should initially be placed on stacks of bricks *(see p. 157)* so leaves can reach the surface. Position ornamental plants like water lilies first, then add submerged plants. *(Continued overleaf.)*

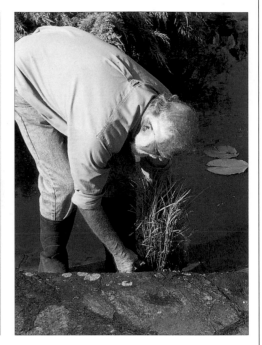

10 ONCE THE DEEP-WATER plants have been installed, add the bucket full of reserved mud and original water *(see p. 143)*. This will help fish and any other pond life resting in the holding container to reestablish themselves quickly when put back in the pond.

11 BEFORE TRANSFERRING THE FISH from the bucket into the pond, examine them carefully. Check that they have not been damaged in any way, and look for signs of fungal growth or other disorders *(see pp. 174–175)*. Then reintroduce them to the pond.

12 UNWRAP THE MARGINALS, divide or thin them *(see pp. 160–161)* if necessary, and repot in their baskets on the marginal shelves. Then refill the pond to its correct level and treat the water for chlorine and other additives. Reconnect and position the pump.

A WELL-TENDED POND
This pond is no longer filled with overcrowded, congested plants, which have either been removed, divided, or thinned. The pond is now refilled with clean water, to which a small quantity of the original water and mud is added to reintroduce the microscopic life that allows a working ecosystem to become established again. The floating-leaved plants have been drastically thinned, retaining only the healthiest portions; while they grow, fish can take advantage of the shade cast by the overhanging juniper. Turn on a fountain, if you have one, to give maximum oxygenation to the water.

POND REPAIRS

POND CLEANING PROVIDES an ideal opportunity to inspect pond linings for structural damage, because a pond must be empty in order repair it. Large holes or cracks are usually obvious, because the water drops to their level. Minimal damage, however, will cause only very slow seepage, and may be hard to locate. Damage may be accidental or caused by extreme weather conditions *(see pp. 138–139)*. Inexpensive flexible and rigid liners are more likely to develop cracks than good-quality ones. Reinforced concrete pools *(see pp. 90–91)* are extremely resilient, but ordinary concrete will deteriorate within a few years.

REPAIRING FLEXIBLE LINERS

The simplest way to repair butyl, EPDM, or PVC liners is with double-sided, adhesive PVC tape *(see right)*, which can be obtained from suppliers of aquatic goods. It is probably not worthwhile repairing an inexpensive polyethylene liner. Before repairing a liner, it is important to clean the surrounding area thoroughly with a scrub brush and water. When the repair work is complete, wait at least 12 hours before refilling the pond.

REPAIRING PREFORMED RIGID UNITS

If a preformed rigid unit is not level, or if the ground underneath and the backfilling around it has not been thoroughly compacted, the unit is likely to crack eventually under the weight of the water. This applies particularly to cheaper plastic units. The crack can be repaired with a motor repair kit containing fiberglass matting. First, roughen the surrounding area with coarse sandpaper and clean it with water. Allow the area to dry, and apply a patch of fiberglass matting that is one-and-a-half times larger than the damaged area. Wait 24 hours for the compound to set. Check that the ground around the unit is well compacted.

REPAIRING CONCRETE PONDS

It is possible to repair cracks and fractures in concrete ponds, although this is not a long-term solution. First, clean the damaged area thoroughly with a scrub brush and water, and

REPAIRING A FLEXIBLE LINER

1 **ALLOW THE DAMAGED** area to dry, and clean with a soft cloth, dampened with alcohol.

2 **PLACE DOUBLE-SIDED** adhesive tape over the puncture and allow two minutes for it to become "tacky."

3 **CUT A PATCH** from a spare piece of liner and press firmly onto the tape, ensuring that the edges are flat.

allow it to dry. Then fill the crack with a commercial, fast-hardening sealant. If there is any likelihood of rain, cover the area with a sheet of polyethylene. Then apply a waterproof sealant and allow at least 24 hours for the compound to dry.

If a concrete pond is irreparable, lining the shell with butyl or EPDM and underlay will prevent the pond from leaking. (These are the most suitable types of lining material for a concrete pond, as they are less likely to be damaged by rough edges than PVC or polyethylene.) Lay the liner and underlay over the shell *(see also pp. 78–79)*, allowing for an overlap of about 4in (10cm); bury the edges of the liner in the surrounding earth. If the pond is surrounded by edging, trim the liner and mortar it to the paving at the point where it meets the edge of the pond.

REPAIRING CRACKS IN CONCRETE

1 **TO MEND A FINE** crack, first use a thin stone chisel and a club hammer to widen the gap, tapping very gently.

2 **CLEAN OFF DUST** and debris by brushing vigorously in the crack and surrounding area with a stiff wire brush.

3 **USING A SMALL** pointed trowel, fill the crack with a concrete sealant. Allow at least two days for the sealant to dry.

4 **BRUSH THE AREA** with a commercial pool-sealing compound. This will prevent toxins from leaking into the water.

PLANTS FOR WATER GARDENS

FOR GARDENERS, the chief excitement of creating water features is the opportunity they provide to use a new range of plants that need special growing conditions, and to grow and display more commonly seen garden plants in a new and attractive environment. The pleasure of watching the birds, insects, and other wildlife attracted by the water and its planting is a valuable bonus.

PLANTING NEW WATER FEATURES

Of all the specialty plant groups, water plants are among the easiest to grow successfully. Given the correct planting site and healthy water conditions, they will thrive with a vigor that is extremely satisfying. Provided that initial stocking is done with care, the majority of water features will look respectably furnished by the end of the first growing season and positively well established by the end of the second.

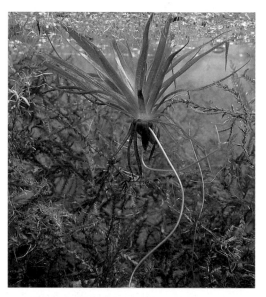

UNDERWATER PLANTS

Submerged plants play an important role in water health and, seen waving under the surface, heighten the effect of a natural pond. The roots and partially submerged leaves of Stratiotes aloides, *the water soldier, provide food and shelter for wildlife dwelling below the water surface.*

FLOATING LEAVES

Water lilies not only have superb ornamental value but also perform a functional role: the floating lily-pads shade the water, helping to restrain the growth of algae.

INFORMAL PLANTING

To create an informal effect, allow plants to spread and mingle. Marginal beds permit grasses, reeds, and sedges to grow freely within the limitations of the site. Free-floating plants form changing patterns on the water, moving gently with winds and water currents. They multiply readily and, like vigorous marginals, need regular thinning.

EXOTIC DISPLAY
If climatic conditions do not allow tropical plants to be used outdoors year-round, they can be used in exotic container displays. Here, the pink of Nymphaea *'Emily Grant Hutchison' contrasts strikingly with pea-green* Pistia stratiotes *(water lettuce).*

FORMAL PLANTINGS
The restrained use of well-tended plants both in and around the pool enhances a formal setting. A raised pool always gives a formal effect, and makes plant care easier too. Here, the plantings soften without subduing the impact of the elegant stonework and a surrounding parterre of formally shaped clipped hedging and topiary.

ESTABLISHED WATER PLANTINGS

Because plants in and around water grow with such vigor if plantings are left untended, soil and water space will become extremely congested and unhealthy. As plantings mature, steps must be taken to ensure that plants do not become crowded. The free circulation of water or air around and within plants is important; a stagnant environment encourages the growth of fungal spores and other harmful organisms. Also, more dominant specimens will stifle smaller plants and upset the balance between different plant types that is so crucial to pond health. Thin floating-leaved plants regularly through the summer, and divide overly vigorous species to keep them contained. In warmer areas, or where water features are sited under glass, care must be taken that evergreen plants do not take over, because of the head start they have over herbaceous plants that must regrow each spring.

THE RANGE AVAILABLE

Although the range of plants that will grow in water is limited when compared to what is available when designing a border, for example, there are an increasing number of plants to choose from each year, particularly as more non-native plants are introduced for sale. Even if you are restricted by climate to only the hardiest of plants, there are still many options to choose from. Consider combining hardy species with tender perennials that can be replaced annually or if necessary overwintered indoors. When it comes to choosing moisture-lovers for the area around a pond, the range is wide enough for any taste, and includes not only traditional favorites such as hostas, iris, and primroses, but increasing numbers of new cultivars of plants such as lobelia and mimulus.

Most general garden centers now have a small section that is devoted entirely to water plants. However, you will find a wider choice of well-grown plants at nurseries specializing in water gardening. Remember that it is, in many cases, illegal to collect plants from the wild, and in all cases most inadvisable. Even though some very common, unendangered species of submerged plants can often be found in natural ponds on farms or public land, they may carry blanketweed, pests, and diseases, all of which will have a detrimental effect on a garden pond and its plant and animal inhabitants.

PLANTING ENVIRONMENTS

Plants used in and around water features may be divided into two broad groups: those that will survive with their roots under water or in permanently saturated soil, and moisture-loving plants that enjoy a high moisture content in soil but must have some drainage to create air pockets in the soil structure. The first category contains two types of truly aquatic plants that are essential to a healthy pond: those that have submerged foliage, and those that have floating leaves. Marginal plants and moisture-loving plants for moist to wet soil around the water's edge are used largely for ornamental effect or to create wildlife habitats.

SUBMERGED PLANTS

Plants that have underwater leaves play a vital role in aquatic ecosystems. These plants usually have fine, feathery foliage to provide a large leaf surface area, which compensates for the reduction in light levels below water (they will tolerate a maximum depth of 3ft/90cm in full sun). The oxygen released from their leaves as a by-product of photosynthesis (the process by which plants gain energy) passes directly into the water. The water is then able to support other life forms, and a healthy ecosystem develops from which the plants also benefit.

Submerged plants also absorb minerals dissolved in the water, competing with algae and suppressing their growth. Their roots play a much less significant role in absorbing nutrients and tend to be shallow, frequently acting as little more than light anchors. There is equipment available that will carry out the purely functional role of submerged plants; however, plants have other

WELL-BALANCED PLANTING
Here, sensitive planting has produced a lush setting that is dense without being too crowded. Deep-water aquatics play a functional role, moisture-loving plants such as astilbes create a soft edge to the pond, and the clump of Iris sibirica *provides color.*

advantages; apart from their attractively textured foliage, they are essential for wildlife ponds, providing cover in which creatures may shelter and breed. They grow rapidly but can be controlled very simply by removing handfuls of surplus stems.

DEEP-WATER AQUATICS

Water lilies are by far the most popular plants among those that root in deep water. While their roots and tough, flexible stems are submerged, their leaves and flowers must be above water,

GUNNERA MANICATA

IRIS ENSATA

CANDELABRA PRIMULA

CALTHA PALUSTRIS

LAGAROSIPHON MAJOR

DEEP ZONE
Most water lilies prefer to be sited where they can enjoy the full depth of the pond.

WAVING STEMS
The long, fleshy stems of pond weed need the support of surrounding water.

WICK EFFECT
Large plants will suck water over liner edges, and regular refilling *(see pp. 158–159)* may be needed.

SATURATED SOIL
Boggy soil beds must be planted with true marginal plants, not moisture-lovers.

SHELF LIFE
Marginal plants in containers are easy to tend.

A POND DESIGNED FOR PLANTS
Not every pond will encompass the full range of planting sites that water plants and moisture-lovers may occupy; the types of plant you wish to grow will influence both the design and choice of construction method of a water feature.

usually floating on the surface. They must be given a planting depth suitable for their size and vigor so that leaf and flower stalks can reach the surface, otherwise the plant will drown. A number of water lilies, such as the vigorous *Nymphaea alba*, thrive in water that is up to 10ft (3m) deep. Those more suited to medium-sized pools generally prefer a depth of 1½–2ft (45–60cm). In all but large informal ponds, the growth of deep-water plants needs to be controlled by root restriction, regular division or, in small ponds, a combination of both.

FREE-FLOATING PLANTS

These plants absorb all their nourishment from the water through fine roots that hang suspended from leaf clusters or rosettes that float on the water surface. They perform the same function as rooted plants with floating foliage, and many that are semi-submerged also play an oxygenating role. If chosen correctly for the prevailing climate, they need virtually no attention, with the important exception that their sometimes invasive vigor and spread will need regular control. Surplus plants can simply be scooped off the water with a rake or net.

MARGINAL PLANTS

Warm shallows and waterlogged soil at the edges of informal ponds can be populated with a variety of plants that thrive with their roots in depths of water up to 6–9in (15–22cm). Submerged plants, most free-floating plants, and some floating-leaved plants, including dwarf water lilies, will thrive in shallow water. Marginal plants, which generally hold their foliage well above water, are more commonly chosen for the vertical interest they bring to the edges of the pool.

Although they do not contribute to the balance of the water chemistry, marginal plants contribute to a pond's ecosystem, providing an excellent refuge for wildlife, especially aquatic insect life *(see pp. 54–55)*; they are also a key ornamental element in most water features. Many marginal plants are vigorous growers; using planting baskets helps restrict growth

FUNCTIONAL PLANTS

SUBMERGED PLANTS
Submerged pond weeds such as Myriophyllum aquaticum *release oxygen directly into the water during daylight hours. They also compete with algae for minerals.*

FLOATING-LEAVED PLANTS
Water lilies are the most popular aquatics for the deep, central areas of a pond. In addition to their ornamental value, their floating foliage provides essential shade.

and protects the pond structure (in particular, flexible liner) from certain species, including *Typha latifolia* and *Glyceria maxima*, which have sharp, penetrating roots.

MOISTURE-LOVING PLANTS

The range of moisture-lovers includes not only traditional waterside species but also a broad variety of plants, such as hostas and astilbes, that may be used in any bed or border that contains well-watered, water-retentive soil. It must be remembered that moisture-loving plants differ from marginals in requiring oxygen at their roots; the majority will not tolerate waterlogged, boggy areas. However, with some form drainage system provided *(see pp. 58–59)*, they bring a welcome variety of plantings to pond edges, and play an important role in blending water features into the garden as a whole.

HOSTA

PISTIA STRATIOTES
Free-floating plants will drift about the pond in winds and currents.

CAMPANULA PORTENSCHLAGIANA

APONOGETON DISTACHYOS

MATTEUCCIA STRUTHIOPTERIS

TRANSITIONAL BEDS
Well-watered beds surrounding the pond will enable broad plantings of moisture-lovers.

ROCK PLANTS
Alpines will grow in dry planting pockets between rocks.

NYMPHOIDES PELTATA

PLANTING DEPTHS
Bricks under younger and less vigorous deep-water plants keep them closer to the surface.

MYRIOPHYLLUM AQUATICUM
In the shallows, submerged plants may grow above the water, rooting lightly in mud or among rocks.

FURTHER INFORMATION

- Encouraging Wildlife – pp. 54–55
- A Balanced Ecosystem – pp. 136–137
- Routine Plant Care – pp. 158–159
- Plant Catalog – pp. 178–207

SOILS AND CONTAINERS

MOST WATER PLANTS are tolerant of a wide range of soil types; it is the quality and the acidity or alkalinity – the pH balance – of the water that is of primary importance. Unlike many other types of plants, water plants do not require a medium rich in nutrients, which will encourage algal growth in the water. Growing mediums, whether for planting beds or individual planting baskets or crates, must be of a certain texture, but if garden soil is unsuitable, it can be improved. Planting baskets or crates are ideal, not only for restricting growth in smaller ponds but also for making it easy to lift, divide, and move plants.

PLANTING MEDIUMS

Ordinary garden topsoil may be used both in integral planting beds and in planting crates, provided that it is of good quality and suitable structure. In a well-cultivated garden the topsoil will be rich in organic matter and will have a consistency that is firm yet porous. Soil that is too light will dissipate in the water and will not allow plants to develop a sound root system, while a very heavy soil will compact and stifle the roots.

SOIL CONTENT

Soil is generally classified according to its clay, silt, and sand content; it can be tested *(see right)* to discover what proportion of each it contains. Most garden plants enjoy a soil that is not dominated by any one type of soil particle, contains a good proportion of humus, and a clay content of between eight and 25 percent. Soil for water plants ideally needs to be heavier, and clay should be added to sandy and silty soils.

SOIL NUTRIENTS

Soil taken from a garden that grows healthy plants will help most water plants off to a good start. Never add fertilizers at planting time or take soil from a bed that has recently been

ORGANIC MATTER
A layer of organic matter floats on the surface.

CLAY
Clay is the last type of soil to settle.

SAND
Sand forms the bottom layer.

SOIL COMPOSITION
Take a small quantity of soil and dry it thoroughly, so that it is crumbly and can be rubbed easily through the fingers. Half-fill a watertight container with water and add the soil. Place a lid on the jar, shake firmly, and leave for three to five days, after which time there will be individual layers of sand, silt, clay, and organic matter. A suitable soil for water plants should have a layer of clay that is twice as deep as the sand.

fertilized; the nutrients will dissolve into the water and provide nourishment for unwanted algae. Concentrated fertilizers in small ponds may also severely disrupt the water chemistry and can be toxic to fish. As soon as microscopic life develops in a new pond, a food chain is set in motion *(see pp. 136–137)* that will give plants supplementary nourishment. As plants mature, soil renewal when dividing *(see pp. 160–161)* or a spring supplement of slow-release fertilizer will replenish nutrient levels. Fertilizer tablets made specifically for feeding water plants on a monthly basis are also available.

SOIL STRUCTURE AND COMPOSITION

CROSS-SECTION THROUGH SOIL
From the surface downward, left: topsoil contains the nutrients plants need; its composition varies (right) according to the locality. Subsoil has little or no nutritional value and consists primarily of compacted stony matter, sand, or solid clay.

SAND
Sand is dry, light, and free-draining.

SILT
Silt is reasonably moisture-retentive, but easily becomes compacted.

GARDEN SOILS
The drainage of different soil compositions varies.

CLAY
This heavy soil is slow-draining.

SOIL FOR MOISTURE-LOVING PLANTS

In planting areas around ponds and in bog gardens, the key quality of the soil is its moisture-retentiveness. Soil that drains too quickly will not provide these plants with the moisture levels they need to thrive. Evaporation from the soil surface is also increased. Improved garden soil is ideal for moisture-lovers. Again, clay should be added to light, gritty soils. With all soils, work in a good proportion of well-rotted organic matter before planting, adding more in subsequent years. Provided that fertilizers cannot leach out into pond water and upset the water chemistry, moisture-loving plants can be lightly fertilized, if necessary.

IMPROVING SOIL STRUCTURE
Using a fork, dig in organic matter such as compost to improve the structure of the soil.

TESTING THE pH

Simple pH kits can be used to check the acidity or alkalinity of soil and, importantly for aquatic plants, pond water. Mix with some of the solution included in the kit. Then check the color of the liquid against the chart in order to find the pH level.

TEST TUBE

CHART
A range of colors indicate different pH values.

TESTING WATER
Mix pond water with some of the solution provided.

PLANTING CONTAINERS

While the effect is never quite as natural as that of plants growing and mingling in soil, growing water plants in containers has many advantages, especially in small and formal ponds. Water lilies, deep-water plants, and marginal plants can be planted in baskets to prevent them from growing too large; plants in containers rarely reach more than half the maximum spread they would attain when grown in soil. Also, plants may need lifting and dividing at different times; the roots of plants growing together in beds will soon become entangled, making it difficult to avoid damaging them. Planting containers make it possible to deal with plants separately.

BASKETS AND CRATES

Plastic planting baskets and crates are readily available in various sizes and shapes. Retailers that stock preformed rigid pool units usually have a range of crates specially tailored to fit the contours of these pools and their marginal shelves. Containers have open-lattice sides in order to allow water and gases to reach the soil. Planting baskets with wide-meshed sides will need to be lined with burlap or polypropylene, otherwise

soil will fall out before the plant's roots have a chance to grow and bind it together. The piece of material used to line the basket needs to be approximately twice the size of the basket. Fine-mesh containers, however, do not require lining.

Always choose a size of basket appropriate to the size of the plant; if the basket is too small, the plant will become top-heavy and may topple over. With taller marginals it may be necessary to anchor the basket *(see p. 157)* with a brick placed in the bottom, or by adding rocks on top of the soil. When established plants grow too large for their containers in most garden ponds it is usually preferable to divide the plant *(see pp. 160–161)*. Only replant the healthiest portion into the same basket, discarding the older, less vigorous parts rather than move the whole plant into bigger quarters.

OTHER CONTAINERS

Although planting crates are not expensive to buy, other containers may be improvised. Submerged plants may be grown in ordinary plastic plant pots, since they take their nourishment directly from the water; the roots merely act as an anchor. Deep-water plants are often planted in solid-sided rubber or plastic tubs. Used nursery pots from trees or shrubs are generally large enough and work well. A shallow plastic laundry basket makes a fine improvised container for a large vigorous water lily, although it would be far too large for less vigorous plants or, at first, for young lilies. Integral planting beds within ponds *(see pp. 78–79)* may also be constructed with bricks, mortared loosely to hold the structure together, yet allowing water to pass through the walls into the soil.

TOPDRESSING THE SOIL
Always topdress the soil with pea gravel or grit in order to prevent it from spilling out into the water.

AQUATIC PLANTING CONTAINERS

ROUND CONTAINER

SHAPED CONTAINER

LARGE, SQUARE CONTAINER

WIDE-MESH CONTAINERS
The wider mesh sided baskets allow the maximum level of gases to exchange through the sides between water and plant roots. They do, however, also let out soil and will require some form of permeable lining. These containers come in a range of shapes and sizes.

LARGE, ROUND CONTAINER

LINING A CONTAINER
Make sure that there is a sufficient overlap of burlap to prevent soil escaping.

ROUND CONTAINER

SQUARE CONTAINER

IRREGULARLY SHAPED CONTAINER

BURLAP LINING
Cheap and effective, burlap is an ideal lining for wide-mesh containers, allowing gases and water through without letting the soil spill out.

FINE-MESH CONTAINERS
Newer plastic containers with fine-mesh sides do not need to be lined, since soil will not fall through the fine holes.

SELECTING PLANTS

DECIDING WHICH PLANTS to choose for a water garden may at first seem a little daunting; there are, however, some fundamental rules to follow, which should make choosing easier. The first priority is to provide an adequate number of functional plants in order to establish a well-balanced pond as quickly as possible. It is important to achieve the correct numbers and balance of these plants, avoiding understocking or overcrowding. Ornamental planting may be more flexible, depending to a large degree on personal taste, but it is important to consider flowering seasons to provide variety and create a long period of interest.

ESSENTIAL PLANTS

In order to develop and maintain a healthy environment within a pond, it is vital to have some submerged plants and floating-leaved plants, whose role is to filter and oxygenate the water and, by competing successfully for sunlight and nutrients, to minimize algal growth in the water. Floating leaves will help to reduce the inevitable greening of the water with algae that occurs in high light conditions when the pool has inadequate surface cover. It occurs temporarily both in new ponds and each spring, before other plants have a chance to grow, but once they do, a balance is restored and the water clears.

To help this process, a third to half of the pond's surface should be covered by the leaves of free-floating and deep-water plants. In established ponds, water lilies are especially important, since they are among the first plants to spread their leaves in spring. However, they and other deep-water plants take time to establish. Free-floating plants are especially useful in the early establishment of a new pool, or in prolonged hot, sunny weather. *Azolla filiculoides*, for example, spreads rapidly and will provide enough cover within three months in a small pond. Its growth will soon need to be strictly controlled, however. In features with limited surface areas you may wish to remove the floaters in favor of the more permanent ornamental plants once water lilies and other deep-water plants have grown.

STOCKING LEVELS FOR NEW PONDS			
Pond size	Oxygenating plants	Temporary cover	Water lilies
Small 8ft x 6ft (2.5m x 2m)	15 bunches	6 free-floaters	1 water lily
Small to medium 12ft x 8ft (4m x 2.5m)	30 bunches	9 free-floaters	2 water lilies
Medium 15ft x 9ft (5m x 2.75m)	45 bunches	9–12 free-floaters	3 water lilies
Medium to large 20ft x 12ft (6m x 4m)	60 bunches	12–15 free floaters	4 water lilies
Large 30ft x 15ft (10m x 5m)	75 bunches	20–30 free-floaters	5 water lilies

Submerged plants, such as *Lagarosiphon* and *Myriophyllum*, also play an essential role. Not only do they compete with algae for nutrients, they also release oxygen into the water, enabling it to support life. In a new pond, it is vital to add enough plants *(see above)* to provide an adequate density of submerged foliage.

OTHER PRACTICAL CONSIDERATIONS

Once functional plants have been chosen, the design and surroundings of the individual feature may be considered in more detail. Certain plants, notably water lilies, do not tolerate

PLANTS FOR INITIAL STOCKING

SUBMERGED PLANTS
An adequate quantity of submerged plants such as Lagarosiphon major *or* Elodea canadensis *should be added to new ponds, so that their leaves may begin to produce oxygen to aerate the water and enable a healthy ecosystem to develop.*

FAST-GROWING FLOATING PLANTS
Small free-floating plants such as Azolla filiculoides *spread rapidly, and are extremely useful for providing initial cover. By mid-summer, they will probably need thinning so that surface cover is not too dense.*

CONSOLIDATING WET GROUND
If your pond is surrounded by boggy areas, plants with creeping, mat-forming root systems, such as Houttuynia cordata *(above),* Carex, *and* Persicaria *will soon grow to hold soil together and reduce surface evaporation.*

moving water, for example, so plants must be chosen with care for streams and around waterfalls. Ponds with informal beds filled with soil require some plants that will root strongly and knit together the edges. For small ponds, marsh marigolds (*Caltha palustris*) are ideal; for larger ponds, *Iris pseudacorus* or *Cyperus longus* could be used. If you want to attract wildlife, this will also affect plant choice *(see pp. 54–55)*.

ORNAMENTAL PLANTING

Although you will be choosing plants for their visual contribution, you must bear in mind their suitability. The plants you choose and the way you arrange them may be restricted by the style of water feature and by climate and site.

Try to keep planting as simple as possible so that the water remains the focus of attention – planting should enhance rather than dominate the surroundings. Avoid using very vigorous plants in proximity to less robust species, and be especially careful in small areas to choose plants that can be kept within their allotted space. Large species can be used as specimen plants, but smaller plants often look better grouped in twos and threes.

SELECTING COLORS

Some gardeners enjoy bright colors, others prefer subdued shades – it is entirely a matter of taste. Color designs can continue a theme throughout the season *(below)*, or become progressively richer: yellow *Ranunculus* and white callas and bogbean (*Menyanthes trifoliata*) will give a fresh look in spring, while in summer, vivid blue *Pontederia cordata* and rich red *Lobelia cardinalis* stand out against a lush, leafy background. Plants with attractive foliage are particularly well complemented by water. Grasses, sedges, and ferns can be used to create both formal and informal looks.

PLANTING FOR STYLE

FORMAL POOL
As demonstrated above, restrained planting is especially important to the clear symmetrical shapes of a formal pool.

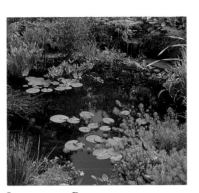

INFORMAL POND
This water garden makes generous use of plants; bear in mind, however, that oxygenators in particular will grow rapidly.

PLANTING FOR COLOR

BOLD COLORS
Dark water and the lush greens of vigorously growing moisture-lovers are perfect backgrounds against which to use rich, bold color.

SIMPLE PASTELS
This low-key planting uses limited space effectively by featuring white flowers, silvery foliage, and pale pebbles to light up a dull corner.

FLOWER COLOR THROUGH THE SEASON			
	Early spring	Late spring to early summer	Midsummer to early autumn
White to cream	Caltha palustris var. alba Leucojum aestivum Petasites japonicus Primula denticulata var. alba	Aponogeton distachyos Calla palustris Menyanthes trifoliata Ranunculus aquatilis	Aponogeton distachyos Filipendula ulmaria 'Aurea' Miscanthus sinensis 'Zebrinus' Sagittaria sagittifolia
Yellow to orange	Caltha palustris 'Flore Pleno' Lysichiton americanum Primula veris Ranunculus ficaria	Iris pseudacorus Narthecium ossifragum Nymphaea 'Odorata Sulphurea Grandiflora'	Inula hookeri Ligularia 'Gregynog Gold' Lysimachia nummularia 'Aurea' Myriophyllum verticillatum
Pink to red	Anagallis tenella 'Studland' Darmera peltata Nymphaea 'Laydekeri Fulgens' Primula rosea	Alisma plantago-aquatica Nelumbo nucifera 'Momo Botan' Nymphaea 'James Brydon' Nymphaea 'Marliacea Carnea'	Astilbe 'Venus' Butomus umbellatus Filipendula purpurea Lythrum salicaria
Purple to blue	Myosotis scorpioides Primula denticulata Trillium erectum	Iris versicolor Hosta fortunei Nymphaea 'Blue Beauty' Nymphaea capensis	Lobelia x gerardii 'Vedrariensis' Phragmites australis 'Variegatus' Pontederia cordata Veronica beccabunga

YEAR-ROUND INTEREST

Foliage plants provide a changing, colorful seasonal display. Most aquatic plants are herbaceous, but evergreen marginal plants include *Thalia, Acorus gramineus, Equisetum hyemale,* and *Carex.* There are many attractive variegated irises and grasses in particular, and for autumn color, *Darmera peltata* and *Lobelia cardinalis* will provide a boost for the garden once the main flowering season is over. The texture of plants can be varied too, from feathery astilbes and swordlike irises and reeds to the broad-leaved gunneras and rheums. The seedheads of many plants can also add a decorative element.

BUYING PLANTS

MOST AQUATIC NURSERIES have a good selection of water plants, although at certain times of the year the choice may be more limited. Any general garden center should have a range of moisture-lovers among its stock. Examine plants carefully before making a choice; good suppliers will have plants on display that are clean, plump, and dense. Aquatic plants will either be sold bare-root or container-grown. They will be packed in plastic bags to make transportation easier. It is advisable to place the plants in another bag to avoid the possibility of leakage. Take plants home as soon as possible, and make sure that they remain moist.

CHOOSING YOUNG PLANTS

Midspring is the best time of year for purchasing plants, when the increasing day length and warmer water will make it easier for them to reestablish in their new environment. There should also be little likelihood of frost. It is possible to add plants until late summer. Cut back plants bought later in the the year that have made more growth before adding them to your garden. They will not be at their best until the next season.

SELECTING DEEP-WATER PLANTS

Most deep-water plants survive winter by storing food reserves in large rhizomes or tubers. The young shoots grow to the surface in spring, and can only manufacture food from sunlight again when the leaves have unfurled. For this reason it is essential to choose plants with a sound, fat tuber or rhizome that will nourish this early stage of growth.

Young deep-water plants are often sold bare-root, having been freshly divided from a parent plant. Buying container-grown plants avoids root disturbance, but water plants generally suffer less transplant setback than other garden plants.

PLANTS ON DISPLAY
Aquatic nurseries should have a range of water plants on display, which will be grouped according to their requirements. This makes it possible to examine the plants thoroughly before making a purchase. It is best to visit aquatic nurseries during spring to midsummer, when there will be a far greater variety of water plants to choose from.

SELECTING HEALTHY PLANTS

FREE-FLOATING PLANTS
Water soldier (Stratiotes aloides) is a semi-evergreen perennial that resembles a pineapple top, with short, stubby roots. The rosette of dark olive-green leaves should be well formed and dense. A well-grown plant will produce creamy white flowers in midsummer.

HEALTHY EXAMPLE

HEALTHY LEAVES
Foliage is dense and well formed.

POOR EXAMPLE

DAMAGED LEAVES

GOOD ROOTS
Roots are clean and undamaged.

NEW GROWTH
Strong central growth is evident.

YOUNG PLANTLET

HEALTHY EXAMPLE

NEW GROWTH
Leaves are sprouting vigorously.

POOR EXAMPLE

SOUND ROOTS
Tuber is plump and firm.

WEAK FOLIAGE
Leaves are small and discolored.

LIMP STEMS

DEEP-WATER PLANTS
Healthy young water lilies will soon put on a fine display. Many water lilies increase by producing small plants that bud off from the main tuber (see above); these can be used immediately to increase stock (see pp. 162–163).

CONTAINER-GROWN MARGINAL
Marsh marigold (Caltha palustris) is particularly useful for wildlife ponds, since it attracts insects early in the year. A healthy plant will be compact, with shiny, dark green foliage. The single, golden yellow flowers appear in spring.

HEALTHY EXAMPLE

HEALTHY LEAVES
Foliage is sound and glossy.

NUMEROUS STEMS

POOR EXAMPLE

WEAK GROWTH

NEGLECT
Weeds suggest poor care.

One reason for buying container-grown plants is to obtain large specimens to create an "instant" effect, but these plants are expensive, heavy, and difficult to transport without damage occurring. Given the right conditions, healthy young plants will soon make plenty of growth. Look for plants with several young folded leaves thrusting from the base – older leaves will probably die shortly after planting.

SELECTING SUBMERGED PLANTS

Most aquatic nurseries or retailers will stock up to six different species of submerged plants, often called oxygenators. Unless you have very strong preferences, buy as many different types as possible: all water conditions are different, and suit different plants. With time you will discover which species are best suited to your garden; excess plants can easily be thinned. Submerged plants are sold as cuttings, in bunches of six to nine stems held together with a small lead clasp near the base. The stems should be 6–12in (15–30cm) in length, have closely spaced leaves, and

look plump and vigorous. Examine bunches carefully: if they are dirty, weak, or contain blanketweed (tiny, bright green strands that clump together like wet cotton) or jellylike snail eggs, do not purchase them.

RINSING NEW PLANTS
Rinse plants in water to wash out and inspect any insects so that you do not introduce harmful ones into the pond.

SELECTING FLOATING PLANTS
Floating plants are generally sold from tanks: the tiny plants such as duckweed (*Lemna*) and fairy moss (*Azolla*) are scooped out of the tank and packed in watertight plastic bags; a small amount of water is added to keep the plants moist while being transported. Larger floaters like water hyacinth (*Eichhornia*) and water soldier (*Stratiotes aloides*) are generally sold individually and packed in plastic bags for transport.

SELECTING MARGINALS AND MOISTURE-LOVERS
Displays of bog and moisture-loving plants in aquatic or garden centers often look tired toward the end of the summer;

KEEPING PLANTS MOIST
If you cannot plant immediately, keep submerged and free-floating plants in a bucket of water (change this daily if the delay is prolonged) and stand young container plants in water. Bare roots of plants may be wrapped in wet newspaper but should be planted on the same day.

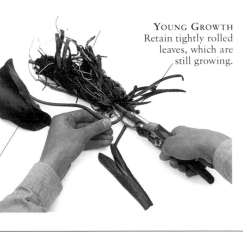

SUBMERGED PLANTS

WATER-FILLED TRAY

late spring is a better time to buy. Use the same criteria to select specimens as you would any garden plant, choosing healthy, compact young specimens with plenty of fresh new growth thrusting up from the base; these will quickly become established in their new quarters. Marginal plants especially may grow at a phenomenal rate; match the vigor of plants to your site, and do not buy too many plants at first.

PREPLANTING CARE
For best results, have your pond filled and planting sites ready before you buy. If you cannot plant immediately, keep the plants moist. Keep marginal and moisture-loving plants in a tray filled with 2in (5cm) of water; check the water level regularly and top up as necessary. Ideally, oxygenators and deep-water plants should be submerged in pond- or rainwater in a large bucket, tub, or garbage can. Also protect plants from extremes of heat and cold until planted. Plants can survive in this state for two to three weeks, then their condition will begin to deteriorate. Before planting, trim plants with a sharp knife to remove any damaged roots, stems, or foliage: water lilies in particular benefit from a little preparation (*see below*) before planting.

PREPARING A WATER LILY FOR PLANTING

1 USING PRUNING SHEARS or a sharp knife, cut back any roots that are either damaged or excessively long to within about 2in (5cm) of the tuber.

OLD ROOTS
Trim back long, coarse roots.

NEW SHOOTS
Young shoots with furled leaves grow from the tuber.

2 CUT OFF ANY leaves that have unfurled close to the base, being careful not to damage any new growth. Retain all of the young, tightly rolled leaves that are still growing; they will soon reach the water surface.

YOUNG GROWTH
Retain tightly rolled leaves, which are still growing.

OLDER GROWTH
Remove any unfurled leaves.

PLANTING TECHNIQUES

WATER PLANTS MAY be planted in aquatic containers, in deep-water beds, or directly into soil on the bottom of a pond or on marginal shelves; some, such as free-floating plants and some submerged plants, are simply placed on the surface of the water. Containers are particularly useful for restricting plants with vigorous growth, although many will rapidly outgrow their containers, especially some of the more vigorous marginals. These will need to be lifted and divided regularly. The condition of the water will influence the health of aquatic plants; check the water quality (*see p. 151*) before introducing them.

PREPARING THE POND
Fill the pond at least three days before planting to allow the water temperature to reach that of the surrounding atmosphere. Aquatic plants absorb nourishment through their top growth as well as their roots, so the condition of the water is important (*see pp. 136–137*). Do not spray water directly onto a soil-bottomed pond or a marginal soil bed – this will disrupt the soil. Cover the soil with a sheet of polyethylene, and rest the end of the hose upon it. The action of the water spreading out over the sheet will help keep the soil in place. As the pond fills, the polyethylene should float up and can be retrieved.

PLANTING UNDER WATER
When planting in submerged soil layers and beds it is generally best to work standing directly in the pond. In fact, when planting marginal beds, standing in the deep zone usually enables you to work at a more comfortable height. Provided that the soil is of a suitable consistency (*see p. 150*) you should be able to firm it down adequately.

PLANTING IN CONTAINERS
Most water gardeners find planting baskets and crates more manageable for deep-water plants than a layer of bottom soil, except in very large informal ponds. Marginals also grow well in containers, which can be positioned in groups to give a more natural, mingled effect. An added advantage is that the plants

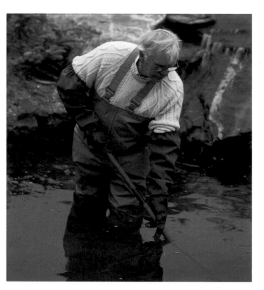

POND ACCESS
In order to introduce planting baskets into the pond, it may be necessary to wade in and place the basket by hand. Thigh or, better still, chest waders will allow you to move in the pond freely. Try to move as gently as possible – any vigorous movement may stir up mud and distress fish.

can be moved around until the desired effect is achieved. Deep-water plants are best spaced evenly around the base of the pond to prevent stems growing through each other and tangling.

Purchased plants may already be in containers, but these can be rather small since display space is often limited in stores. It is worth moving them to a larger pot to allow their roots to develop well. Any aquatic plant sold in an ordinary pot should be transferred into one with openwork sides. Choose a basket appropriate to the size of the plant (as a guide, a vigorous water

PLANTING SUBMERGED PLANTS

PLANTING METHODS
Submerged plants can be planted directly into the soil beds of large, natural ponds; they will be able to root freely and their spread will be unrestricted. In smaller ponds, it is better to plant in containers (right) so that their growth can be controlled.

LEAD CLASP
The weight of the lead pulls the submerged plant down to the bottom of the pond, where it can root.

1 **LINE A PLANTING** container with burlap and fill with damp soil. Firm down lightly. Make evenly spaced holes 2in (5cm) deep and insert bunches of cuttings (here *Lagarosiphon major*).

2 **FIRM IN THE PLANT** with your fingers and trim off any excess burlap. Topdress the plants with a ½in (1cm) layer of pea gravel to keep the soil in place. Lower the basket gently into the pond.

lily needs a crate that is 16in/40cm across and 8in/20cm deep). If you need to add ballast to a container in order to keep large marginals stable *(see below)*, then choose a larger container to accommodate the extra material. Line the baskets if necessary *(see p. 151)*, fill with well-dampened soil *(see pp. 150–151)*, firm lightly and make planting holes. Container-grown plants should be planted at the same depth they were growing in their original containers; most bare-root plants are tuberous or rhizomatous, and these need to be positioned fairly near the soil surface *(see right)*. Firm them in well, and add a layer of stones or pea gravel that is approximately ½in (1cm) thick to prevent soil from drifting away. This layer of gravel is particularly necessary in ponds containing koi and other bottom-feeders, which can uproot plants as they nose around for food.

Either position containers by hand or, if you have a helper, thread two lengths of string through opposite sides of the basket. Holding the ends, you and your partner can stand facing each other across the pond and lower the plant into position. Depending on the depth of your pond, young deep-water plants may need a temporary stack of bricks *(see right)* or an inverted basket to allow the new shoots to reach the surface quickly.

SUBMERGED AND FREE-FLOATING PLANTS

In ponds with a layer of bottom soil, bunches of submerged plants can simply be dropped in the water. The lead clasp around the bunches will pull them down to the bottom, where they will root. They may also be planted in containers. A 12in (30cm) crate will accommodate several bunches. If several species are planted, keep each one in a separate crate.

For free-floating plants such as *Azolla filiculoides* and *Stratiotes aloides* simply float the plants from your hand on the surface of the water.

PLANTING IN SURROUNDING SOIL AND IN BOG GARDENS

Planting in permanently moist soil is no different from planting in any bed or border. Planting crates are not necessary; plant directly into the soil. Do not add fertilizer or handfuls of rotted or concentrated manures where they may leach into water, and be careful not to compact the wet ground when working. Remember that in permanently moist soil plants will grow very vigorously: give them plenty of room to spread, especially giants such as *Gunnera manicata* and *Rheum*, which will develop extensive root systems.

PLANTING BARE-ROOT DEEP-WATER PLANTS

1 LINE THE BASKET if needed and fill three-quarters full with dampened soil. Trim the tuber or rhizome, if necessary *(see p. 155)*, then position it so that it is within 1½in (4cm) of the rim.

2 ADD MORE SOIL and use your fingers to firm the soil, being very careful not to damage new shoots. Topdress with stones or pea gravel to prevent soil floating off the container once under water.

3 PLACE THE CONTAINER on a stack of bricks so that it is initially supported close to the water surface. As new leaves appear, remove bricks gradually until the plant sits on the bottom of the pond.

PLANTING IN MOIST AND WET SOIL

1 DIG A HOLE in the soil bed large enough to accommodate the root ball of the plant. Support the plant (here *Caltha palustris*) with one hand, and gently ease the root ball out of the container.

2 PLACE THE PLANT in the hole at the same depth as it was in the container. Using your hands, thoroughly firm the soil all around the crown of the plant. Soak the entire area with water.

STABILIZING PLANT CONTAINERS

USING A BRICK
If a planting basket is to be used to house a tall, top-heavy marginal, place a brick or half-brick in the bottom of the container before introducing soil. This will anchor the basket so that it will be less likely to tip over.

USING PEBBLES
Pebbles placed on top of the soil in the planting basket are even better than bricks for weighting down plants. This method does not use up soil space and provides a decorative finish.

ROUTINE PLANT CARE

PLANTS MUST BE WELL cared for in order to ensure healthy and vigorous growth. Routine maintenance includes many tasks common to all garden plants, although the techniques used may be modified. In this special environment, it is very important to remove any dying plant material or it will decompose and cloud the water, affecting other life. Regular pond care (see pp. 140–141) will also help maintain clear, well-oxygenated water, essential to successful growth. If you have to enter the water to work, try to accomplish several tasks in one session: repeated excursions into the water, however careful your movements, will disrupt it and its inhabitants.

WATER PLANTS THROUGH THE YEAR

Spring is the busiest time of the year for the water gardener, with many key tasks to be performed. If attended to now, plants are more likely to be vigorous and trouble-free during summer, when they can be enjoyed at leisure. Remember that algae are among the first "plants" to grow, and pond water will temporarily be green and cloudy each spring until the pond's ecosystem adjusts itself to the start of a new growing season.

CUTTING BACK AND THINNING

Most plants used in and around water are herbaceous. In cold climates, where old foliage has been left to shelter the crown of the plant over winter, spring is the time to cut all dead and dying leaves and stems back, together with remaining seedheads of grasses and similar plants. Be sure not to damage the growing points of new, emerging shoots.

Spring is also a good time to thin or divide many plants (see pp. 160–161) if they have begun to outgrow their allotted space. Submerged plants may be thinned at any time they begin to choke the pond. Hardy, free-floating plants sink to the bottom of the pond during the winter, reappearing in spring. Divide the clump-forming ones such as *Stratiotes aloides* when they return to the surface. Most floaters grow rapidly, and may need thinning again by summer. Water lilies and deep-water plants

WORKING IN WET SOIL
Fork over footprints made in damp soil to prevent compaction, being careful to avoid plant roots. In very wet conditions, work as much as possible from a wooden board laid over the soil, in order to distribute body weight evenly.

will need to be divided every three to four years – this will be evident the preceding summer when leaves become congested, with far fewer flowers appearing. Marginal plants will require more regular division, perhaps every other year, or they will outgrow containers and crowd the limited space on the edge of the pond. Moisture-lovers will also need to be divided quite frequently; if not, they will weaken and produce fewer flowers.

INTRODUCING PLANTS

Mid- to late spring, as growth begins and any danger of late frost is past, is an ideal time to introduce new plants to the pond (see pp. 156–157) and to the surrounding soil, so that they are able to benefit from the full growing season. Also, reintroduce any plants that have been protected from cold during winter (see overleaf). When planting moisture-loving and marginal plants, it may be necessary to stand on the soil. Be sure to fork over any footprints afterward; this will prevent the earth from compacting, thereby making it more accessible to growing roots.

FEEDING

Established water plants will benefit from the addition of slow-release fertilizers in spring; water lilies in particular need large amounts of nutrients in order to thrive. Some garden centers and all water garden specialists will stock suitable slow-release fertilizers. These are generally sold in pellet form, and the pellet is pushed well into the soil to prevent its contents from leaking into the water. The fertilizer is released only at the rate that the plant can absorb it; very little surplus enters the water to nourish the growth of algae.

CUTTING BACK GRASSES
Grasses and sedges will benefit from annual pruning in spring: cut the whole plant close to the base, and remove any debris to let light and air into the center of the plant. Many species have sharp leaves, so wear thick gloves.

REMOVING UNWANTED GROWTH

CUTTING OFF DECAYING LEAVES
Hold the plant firmly and use a sharp knife to remove any yellowing or dead leaves, until you reach healthy, green stems. If yellowing is excessive, lift the plant to see if it is diseased in any way (see pp. 164–165).

DUCKWEED AND SURPLUS FLOATERS
Hold a plank vertically and draw it across the surface of the water to skim off duckweed, which is often naturally introduced into the pond by birds or on new plants. Dispose of the weed carefully, as it spreads easily.

PROTECTING POND LIFE
When thinning pond weed, drape it for a while on an edge or rock to allow small creatures to crawl or fall back into the water before disposal. In modest quantities, it can usefully be added to compost heaps.

SUMMER TASKS
Lushly growing plants may renew their leaves frequently, and it is important to regularly pick off or trim with a sharp knife at the stem base those that are yellowing and dying. Deadhead all flowering water plants: in some, this encourages further flowers while in others it removes potential decaying material.
If you wish to collect seed for propagation *(see pp. 162–163)* remember that seeds of aquatic plants need to be sown when freshly gathered, so collect the seed when there is still sufficient warmth for germination to occur, preferably in mid- to late summer. In moist soil around the pond, do not deadhead plants with decorative seedheads unless self-seeding plants are problematic. Weed regularly. Watch water level for any fall in long dry spells. Be sure that the floating plants do not smother the crowns of containerized marginals. Examine plants for signs of pests and diseases *(see pp. 164–165)*; they are susceptible to infections in summer, encouraged by the warm, humid conditions, and recognizing symptoms at an early stage is necessary for effective control.

PREPARING FOR WINTER
As the growing season ends, collect any young plantlets, plant material, or winter buds *(see pp. 160–163)* intended for propagation purposes that require shelter during the winter months. Store in moist soil in frost-free conditions.

Tender aquatics will also need to be lifted from the pond in the autumn. Remove any dying foliage and insert the plants in containers filled with moist soil or sand, which will prevent them from rotting when daylight intensity is low. Place them under glass in a frost-free place until the following spring.

Once winter sets in, take any precautions necessary to protect the pond and its plants from freezing weather *(see pp. 138–139)*, such as installing a stock tank deicer. A thick mulch of clean straw around bog-garden and moisture-loving plants will help to protect their roots.

AUTUMN NETTING
In autumn, lay fine-mesh plastic netting over the pond, securing the edges with bricks or stakes. This will prevent leaves that are shed by the plants surrounding the pond from entering the pond and decomposing. Every week or so, remove the netting, dispose of the leaves, and replace securely.

PLANT PROTECTION
Damp soil or sand will prevent plants from rotting.

FROST-TENDER PLANT

WATERTIGHT CONTAINER

TENDER PLANTS
Overwinter tender plants in a container filled with damp sand. Do not close the lid, but cover with a polyethylene bag with a few holes in it to allow air to enter.

PLANT PROPAGATION

DESPITE CAUTIOUS INITIAL planting, it is likely that plants will outgrow their sites. In a container or small pool this can happen in a single season; in a large informal pond it can take years. Division is one of the most common propagation techniques both in water and out. Use it to control plant size by digging an overgrown clump and discarding the older, less productive growth in favor of young, healthy portions of the plant. This is perhaps the easiest method of propagation. Other methods of propagating water garden plants (*see pp. 162–163*) include taking root or stem cuttings or, provided that the plant breeds true, growing from seed.

THINNING AND DIVIDING PLANTS

Many of the plants used in and around water features spread and multiply readily by vegetative means, producing new plantlets either from the rootstock or on runners. Sometimes these detach naturally from the parent plant, often sinking to the bottom to remain dormant over winter where they are hardy, then growing the next spring (these may be known as "winter buds"). Sometimes they must be physically separated. Clump-forming plants that have a mass of roots may also be physically divided; provided each has a portion of root and one or more shoots, small parts of the plant will grow independently of the parent. Whether these methods are used to control size, or to produce several new plants, depends entirely on how much space is available. If you do not have space to replant all the pieces, discard the older portions and retain the new growth.

Thinning and division should take place when plants are in active growth, ideally in spring so that any cut surfaces will heal quickly. Some moisture-lovers may also be divided in late summer or autumn (*see pp. 196–207*). Dividing water plants in the dormant season is not recommended, as low water temperatures may cause the newly divided plants to rot.

THINNING OXYGENATORS AND SMALL FLOATERS

1 IN SPRING OR AUTUMN, thin out overgrown submerged and small floating plants by "combing" the water with a rake. For containerized plants, lift out the basket and trim some stems off with a sharp knife.

2 BE SURE TO leave enough of the plants so they can regrow. If possible, thin little and often. Drape surplus plants on the side temporarily (*see p. 159*) to allow any inhabitants to escape.

SEPARATING RUNNERS AND PLANTLETS

1 IN SPRING, remove young vigorous plantlets from the parent, either snapping them off carefully from the perimeter of the parent, or severing the connecting stem on each side of the plantlet.

2 PLACE THE PLANTLET directly on the water surface, supporting it gently with your hand until it floats upright. Air sacs in the spongy leaf bases of water hyacinths keep plants buoyant. Roots will soon develop.

DIVIDING WATER LILIES

CONGESTED CROWN
Young stems and leaves have difficulty reaching the water surface when crowded by older foliage.

OVERGROWN PLANT
A water lily in need of thinning has few flowers and crowded leaves that thrust out of the water, rather than floating on it. Its roots have exhausted the soil nutrients, so it produces more leaves and stems, which in aquatic plants can absorb food from the water.

1 CAREFULLY LIFT THE plant and rinse off the soil. Remove all opened leaves, and cut the rhizome in two, retaining the part with the most vigorous young, emerging shoots. If desired, remove any suitable bud cuttings (*see p. 162*) for propagation.

TOP-DRESSING OF PEA GRAVEL

VIGOROUS NEW GROWTH

2 TRIM LONG COARSE roots, replant with the crown just below soil level, and reposition the water lily in the pond just as for a new young plant (*see pp. 156–157*). Discard the old portion of the rhizome.

DIVIDING RHIZOMATOUS PLANTS

1 LIFT THE PLANT (here, *Iris pseudacorus*) and rinse soil off the roots. Large masses of fleshy rhizomes can be split apart with your hands; otherwise, use a knife to separate vigorous portions of the rhizome, each with a number of fibrous roots, strong young leaves, and shoots.

2 USE A SHARP KNIFE to trim the rhizome neatly, removing any isolated portions that do not show any new shoot growth *(inset)*. Trim all of the top growth back to 3–4in (6–9cm), and cut back long roots so that they can be comfortably accommodated in the container.

3 REPLANT CAREFULLY, filling fresh soil around the rhizome, rather than pressing it into a hole, so that the roots are not compressed. Top-dress with pea gravel and reposition in the pond, on bricks if necessary to raise the trimmed top growth just above water.

SUBMERGED AND FREE-FLOATING PLANTS

Submerged plants are very easy to thin. Surplus stems can either be pulled out by hand or raked out *(see facing page)*. These plants are extremely resilient, and will regrow no matter how roughly they are treated. If they are in containers, lift the container out of the pond and remove old growth with a sharp knife. The smaller free-floating plants can also be raked off, or hosed to the edge of the pond and scooped out. The larger, more succulent floaters such as *Pistia* and *Stratiotes* are worth handling with more care. Separate and refloat only as many young plantlets as are required.

TUBEROUS AND RHIZOMATOUS PLANTS

Plants such as water lilies and most irises have tuberous or rhizomatous roots: that is, shoots grow up and fibrous roots grow down from a swollen, fleshy storage organ just below the soil surface. These organs grow and branch, developing new growing points at their tips from which fresh shoots emerge. As the new leaves grow to maturity, energy is stored in the new portion of the rhizome or tuber until it is capable of surviving independently of the parent root system. The plants are easy to divide *(see above and facing page, below)*. Either replant the best new portion and discard the rest, or retain more than one piece for replanting elsewhere in your pond.

FIBROUS-ROOTED PLANTS

The majority of moisture-loving plants form thick clumps that expand in rich, moist soil to form a circular mass of fibrous roots. The older roots inside the clump become progressively less productive, and flowers appear only on the young growth around the edges. The whole clump may be lifted and divided into sections. Grasses and sedges often have quite shallow root masses that can be pulled apart by hand *(right, above)*; other herbaceous plants form dense, bulky root balls *(right)* that must be separated with a garden fork or with a knife.

DIVIDING CLUMP-FORMING PLANTS

DIVIDING GRASSES

Cut down taller grasses to 6–8in (15–20cm), then lift the clump with a mass of soil adhering to the root ball. From the edge of the clump, where growth is youngest and most vigorous, pull away sections with a root ball of about a handful in size. Discard the older, tired central portion, and replant the new portions.

ORIGINAL PLANT

NEW GROWTH
Take a handful of the root mass, not the top growth, and pull away firmly.

DIVIDING DENSE CLUMPS OF TOUGH ROOTS

Plants such as hostas develop into substantial clumps (left) that may be too tough to divide by hand. Use a garden spade (or lever with two forks back to back) or cut through the mass with a sharp knife. With the root ball in pieces of a more manageable size, carefully separate small sections (right) with a good root system and several plump buds or shoots and replant.

OTHER METHODS OF PROPAGATION

THE CONVENIENCE OF PROPAGATION by division *(see pp. 160–161)* is that the young plants obtained can immediately be planted out into the garden. Propagation by other means, such as by taking root or stem cuttings, or from seed, tends to produce very young plants that, with a few exceptions, will not survive if planted directly into the pond. They must be cared for in a separate environment, usually under glass, until they have grown sufficiently to survive. If you have the facilities to care for these young plants, however, the techniques involved are not difficult and can produce a great many new plants.

WINTER BUDS

Some water plants, such as frogbit (Hydrocharis morsus-ranae), produce swollen buds on their roots that naturally detach at the end of the growing season, over-wintering at the bottom of the pool and developing into plants in spring where they are hardy; some float to the surface and grow roots downward, while some root into bottom mud and send shoots upward.

WINTER BUD

ROOT BUD CUTTINGS

When tuberous or rhizomatous plants are lifted in spring, or bought bare root, there may be tiny new growing points visible on the rootstock where shoots are only just emerging. While a section of the rootstock with only this growing point is unlikely to survive if planted out, it can be potted up and grown on. On rhizomes, cut off a 3–4in (7–10cm) portion of the rootstock behind the growing point. On tuberous water lilies, and at the base of plants such as flowering rush *(Butomus umbellatus)*, the new growth may be emerging from a protruding nodule, or root bud; in this case, snap off the entire bud.

Root buds and cuttings should be planted either individually in small pots or in seed trays with the growing tip just visible. The pots are then placed in a greenhouse or under lights in a shallow tray with enough water in it to cover the soil. As the shoots grow they will need to be potted on, and the water level will need to be raised accordingly. The young plants should be kept in cool but frost-free conditions over winter, and may be introduced to the pond as growth begins the following spring.

On some plants, such as *Hydrocharis morsus-ranae* and *Hottonia palustris*, pebble-like root buds *(see above right)* detach naturally and sink to the bottom of the pond and stay dormant over winter where they are hardy; otherwise they are winter-killed (they are known as "winter buds"). These root buds may also be collected, potted up, and grown on in the same way as for root buds and cuttings.

PROPAGATION BY ROOT-BUD CUTTINGS

1 CUT OUT THE swollen bud with its growing point from the rootstock. It may be necessary to cut through neighboring leaf stalks to obtain all of the bud. Use a sharp knife; fungal infections are less likely to enter clean cuts. Rinse the bud thoroughly.

2 FILL A 4IN (10CM) pot with potting soil or sifted topsoil, and firm. Firm the bud into a small indentation so that it sits securely on, rather than in, the soil; topdress with pea gravel to hold the bud in place.

3 STAND THE POT in water that just covers the gravel. Keep in a greenhouse and repot as necessary. Gradually stand the pot in deeper water, but keep the shoot tips above water. Plant the following spring.

TAKING SOFT STEM CUTTINGS

SHARP CUT
A clean cut decreases the likelihood of fungal growth.

ROOTING AGENT
Plants will benefit from rooting powder.

1 WITH A SHARP KNIFE, detach a non-flowering shoot about 6in (10cm) long from the parent plant (here *Veronica beccabunga*). Carefully remove the lower leaves and any low sideshoots.

2 WITH THE LOWER portion of the stem clear of leaves and sideshoots, cut the stem squarely across with a sharp knife to just below a node, or swollen area, where a leaf was removed.

3 DIP THE PREPARED cutting into hormone rooting powder, which will encourage roots to grow from the nodal area. The cut surface will be sufficiently moist to allow enough powder to stick.

4 TAKE A FINE MESH container, approximately 4in (10cm) square, and fill it with potting soil. Insert the cutting into the container, firm it in, and keep under glass until rooted.

STEM CUTTINGS

New submerged plants can easily be obtained from cuttings if they are looking ragged after winter, after emptying and cleaning a pond, or if more plants are required. They do not need to be rooted before being introduced into the water. Simply cut or pinch off healthy young shoots, 4–6in (10–15cm) long, and tie them in bunches of six to eight with florist's or garden wire. As with purchased submerged plants *(see p. 155)*, either weight the bunches and throw them into the water, or plant several bunches in a container and immerse it.

Many marginal and moisture-loving plants may also be propagated from individual soft stem cuttings *(see facing page, below)*. These cuttings should be rooted under glass, with the soil kept either moist or wet, depending on the plant's needs. Cuttings from creeping bog plants such as *Veronica beccabunga*, *Ludwigia palustris*, and *Mentha aquatica* root particularly easily and should take only two to three weeks.

PROPAGATION BY SEED

Most moisture-lovers and some deep-water plants, including *Aponogeton distachyos*, *Orontium aquaticum*, and some lotus and tropical water lilies, may be grown from seed *(see right)*. Plants will take some time to develop and flower, so this method of propagation it is recommended only for the patient gardener or where lots of plants are required. Seed of most aquatic plants must be collected when ripe in summer or autumn and if not sown immediately, should be stored in jars of water. The seedlings must be grown in moist or permanently wet soil depending on the plant's natural growing environment.

Seeds of cultivars may not grow true to type; variation in offspring is likely unless precautions have been taken to prevent cross-pollination. This is difficult in open environments. However, many species grow well from seed, particularly native plants. Marginals such as the water plantain (*Alisma plantago-aquatica*) are prolific seed producers, whose seed often floats for some distance to achieve effective spread.

PROPAGATION BY SOWING SEED

1 FILL A STANDARD seed tray with heavy garden soil or sifted garden loam, and water and compress it. Use a piece of folded paper to distribute the seeds evenly on the soil surface.

2 SIEVE A LAYER of fine sand or peat over the seed. This will help to retain moisture around the seed coat. For aquatic plants, stand the seed tray in a deep tray of water, keeping it filled up to just below soil level. Keep seed of moisture-lovers well watered.

3 PLACE THE TRAY in full light in a greenhouse until the seeds have germinated. When seedlings have two or three leaves, prick them out into individual pots. Pot on again when a good root system has developed. Keep young aquatic plants immersed in water as they grow. Overwinter in frost-free conditions and plant out the following spring.

PLANT CARE THROUGH THE YEAR			
Spring	**Summer**	**Autumn**	**Winter**
• Trim off all dead and winter-damaged foliage from perennial plants. • If removing winter casualties, check first that there is no new growth at the base of the plant. If not, remove, and work compost into the soil before replanting. • Once the danger of frost has passed, introduce new plants, and reintroduce plants that were removed for protection over winter. • Divide crowded or overgrown plants as necessary *(see pp. 160–161)*. • Feed aquatic plants, especially water lilies, with slow-release fertilizer. Ordinary garden fertilizers may be applied only where they will not leach out into water. • Once all planting, replanting, and feeding has been done, mulch boggy areas of soil to conserve soil moisture. • Remember that a temporary "greening" of the water is natural in spring; do not take action unless it persists.	• Deadhead flowering plants where decorative seedheads are not desired. • Where plants are in containers, move them around if large plants grow to dominate smaller specimens. • Remove any dying or disease-affected foliage *(see p. 159)*. Congested foliage may be lightly thinned. • Make a note of plants that are becoming overgrown and congested, so that they may be thinned in autumn or the following spring. • Note gaps in plantings where new plants could be accommodated when dividing crowded plants. • Check plants for symptoms of pests and diseases, and treat as necessary *(see pp. 164–165)*. • If algal growth is a problem, consider whether there are enough submerged and floating-leaved plants in the pond; it is not too late to introduce more.	• Collect and either plant or store any material for propagation, such as ripe seed or winter buds. • Check plants for symptoms of pests and diseases, and treat as necessary *(see pp.164–165)*. • If you have a greenhouse (or indoor light garden), take cuttings of tender and borderline hardy perennials, in case the parent plants do not survive the winter. • Remove frost-tender plants for overwintering *(see p. 159)*. Wash, dry, and store any containers from which plants have been removed. • In extremely exposed areas, cut back tall grasses, reeds, and other plants, reducing their height by about half, to prevent wind damage. • Protect moisture-loving plants against cold weather with a mulch of straw.	• As severe weather sets in, take measures *(see p. 139)* to protect plants. • Float an electric stock tank deicer in ponds to keep the water from freezing over completely. • If you have a cool, light place where plants may be stored over winter, bring in marginally hardy plants and keep them evenly moist over winter in trays of water. • Leave dying and frost-damaged foliage on perennial plants until spring to protect new growth below. • To make sure that the water environment remains healthy for dormant plants, make holes in ice sheets, and brush off snow to let light in. • Browse through plant catalogs and order attractive new plants for your pond.

PLANT PESTS AND DISEASES

Wᴀᴛᴇʀ ᴘʟᴀɴᴛꜱ ᴀʀᴇ vulnerable to a number of pests and diseases that invade leaves, stems, and roots, especially during summer. Dividing and thinning plants *(see pp. 160–161)* will reduce the problem considerably; for example, most of the pests of water-lily foliage attack when the leaves are held well above water, often an indication of an overgrown plant. Also, be sure to remove aging or dying floating leaves. Creating an environment that will accommodate fish and frogs is worth considering, since these creatures are very efficient pest predators.

PLANT DISEASES

BROWN SPOT

PLANTS AFFECTED Water lilies and lotuses *(Nelumbo)*. **CAUSE** A fungal infection that gains entry through insect bites or wounds on the leaf. As with many fungal leaf spots, older leaves are more susceptible, especially if infected leaves are promptly removed. **SYMPTOMS** Dark patches appear on the leaves; the patches become far more pronounced in cool, wet summers. In serious cases, the leaves can become so badly infected that they eventually disintegrate. **TREATMENT** Remove and discard infected leaves immediately, cutting through the leaf stalk at the base. Although fungicides will control the disease, it is seldom serious enough to require chemical control measures. Make sure that the plant is kept in full vigor by thinning when necessary *(see pp. 160–161)*. It is also important to regularly remove any dying or yellowing leaves *(see pp. 158–159)*.

PRIMROSE LEAF SPOT

PLANTS AFFECTED Primroses growing in moist ground. **CAUSE** A fungal disease that attacks aging leaves that have been wet for several hours, allowing spores to germinate and penetrate the leaf. **SYMPTOMS** Small, circular spots, usually brown, appear on the leaves of older plants, or on plants that are starved of nutrients or lacking in vigor due to root weakness. These spots may coalesce. **TREATMENT** Control involves good garden hygiene and adequate feeding. Where fertilizers may leach into pondwater, use a slow-release type or incorporate compost at planting time and mulch annually. It is especially important to remove old leaf debris. Remove and discard affected leaves, then spary a wide-spectrum fungicide safe for use around water gardens over the entire plant, including the undersides of leaves. Repeat the application after 14 days. Avoid frequent and heavy overhead watering.

IRIS LEAF SPOT

PLANTS AFFECTED Bulbous and rhizomatous irises. **CAUSE** The fungus *Mycospharella macrospora* is attracted by mechanical injury to the leaves of the plant, and by wet weather. It produces spores that are spread on air currents and by rain and splashing water. This disease usually develops after the leaf has been wet for several hours. **SYMPTOMS** Brown oval spots scattered at random; the spots become elongated as they stretch in the direction of the leaf veins. The center of the spot is often lighter in color, and may show the spores of the fungus. The spots sometimes coalesce. **TREATMENT** If spots occur early in the season, spray the affected plants with a wide-spectrum fungicide safe for use around water gardens. Make sure there is no risk of spray drift into the water. If infection occurs after flowering, remove affected leaves.

ARMILLARIA ROOT ROT

PLANTS AFFECTED A large range of plants, especially trees and shrubs. **CAUSE** A damaging fungus produces discoloration of the foliage and progressive dieback of shoots. It then penetrates root tissue, affecting the plant's ability to transport water to its leaves. The fungus spreads through the soil by means of dark brown, rootlike structures. **SYMPTOMS** White streaks of fungal growth develop within the dead tissue of the roots and crown. Plants may die rapidly or may take several years to die. **TREATMENT** Dead and dying plants should be removed immediately and, if possible, the soil should be changed in the vicinity of the infection. Chemical control is not practical on herbaceous material near water, which it may contaminate. Do not replant any herbaceous or woody specimens for a year; this will allow any remaining portions of fungus surviving on root fragments to die.

POWDERY MILDEW

PLANTS AFFECTED Some soft-stemmed marginals and moisture-loving plants, particularly *Caltha palustris*. **CAUSE** A fungal infection that is encouraged by overcrowding, and by humid or damp air around the top growth and dryness around the roots. **SYMPTOMS** A white, powdery fungal growth develops on the leaf surface and can spread to the underside. The mildew may kill off small areas of leaf tissue, which then drop away. **TREATMENT** Remove the infected leaves promptly, and spray the plant with a suitable fungicide. New growth will regenerate from the crown.

LOTUS BLIGHT

PLANTS AFFECTED Lotus *(Nelumbo)* species and cultivars. **CAUSES** There are two disorders referred to as blight, both of which attack leaves: one a fungal blight, and the other a bacterial blight. **SYMPTOMS** Brown patches appear near the edges of the leaf, which later disintegrates. **TREATMENT** Treatment for fungal blight involves spreading the entire surface of the growing bed with a fungicide in powder form. The bacterial blight is more resistant to chemicals and therefore less easy to control. Treatment for this strain should include removing all infected tissue immediately.

OTHER DISEASES

Water lily leaf spot Dark patches form on water-lily leaves, which eventually rot and disintegrate. Leaves should be removed and discarded. Spray with fungicide after new leaves appear in spring; repeat every 10 to 14 days until flowering begins. *Rhizome rot* A widespread disease that causes the leaves of rhizomatous irises to die back. Cut out any rotting parts of the rhizome and dust the cut surfaces with a fungicidal powder.

PLANT PESTS

SNAILS

PLANTS AFFECTED
Marginals and moisture-lovers (garden snail); most species of submerged plants (water snail).
CAUSE Garden snails and water snails eat small pieces of tissue from the leaves and stems of plants.
SYMPTOMS Irregular, unsightly holes appear on leaves and stems. Snails are mostly active after dark or during wet weather.
TREATMENT Stocking fish can be useful, since they may eat the jellylike strands of water snails' eggs, laid on the underside of floating leaves. Adult snails can be lured on to lettuce leaves left to float on the water in the evenings; they can then be netted off the following morning. Non-chemical controls for garden snails include laying traps overnight (*see* Slugs, *right*).

CADDIS FLY

PLANTS AFFECTED
Young water lilies.
CAUSE Adult caddis flies that lay their eggs on or near water. The eggs swell up rapidly on contact with water, and hatch in about 10 days. The larvae spin protective cases that they cover with pieces of leaves, small stones, or pebbles, to form shelters. They float or swim around in their structures, feeding hungrily on any vegetation present, and are quite capable of destroying young water lilies whose foliage is underwater. They later pupate at the water's edge.
SYMPTOMS Damaged water-lily leaves.
TREATMENT Stocking the pond with fish can be very useful, since they are a major predator of these pests. Remove by hand any of the well-disguised larval cases.

CHINA MARK MOTH

PLANTS AFFECTED
Mainly water lilies, but occasionally other water plants.
CAUSE This pest lays eggs on floating foliage in late summer; the eggs hatch into leaf-eating caterpillars that eat the undersides of leaves and form shelters by weaving silky cocoons with the pieces of foliage.
SYMPTOMS Extensive damage, manifested by leaves with oval shapes cut from the leaf margins. It is common to see pieces of decomposing foliage floating nearby.
TREATMENT Remove the caterpillars' cases from the underside of the leaves. Remove severely damaged leaves and discard them, or spray with *bacillus thuringiensis* (BT), a biological spray that will control the larvae without harming the pond environment.

SLUGS

PLANTS AFFECTED
Any number of soft-leaved plants growing in moist ground, particularly hostas.
CAUSE Several species of slug that feed on plant tissue.
SYMPTOMS Irregular holes appear in the foliage, and in severe cases whole stems can be stripped.
TREATMENT As slugs can never be completely eliminated from gardens, control measures should be concentrated on protecting vulnerable plants. Avoid heavy organic mulches. Cultivating soil regularly will destroy eggs. Encourage predators such as frogs, toads, and birds. Non-chemical controls include laying overnight traps such as hollowed-out potatoes or grapefruit skins. Half-filled jars of beer sunk in the ground will attract slugs, which fall in and drown.

IRIS SAWFLY

PLANTS AFFECTED
Water-loving irises, particularly *Iris pseudacorus*.
CAUSE Bluish gray larvae, up to ¾in (2cm) long, eat the edges of the leaves in summer.
SYMPTOMS Large chunks of foliage are eaten from the sides of the leaves, with noticeable saw-edged margins to the cut surfaces. In severe attacks, the leaves can be reduced to a skeletal central vein.
TREATMENT The most effective measure of control is the diligent hand removal of cater-pillars as soon as the first signs of attack are seen. The caterpillars are quite conspicuous – slide the leaves through finger and thumb to collect and dispose of them. Remove any severely damaged leaves by cutting through the leafstalk at the base, and destroy.

FIGWORT WEEVIL

PLANTS AFFECTED
Figwort (*Scrophularia auriculata*), *Phygelius*, *Verbascum*.
CAUSE Small beetles infest the shoot tips of plants. The beetles have a snoutlike projection that makes incisions in plant tissue, into which the females sometimes lay their eggs. The larvae that develop are sluglike in appearance; they attack leaves and occasionally flowers. They then envelop themselves in a brown cocoon attached to the top of the plant.
SYMPTOMS Holes and brown patches appear on the affected plants' leaves.
TREATMENT If possible, remove the weevils by hand. In severe cases, it will be necessary to remove all wildlife from the pond and treat the water with an insecticide.

WATER-LILY BEETLE

PLANTS AFFECTED
Water lilies.
CAUSE On emerging from hibernation, small brown beetles migrate to water-lily pads and lay their eggs.
SYMPTOMS The beetle larvae create holes by stripping the surface layer of tissue from the leaves; the leaves will eventually shrivel and rot. Adult beetles also feed on flowers.
TREATMENT Since the beetles hibernate in poolside vegetation, cutting down herbaceous plant material in autumn (*see pp. 158–159*) will remove the beetles' winter protection. Water-lily leaves should be sprayed frequently throughout the summer with a strong water jet in order to dislodge the larvae, which will be devoured by any fish present. Adult beetles and larvae may be removed by hand.

LEAFHOPPERS

PLANTS AFFECTED
Soft- or fleshy-leaved marginals, whose leaf tissue is vulnerable to attack.
CAUSE Small, green leafhoppers, which can transmit viral diseases. Adults and their creamy yellow nymphs suck the sap from the undersides of plant leaves.
SYMPTOM Small, pale green or yellow spots appear on the upper leaf surfaces. Severe infestation causes the leaves to turn brown.
TREATMENT Hose the leaves frequently with a jet of water to dislodge the leafhoppers. If there are fish present, the pests will be eaten. To minimize the risk of attack, make sure that plants do not become congested, allowing insects to move easily from leaf to leaf; divide the rootstock of water lilies (*see p. 160*) every two to three years.

OTHER PESTS

Iris flea beetle Bluish black beetles attack waterside irises in midsummer. Small leaf areas lose their tissue. Control by frequent spraying with a strong jet of water.
Vine weevil These dull black beetles attack several moisture-loving perennials, such as hostas, primroses, and astilbes. Irregular notches are eaten out of the margins of the leaf. However, most damage is done by the larvae, which eat the roots until the plant wilts. Remove the weevils by hand.
Spider mites In hot, dry summers, these tiny mites congregate on the undersides of water-lily leaves and other aquatic foliage held above the water. Remove by hand or drown by weighting down the leaves for a day or two with nets.

FISH FOR WATER GARDENS

THE ORNAMENTAL ATTRIBUTES of fish have been recognized and appreciated for centuries. The first people to keep and breed fish for their decorative qualities were the ancient Egyptians. There is also strong evidence to suggest that the most popular of ornamental fish, the goldfish – which is closely allied to the carp – was selectively bred in China as far back as AD 970.

CREATING A BALANCED ENVIRONMENT FOR FISH
With the availability of exotic fish from habitats all around the world, it has become even more important to create an environment suitable for mixed populations of fish *(see pp. 168–169)*. Whether a garden water feature is large or small, formal or informal, the basic requirements for keeping fish remain the same – clear, well-oxygenated water, varied depths, adequate shelter and shade, and food.

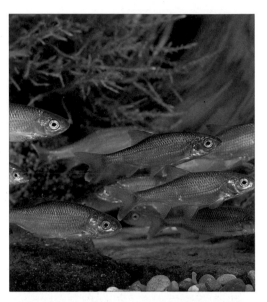

WILDLIFE POND
Much of the charm of a wildlife pond lies in the sheer variety of wildlife it attracts. Unfortunately, this variety means that the inhabitants of such a pond, including its fish, are susceptible to a range of predators. Because they are not highly colored ornamental fish – and hence cheaper to replace – native varieties such as minnows and sunfish are ideally suited to wildlife ponds.

GOLDFISH FEEDING
Although a well-planted pond should guarantee that these goldfish obtain most of the food they need, some supplementary feeding will be necessary. Fish that become used to regular feeding at the same place each day will soon learn to assemble at the surface of the water at the right time and in the right spot.

FISH IN FORMAL POOL
Much of the pleasure of fish-keeping derives from viewing the fish at close quarters. This raised formal pool with its submerged and floating-leaved plants provides an ideal environment for fish, as well as an ideal platform from which to view them.

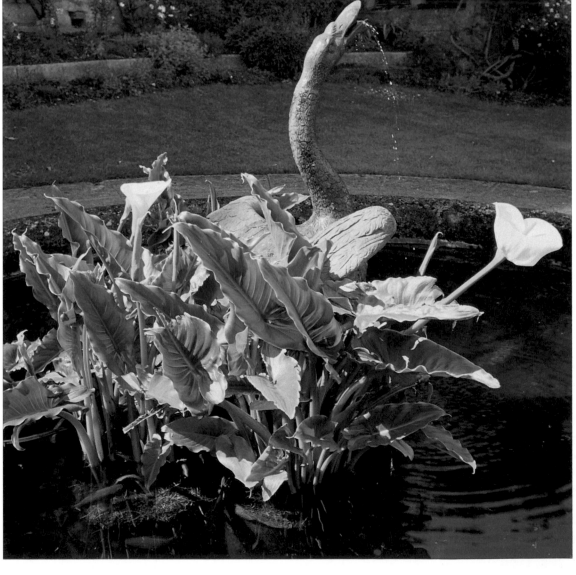

INFORMAL POND
Although clear water allows an unimpeded view of fish, crystal clear water is not necessarily the kind of environment fish prefer. Many species feel insecure in water that leaves them clearly visible to aerial predators such as herons and kingfishers. Carp, for instance, will disturb mud at the bottom of a pond in order to create a more opaque habitat.

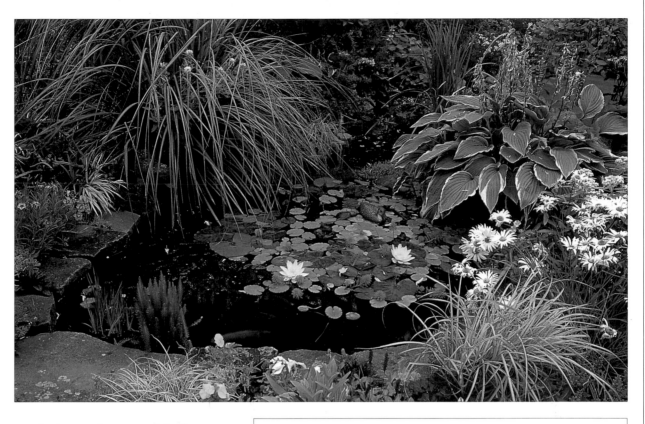

Although fish need room in which to swim around freely, even a barrel will accommodate one or two small goldfish. Deep-water ponds have distinct advantages over shallow ponds: not only are they suitable for fish that feed at different levels *(see pp. 168–169)*, but the water remains at a more constant temperature and retains more dissolved oxygen during hot weather. If a pond is too shallow, and there are no places to hide, fish will become stressed and dart about, stirring up mud at the bottom of the pond and disturbing plants.

Provided that fish are fed, a suitably constructed pond without plants, but with a sophisticated filtration system *(see right, below)*, will give fish all they need. However, most gardeners prefer a more natural, "planted" environment in which the plants themselves fulfill the fish's requirements for clear water, food, shelter, and shade *(see right, above)*. Even algae, which can become a problem if allowed to spread unchecked, are useful components in the ecology of a fish pond; not only are algae the first link in the food chain, they also provide a breeding ground for creatures on which fish can feed.

FISH BEHAVIOR

Like all vertebrates, the behavior of fish comprises two components: instinct and learning, the latter demonstrated by a fish's ability to appear at the same time and in the same place for feeding – one of the pleasures of fish-keeping. Although many species prefer to remain solitary – except in the spawning season – other species, such as minnows, form schools and must spend their lives in the company of their own species. Solitary species tend to be predatory and are often large. In contrast, schooling species tend to be smaller and, most commonly, omnivorous. They gather together for mutual protection and to share food.

KEEPING THE WATER CLEAN

USING PLANTS AS NATURAL FILTERS
Plants can be used to create a healthy environment for fish. Aside from their "filtering" qualities, submerged plants (see pp. 148–149, 178–179) and floating-leaved plants provide vital shade for fish.

SUBMERGED PLANTS
Oxygenators absorb carbon dioxide and produce oxygen to replace the oxygen used by fish.

TERRA-COTTA PIPE "HIDE"

MARGINALS
These plants absorb nutrients in fish waste that would otherwise feed algal growth.

FLOATING-LEAVED PLANTS
These help prevent the buildup of algae by blocking out the sun.

ARTIFICIAL FILTRATION SYSTEM
If a crystal-clear, heavily stocked pool is desired, supplement a biological filtration system (see pp. 70–73) with a UV clarifier (to keep the water clear of algae), which has a magnet designed to prevent the buildup of mineral deposits on which algae thrive.

SHADE
Coping stone with over-hang gives shade and shelter.

FILTER OUTLET

FILTER

UV CLARIFIER
(SEE P. 71)

MAGNET
(SEE P. 71)

SUBMERSIBLE PUMP

HIDING PLACE
Brick provides fish with shelter.

DELIVERY PIPE

FISH SPECIES AND THEIR REQUIREMENTS

D IFFERENT SPECIES OF FISH have different environmental preferences. Wildlife ponds, for example, are more suitable for hardy, native fish, while exotic fish will look their best in the sheltered environs of informal or formal ornamental ponds. Since fish feed at different water levels, establish the preferences of your chosen fish before buying and introducing them to the pond. Koi, which require a water depth of at least 3ft (1m), would be unsuited to a shallow pond, while orfe, which swim in the upper layers of the water, require a pond with a large surface area. A pond with adequate depth and surface area can accommodate several species.

VARIETIES OF GOLDFISH

The many types of goldfish all belong to the same species, *Carassius auratus*. They like rich, weedy ponds that have plenty of cover and a muddy bottom. They breed easily and can often live for more than 10 years. The single-tailed varieties are the hardiest, but all can live in 39°F (4°C) water provided adequate oxygen is available. A pond heater *(see p. 139)* or running pump in winter will provide this.

SINGLE CAUDAL FIN (TAIL)

COMMON GOLDFISH
Usually orange-red in color, this fish feeds at all levels. It is generally no longer than 6in (15cm), and is easily bred. Being hardy, it is ideal for most garden ponds, and will tolerate water as warm as 95°F (35°C), but not for extended periods.

HIGH DORSAL FIN

FANTAIL GOLDFISH
The metallic orange Fantail has an egg-shaped body and seldom exceeds 3½in (9cm) in length. It is less hardy than the Common Goldfish, although just as easily bred. It feeds at all levels.

DOUBLE CAUDAL FIN

MOTTLED COLORS
The coloration of shubunkins depends on both their strain and on the formation of their scales.

DEEPLY FORKED, SINGLE CAUDAL FIN

RED "CAP"

EXOTIC GOLDFISH

For the more adventurous fish-keeper, there are many exotic forms of goldfish to choose from. Originally bred in China and Japan, they are available in many different shapes, sizes, and colors. The more popular varieties include the Celestial, with its peculiar upturned eyes, the Bubble-eye, with enlarged fluid-filled sacs beneath its eyes, the Oranda, with a "hood" that covers its entire head, and the short, plump Pearlscale. All these fantails prefer very clean water. They should be brought indoors during the winter.

BRISTOL SHUBUNKIN
Shubunkins can grow to lengths of 15in (38cm). The popular varieties, like this one, feature black, red, purple, blue, and brown scales beneath pearly scales. Most shubunkin types are hardy, and feed at all levels. They also breed easily.

SARASA COMET (RED CAP)
A comet's colors depend on its strain. Sarasas have a white or silver base color, feed at all levels, and breed easily. Although hardy, they thrive best in temperatures of 46–68°F (8–20°C).

DORSAL FIN

FORKED TAIL
All comets have one deeply forked caudal fin, which may be almost as long as their bodies.

"TELESCOPIC" EYES

MOOR
The egg-shaped Moor should ideally have a velvety, jet-black body with no silver showing through. Some Moors have normal eyes, and some have "telescopic" eyes, which protrude on conical supports. They grow to approximately 4½in (11cm), feed at all levels, and are easily bred. They should be kept indoors in winter.

DOUBLE CAUDAL FIN

GOLD COMET
Growing to lengths of up to 15in (38cm), the Gold Comet needs a lot of space to swim in. It is very hardy, and can tolerate temperatures as low as 32°F (0°C) and as high as 104°F (40°C). Comets breed easily and, like most goldfish, feed at all levels.

THE CARP FAMILY

The size and shape of carp vary enormously, as do their habits, habitats, and choice of food. Most carp will eat small invertebrates rather than other fish, while some are omnivorous, eating both plants and invertebrates. Others, including the popular Grass Carp, are completely herbivorous.

SPECIALITY KOI

The more exotic, highly bred koi carp are classified by scale types, patterns, and colors – single-color, two-color, and multicolor. Because koi are viewed from above by show judges, their colors and patterns have been specifically developed for this purpose. To house and display koi well, pools must be deep, with crystal-clear water.

ORNAMENTAL KOI

CRUCIAN CARP
(Carassius carassius)
This boisterous fish is not suited to small ponds. It is a bottom-level feeder that can grow up to 24in (60cm) long. It thrives in weedy habitats, is easily bred, and will tolerate temperatures of 32–68°F (0–20°C).

PLANT EATER
The wide-mouthed Grass Carp feeds on vegetative matter.

REFLECTIVE SCALES
This carp boasts unusually large, shiny scales.

LATERAL LINE

GRASS CARP *(Ctenopharyagodon idella)*
The silver-gray Grass Carp has a wide mouth adapted for feeding on plants. It has a huge appetite, and grows very quickly up to a length of 24in (60cm). A middle- to bottom-level feeder, it is easily bred, and will thrive in large ponds in temperatures of 32–68°F (0–20°C).

MIRROR CARP *(Cyprinus carpio)*
This domesticated form of Common Carp has very large scales on parts of its body. Up to 24in (60cm) long, it is unsuitable for small ponds. It is a bottom-level feeder, easily bred, and tolerant of temperatures of 32–68°F (0–20°C).

KOI *(Cyprinus carpio)*
Not all koi are expensive, only those intensively bred for special colors and patterning (see box, left). Because they grow to 24in (60cm) in length, koi are unsuitable for very small ponds. Hearty eaters, especially of plants, they need an efficient filtration system to deal with their waste. Koi feed at all levels, are easily bred, and prefer temperatures of 39–68°F (4–20°C).

OTHER FISH

Decorative alternatives to goldfish and koi include lively orfe, while more subtly colored fish for large, natural ponds include comets (*Carassium auratus*), which dart about just beneath the water's surface. Smaller wildlife ponds can accommodate a variety of species including minnows, sunfish, bluegills, all of which are popular with children; minnows, best introduced in groups of at least 8 to 10 also will thrive in a stream if the water is deep enough.

ROACH *(Rutilus rutilus)*
Roach, which grow to a length of 10in (25cm), are a European species not found in North America. They tolerate clear and muddy water, but prefer well-oxygenated water. They are middle-level feeders, and spawn when the water temperature rises above 54°F (12°C).

RUDD *(Scardinus eryphtyhrophthalmus)*
This lively gold or silver fish reaches 10in (25cm) in length. This European species will breed freely in a spacious pond that has plenty of under-water foliage. It is a surface-feeder and tolerates a wide range of temperatures, up to a maximm of about 102°F (38°C).

GOLDEN ORFE *(Leuciscus idus)*
Unsuitable for small ponds, these hardy fish grow to 18in (45cm) or larger. Active surface-feeders, orfe spawn when the water temperature rises above 50°F (10°C).

BITTERLING *(Rhodes ceriseus)*
This bottom feeder grows to 2–3½in (5–9cm) in length, and prefers temperatures of 50–68°F (10–20°C). Breeding is complex, as the female needs a freshwater mussel in which to lay her eggs.

SCAVENGING FISH

All pond fish, including koi and carp, are scavengers and will clean filamentous algae from the pond. A good filtration system should be able to remove debris. Clams or mussels, if placed in a tray on the bottom, can help keep the water clear. Be wary of adding the carnivorous catfish, which can grow up to 12in (30cm) long. Catfish are aggressive and will eat other decorative pondfish.

BUYING AND INTRODUCING FISH

THE IDEAL TIME TO buy fish is late spring or early summer, when the water temperature reaches about 50°F (10°C). The conditions under which the fish are transported and introduced into the pond, and the readiness of the pond itself, are as important as the selection of healthy fish. Always test the acidity or alkalinity of pond water with a pH test kit *(see p 151)*, and use a pH adjuster, available in powder form, to remedy any imbalance. As a precaution, fish can be disinfected with a commercial fungal cure before introducing them.

SELECTING FISH

The first step to buying healthy fish is to choose a reputable supplier, who will allow you to pick out and inspect individual fish, and who will have an oxygen cylinder on site to inflate a carrying bag with enough oxygen *(see facing page)* for the journey home. Avoid buying fish from tanks that are connected to each other; this exchange of water increases the risk of waterborne diseases. Also avoid buying fish from a crowded selling tank, as this environment provides ideal conditions for the incubation of many pests and diseases *(see pp. 174–175)*. If possible, buy fish that are no more than 3–5in (7–12cm) long. Bigger fish not only cost more; some may find it harder to acclimatize to a new environment. Inexperienced fish-keepers should not invest in exotic and expensive varieties of fish at the outset, as these fish often have special requirements. If a fish becomes ill, a good supplier or a water garden center will be able to offer advice; failing this, they will be able to recommend a veterinary practice specializing in fish.

BRIGHT EYES
Always choose a fish with bright eyes. Cloudy eyes are indicative of ill health.

DORSAL FIN
A healthy fish should carry a sturdy dorsal fin that is fully erect.

CAUDAL FIN
Make sure that the delicate tail fin is intact.

CHOOSING A HEALTHY FISH
Always select a fish with bright eyes and a sturdy body. The fish should be lively, its large dorsal fin erect, and its two ventral fins well expanded. A healthy fish will swim effortlessly, with its fins erect; it will also be able to remain perfectly still in the water. If a fish regularly sinks, or bobs to the surface of the water, it may have a swim-bladder disorder. Highly colored fish may not be ideal purchases, as the strong coloration could mean that they have been freshly imported. More subdued colors are an indication that the fish has been in quarantine for some length of time – probably under cover – and will therefore be less prone to disease.

FLAT SCALES
The scales of a healthy fish lie flat against its body.

VENTRAL FINS
When swimming, a fish's fins should be held away from the body.

FIN ROT

FUNGUS (COTTON DISEASE)

INTERNAL AILMENT
Fish with an internal ailment may trail colorless excreta.

DROPSY
Bristling scales are one indication that a fish has dropsy.

WHITE SPOT

DULL EYES

MOUTH FUNGUS

SIGNS OF AN UNHEALTHY FISH
Check that small fish in particular do not have damaged or missing scales, as the exposed tissue beneath the scales will be vulnerable to secondary fungal infection. Because larger fish are more aggressive, it is more common for them to have some missing scales. If the spine of a fish appears to be bent, it could be the result of damage to its nervous system. A bloated body, bulging eyes, and bristling scales are indicative of dropsy (see pp. 174–175).

TRANSPORTING AND INTRODUCING FISH

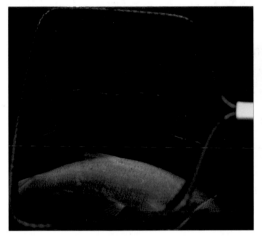

1 TRAWL A WIDE, soft mesh net underneath the selected fish. To prevent the fish from panicking and damaging itself, be as gentle as possible. Do not take the fish out of the water.

2 TO MAKE THE plastic bag more manageable, roll down the top as shown. Fill the bag with 2–3in (5–8cm) of water from the holding tank. Tip the fish gently from the net into the bag.

3 IF THE JOURNEY HOME will take more than four hours, ask the dealer to inflate the bag with oxygen from a cylinder, then seal. Do not leave fish in a sealed bag for more than 36 hours.

4 TO SUPPORT THE BAG and maintain the level of the water inside it, place it in a cardboard or styrofoam box for the journey home. Cover the box: light can cause the fish stress.

5 FLOAT THE UNOPENED bag on the pond until the water temperature in the bag matches that of the pond. To further acclimatize the fish, add a little pond water to the bag a few times, and reseal.

6 BY NOW THE POND WATER should have the same chemical composition as the water in the bag. Release the fish. Once it swims around happily, give it small quantities of food.

GUIDE TO STOCKING LEVELS

To achieve a healthy balance of submerged pond life, stock with a number of small fish rather than a few large ones that will swiftly devour other members of the food chain.

The number of fish your pond will support depends on its surface area (because it is this factor that chiefly determines how much oxygen will be available to them) and the length of the fish when mature (because their size determines their oxygen needs). An area of 1ft x 1ft (30cm x 30cm) will support a fish 2in (5cm) long, from nose to tail. While an area three times as big will accomodate three such small fish, it could instead be allocated to one 6in (15cm) fish. You can therefore divide your pond into equal portions to support a number of same-sized fish, or, for a mixed population of differently sized fish, allocate an appropriate area to each (*see right*) as space allows.

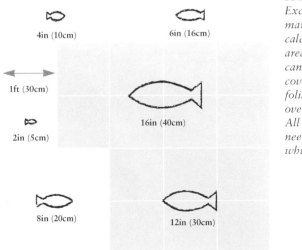

4in (10cm)

6in (16cm)

1ft (30cm)

16in (40cm)

2in (5cm)

8in (20cm)

12in (30cm)

HOW MANY FISH?
Exclude areas of marginal planting when calculating the surface area of clear water (this can include areas covered by floating foliage). Never overstock a pond. All fish, large or small, need enough space in which to swim freely.

ROUTINE FISH CARE

THE NATURAL ECOLOGY of a pond takes months, if not years, to establish itself *(see pp. 136–137)*. However, while it is advisable to wait several weeks before putting fish into a newly constructed pond, the addition of a dechlorinator and water conditioner, stocked by fish suppliers, can eliminate any wait.

AN IDEAL HABITAT

A well-planted pond makes an ideal habitat for fish. Submerged plants provide a spawning ground, cover, and food, as well as oxygen during the daylight hours, while floating-leaved plants create shade. Additional cover can be provided by placing corrugated tiles or terra-cotta piping on the bottom of the pond. The pond should not have any rough edges that fish could rub themselves raw against; this could lead to infection. If planning to keep boisterous fish such as koi, which tend to stir up mud at the bottom of the pond, it is essential to install a mechanical filter *(see pp. 70–73)*. In hot weather, a hose with a spray attachment or sprinkler can be used in an emergency, if fish are distressed and gasping for air. The pH levels of pond water should be maintained between 6.8 and 7.5 *(see p. 151)*. To lower the risk of diseases being transmitted, avoid overstocking.

FEEDING FISH

During winter, fish are semi-dormant and will not require feeding. They will live off reserves of fat and occasional stray food items. As spring advances and fish become more active, they will need an increasingly rich diet. If the pond is not yet well-enough established to satisfy their food requirements, most good-quality, prepacked fish food will adequately supplement any diet deficiencies. Feed fish once a day as the temperature rises and the fish begin to actively search for food. This frequency can be reduced gradually to several feeds per week as the season progresses. Foods such as frozen or freeze-dried shredded shrimp, which are rich in protein, will provide a dietary boost during the breeding period. Never overfeed fish, since uneaten food will decompose and pollute the water.

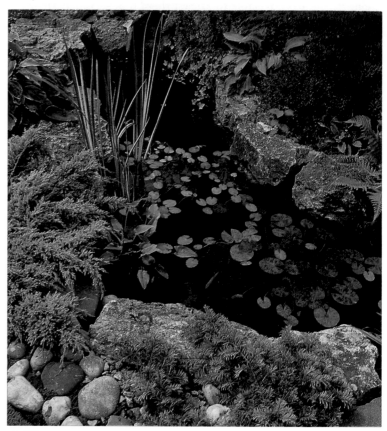

A WELL-PLANTED POND
Fish are happiest in a pond that provides shade and shelter and has a variety of submerged, floating, and deep-water plants. The pond should not be overstocked and should be well maintained so that the fish are less susceptible to waterborne diseases (see pp. 174–175). Clean water is not only beneficial to their health; it also allows them to be seen.

PREPARED FISH FOODS

FROZEN FOOD

Frozen or freeze-dried natural aquatic foods such as shredded shrimp, dried flies, and ants' eggs are rich in protein and contain all the nutrients that fish need.

DRIED FISH FOOD
Floating pellets and flakes are prepared to provide a balanced and nutritious diet for fish. Crumb food, although less nutritious, does give fish essential roughage.

PELLETS

CRUMB FOOD

FLAKED FOOD

EATING HABITS
A useful rule is to provide fish with no more food than they can eat within 10–15 minutes per day. All fish, even bottom-feeders, can be tempted to the surface with floating pellets of food. Even if fish are fed regularly, they will supplement this diet with live foods including gnats and mosquito larvae.

INSPECTING FISH

To remove a fish from the pond, always have a large bowl or bucket ready. Rather than chase fish around the pond, causing them stress, it is advisable to attract them to a secluded area with a sprinkling of food. If the fish is a small specimen – say, 4in (10cm) long – gently trap it in a soft net, then lift the net out of the water and release the fish into a bowl filled with pond water. Alternatively – and preferably – scoop the fish out of the net with a small bowl, without removing the net from the water, and release it into the larger holding bowl.

Under no circumstances should large fish (carp, for example) be lifted out of the water in a net. First net the fish gently, then lower the holding bowl into the pond and guide the fish into it.

BREEDING FISH

Whether or not fish breed depends on the population of the pond. If it is overstocked, the female will reabsorb her own eggs; if fry develop, most will not survive. The breeding season occurs between spring and midsummer, but unless they have reached a certain size, fish will not breed. Goldfish, shubunkin, and carp, for instance, must be at least 3in (8cm) long. Most pond fish lay and fertilize their eggs externally. Three or four days after the male has fertilized the female's eggs by spreading his milt over them, the fry begin to develop. During summer, professional fish breeders use a method known as hand-stripping to selectively breed fish. This should not be attempted by novice fish-keepers, as it involves the delicate task of removing the female fish's ova and the male's milt.

LIGHTING AND FISH

Only use lighting in a fish pond if the pond is large enough to allow fish to take refuge in other, unlit nooks and crannies in the pond if disturbed by the light. Never light up the entire area of a fish pond, or leave the lights on all night.

SIGNS OF ILL HEALTH
When inspecting a fish for signs of ill health, it will be necessary to look at it closely and in reasonably clear water. Small fish may be lifted out of a pond in a soft net and placed in a holding bowl filled with pond water. Net large fish, but rather than lifting them out of the water, guide them into a holding bowl.

BABY FISH
Baby fish, called fry, start out as minute and transparent organisms, and only begin to look like fish after two or three weeks. Depending on her size, a female may lay between 5,000 and 200,000 eggs, which hatch in 5–10 days depending on the temperature of the water. Males usually mature in their second or third year, females in their third or fourth year.

SEASONAL CHECKLIST FOR FISH CARE			
Spring	**Summer**	**Autumn**	**Winter**
• Use a testing kit *(see p. 151)* to evaluate the water's pH levels. • Introduce new fish *(see pp. 170–171)*. • When the water temperature reaches 50°F (10°C), begin feeding high carbohydrate diet (wheat germ etc.). Do not begin feeding high protein diet until the water temperature is 60°F (15°C). • Reintroduce fish overwintered indoors *(see p. 139)*. • Inspect fish for parasites or disorders they may have picked up during the winter *(see pp. 174–175)*. • Remove algae *(see pp. 140–141)*. • Keep an eye out for herons, which become active in the spring when food is not yet plentiful *(see p. 174)*. • Take precautions against predators by erecting a netting fence, approximately 18–24in (45–60cm) high, around the perimeter of the pond *(see p. 174)*.	• Introduce new fish *(see pp. 170–171)*. • Replace water lost through evaporation *(see pp. 138–141)*. • Check water-lily leaves for pests, then hose them into the water for the fish to eat. • Regulate feeding, since more natural foods are available to the fish. • Check fish regularly for pests and diseases, especially in very hot weather *(see pp. 170–171, 174–175)*. • If necessary, remove fry to a separate pond or to a bucket of water taken from the pond until they grow larger. • In hot spells, if fish are surfacing and gasping, use a hose with a spray attachment or a sprinkler to rapidly increase the oxygen content of the water.	• Feed fish when the weather is warm and bright *(see p. 172)*. • To build up fish for the winter months, supplement their diet with high-protein foods *(see p. 172)*. • Remove tender species of fish and keep under cover for the winter *(see pp. 168–169)*. • Net the pond to protect it from falling leaves and debris. Keep an eye out for herons as they prey more heavily on fish to build up their own reserves for the winter months *(see p. 174)*.	• Cease feeding fish as they become semi-dormant. • Place terra-cotta pipes at the bottom of the pond to provide fish with shelter from predators. • If freezing temperatures are forecast, install a stock tank deicer, pool heater *(see p. 139)*, or place one or more floats in the water, or cover a section of the pond *(see pp. 138–139)*. • If a pond ices over, make an air hole by placing a pan of boiling water on the ice. Never break ice with a hammer; the shock vibrations are harmful to fish.

FISH PESTS AND DISEASES

Lthough fish are vulnerable to a range of pests and diseases, a healthy pond environment can minimize these hazards. Be sure that the pond has different depths and varied planting, and avoid overstocking with fish *(see pp. 170–171)*. Cleaning the pond regularly *(see pp. 140–141)* and maintaining a balanced ecosystem *(see pp. 136–137)* are equally important. Most fish diseases are curable, and treatments for many are available from pet shops or garden centers. If a fish displays symptoms or behaves abnormally, move it into a separate container *(see p. 171)* away from other fish, while you seek advice and treatment.

FISH PESTS

DRAGONFLY AND DAMSELFLY LARVAE

Dragonflies can spend up to five years as nymphs (larvae) underwater, but only have one or two months of adult life. The color of these scorpion-like nymphs *(right)* varies from green to brown and gray. They spend most of their time at the bottom of the pond, where they prey on small fish and insect larvae. They catch the fish by shooting out their "mask," an extension of the lower jaw that resembles the claws of a lobster. These claws grip the prey and draw it back into the mouth, where it is injected with digestive fluids. Although both dragonfly and damselfly larvae prey on small fish, they themselves are important food for larger fish and birds. The adults are an attractive and interesting addition to the life of a pond.

HERON

A variety of herons, including great blue herons and green herons, will eat pond fish. Herons obtain food by wading in shallow water or standing in the water on one leg, head hunched into the tops of their wings. Without warning, these birds will stretch out their long necks and stab passing fish and other aquatic animals with their long, sharp, daggerlike beaks. Having identified a fish pond, stream, or bog garden as an excellent source of food, a heron will hunt relentlessly. Control is not easy, and if visits persist, it may become necessary to erect a netting fence, 18–24in (45–60cm) high, around the edges of the pond. The fence should be strong enough to keep these large birds out; a netting roof spread across it will also stop small diving birds getting through. Koi keepers often build ornamental pergola-like structures over their ponds; this structure can then easily be covered with netting when necessary.

FISH LICE

Fish lice can affect most pond fish, irrespective of size. Lice attach themselves to the body of the fish and cause damage to the tissues. Sometimes this results in death. It is possible to remove the clearly visible parasites by lifting them off gently with a pair of tweezers. Another method of removing them is to hold the fish in a soft net and dab a little kerosene on the lice with a small paint brush. Dip the fish in a solution of appropriate antiseptic to reduce the risk of secondary infection.

WATER BOATMAN

The most common species of water boatman is oval, with a brown back and a black underbelly with a conspicuous brown triangular mark in the center. The water boatman is often called a back-swimmer because of its habit of swimming upside down. Although it is only ⅕in (1.5cm) long, it can kill a small fish by injecting poison through its piercing mouthparts. Control is very difficult because the adults fly from pond to pond on summer evenings. Regular netting is the only effective control.

WHIRLIGIG BEETLE

Only ⅛–¼in (3–6mm) long, these black, oval beetles congregate in groups and gyrate on the surface of the water. Although they are air-breathing insects, they spend nearly half their lives in water and can, when necessary, create an air bubble to keep themselves supplied with oxygen as they dive to the bottom of the pond in search of food. They feed on other aquatic insects, but will also attack fish fry. The only method of control is to net off the adults from the water surface.

GREAT DIVING BEETLE

This insect, which is capable of storing oxygen in its wing cases, spends most of its three-year lifespan in water. It flies at night, and swims on the surface of the water before diving for prey. It has a dark brown body with a distinctive yellow or gold edge, and reaches a length of 2in (5cm). In addition to preying on newts and tadpoles, this beetle can kill small fish with its ferocious bite. There are no effective methods of control; if a beetle is seen, remove it with a net.

WATER SCORPION

Although these creatures resemble land scorpions, the tail of a water scorpion is a harmless breathing tube. About 1in (2.5cm) long, the water scorpion lives in shallow water and watches for prey from the leaves of plants. When a small fish passes by, the insect grabs and holds the victim with its pincerlike front legs, while its sharp mouthparts pierce and kill it. Rigid pond hygiene is one method of control; the other is to remove the insect by hand when its tail is seen on the surface.

> ### OTHER PESTS
>
> Amphibians such as frogs will eat fish. A bullfrog can eat a fish up to one-third its size. Various snakes also will prey on fish, including water snakes and the normally land-dwelling garter snake. Small, airborne predators such as kingfishers will also prey on fish. It is advisable to construct a strong netting fence around the pool approximately 18–24in (45–60cm) high. This will help to keep out herons as well as fish-loving cats and, in certain areas, "escaped" pests such as mink and turtles.

FISH DISEASES

DROPSY

FISH AFFECTED Dropsy is an uncommon disease, but it is, unfortunately, one that can affect most pond fish.

SYMPTOMS The body of an affected fish becomes severely bloated and the eyes protrude. The most distinctive symptom to look for is bristling scales that, once the disease has taken hold, resemble an open pine cone.
TREATMENT Treatment is difficult to prescribe, owing to the many possible causative agents. One of the most common causes of dropsy is bacterial septicemia. Broad-spectrum type antibiotics – prescribed by a vet specializing in fish – administered to the affected fish and its contacts may be beneficial in some cases. Improved water quality, reduction of stress, and good-quality food also sometimes help.

WHITE SPOT

FISH AFFECTED A widespread disease affecting most pond fish, especially newly purchased fish.

SYMPTOMS A number of white spots resembling grains of salt will be found on the body, fins, and tail of the fish. The spots are caused by tiny parasites burrowing into the skin of the fish. However, do not confuse this with the white pimples that appear on the gill plates of male fish during the mating season. Because of the itchiness caused by white spot, fish will rub themselves against objects.
TREATMENT Treatment is only effective in the very early stages of the disease. Place the fish in a holding tank and, by adding warm water, gradually raise the temperature to 60–65°F (16–18°C) to encourage the parasites to swarm. Then add a commercial remedy to the water. Change the water every three days and continue treatment until the fish is healthy. Effective and easy-to-use "whole-pond" treatments against white spot are now available; these present more practical alternatives than the treatment of individual fish, especially if more than one specimen in the pond is affected.

FIN OR BODY ROT

FISH AFFECTED This is a fairly common disease that mainly affects long-finned goldfish and shubunkins.

SYMPTOMS A whitish line develops along the outer fin and tail. The area also becomes ragged and bloodshot. This is due to the disintegration of the soft tissue between the bony rays of the tail. The condition may be complicated further by a fungal attack.
TREATMENT The disease is progressive and will cause death if the condition reaches other parts of the fish's body. However, treatment is effective if administered at the early stages of the disease. Capture the fish in a soft net then remove the damaged tissue carefully with a pair of sharp scissors. Afterward, use a fungal cure based on malachite green or methylene blue.

SKIN AND GILL FLUKES

FISH AFFECTED All types of fish.
SYMPTOMS Invisible to the naked eye, flukes are microscopic flatworms that use hooks to attach themselves to the fish.

The skin fluke causes irritated patches on the skin and fins, while the gill fluke causes inflamed gill tissues and loss of color. Both lead to excessive production of mucus and scratching against objects. The breathing rate of the fish will increase, its fins will twitch, and it will swim about in an agitated state, often rushing to the surface of the water as if short of air.
TREATMENT Commercial medications are available, including a parasite cure based on dimethyltrichlorohydroxyethyl-phosphonate. Salt baths containing ¼–½oz (10–15g) salt (pure sodium chloride or rock salt, *not* household salt) to 35fl oz (1 liter) of water are also effective, as is immersion in a very dilute formalin solution: 7fl oz (20ml) formalin in 11 gallons (100 liters) of water. Formalin is stressful to fish; they should only remain in the solution for 30–40 minutes. Immersing fish in a dilute methylene blue solution over an extended period may also produce results.

ULCER DISEASE

FISH AFFECTED All types of fish are susceptible to this bacterial disease.

SYMPTOMS Pathogenic bacteria are very common in pond water and will cause disease if the fish are at all vulnerable. The bacteria associated with ulcer disease can produce a wide range of symptoms that are easily detected, from shredded dorsal, tail, and ventral fins, to ulcers on the body, hemorrhagic (bloody) spots, and a "pop-eye" appearance.
TREATMENT Like many of the diseases that affect pond fish, this one can be cured if it is caught early enough and treated – under the guidance of a vet specializing in fish – with antibiotics such as tetracyline or chloramphenicol. Fish foods that contain antibiotics are also available from vets and good fish stockists.

FISH TUBERCULOSIS

FISH AFFECTED All types of fish.

SYMPTOMS This common fish disease is caused by bacteria. Symptoms can range from the development of ulcerated swellings and "rotting" fins, to the loss of coloration. Gradual consumption, causing the fish to lose weight and condition progressively, is also symptomatic of the disease.
TREATMENT The tuberculosis bacteria will spread very quickly through the pond; it is essential, therefore, to remove affected fish from the pond as soon as the symptoms become evident. In cases of suspected tuberculosis, always consult a vet specializing in fish. Some commercial antibiotics may produce a cure during the early stages of the disease. However, in the long term, fish almost invariably die.
WARNING When treating fish affected by this disease, always wear protective gloves, especially if there are cuts or scratches on your skin. Fish tuberculosis can, albeit rarely, affect humans, resulting in localized nodular growths that, while not normally presenting a major health problem, can nevertheless prove stubborn to treat.

OTHER FISH DISEASES

Mouth fungus affects all types of fish. The area round the mouth develops white or cream-colored growths that, in severe cases, can extend to the jaw bones, killing off tissue as the disease progresses. Treat with a medication based on malachite green, phenoxethol, and acriflavine. Antibiotics can also be effective; always consult a vet specializing in fish before using them.

Fungus or *cotton disease* affects all types of fish, but usually only fish already weakened by stress, injury, or infection. Cottonlike growths appear on the fins, gills, eyes, and mouth of the fish, usually at a point where damage to the tissues has already occurred. Commercial treatments are available, but these are only effective for large fish. Follow the instructions carefully.

FURTHER INFORMATION

- Fish Species and their Requirements – pp. 168–169
- Buying and Introducing Fish – pp. 170–171
- Routine Fish Care – pp. 172–173

THE PLANT CATALOG

Submerged Plants • Floating-leaved Plants
Water Lilies • Lotuses • Marginal Plants
Moisture-loving Plants

Throughout the catalog, symbols are
used for a quick reference to plants' growing
requirements; a key to these plant symbols can
be found on page 4. Detailed descriptions of a
number of other plants can be found in
Water Garden Designs (pp. 16–44).

Blending into the Garden (*LEFT*)
*Carefully chosen and positioned plants will soon make a water
feature look established. A wide range of moisture-loving
plants can be used to soften and disguise pond edges.*

SUBMERGED PLANTS

Unless an advanced filtration system is to be installed in a pond, plants whose leaves are at least partially submerged in the water are essential to maintain clear, well-oxygenated water *(see pp. 152–153)*. These plants are often listed as "oxygenators" in plant catalogs. Most such plants root at the bottom of the pond in a soil layer or in baskets and are entirely submerged. Their stems are not robust enough to be self-supporting out of the water although they occasionally thrust flower spikes above the surface. Others, such as *Myriophyllum aquaticum*, are able to grow above and below the water. An oxygenating role also can be performed by certain free-floating plants that float not on, but just below the surface, with only part of their leaves above water. Their floating leaves provide valuable shade, and their suspended roots absorb nutrients from any fish waste, thus helping to prevent a build-up of toxic material in pond water. All plants in this category can be fast-growing, and must be regularly thinned *(see pp. 160–161)* so that they do not dominate the pond; during the night, they deplete the water of oxygen and produce carbon dioxide. A fountain or waterfall running at night can effectively combat this effect.

Fontinalis antipyretica (water moss)
Mosslike evergreen perennial with branched stems bearing olive-green, scalelike leaves. Best in cold streams (it is much less vigorous in still water). Plant by weighting the plants between boulders, on which roots will cling. Propagate by division in spring. Zones 4–10. H 3in (8cm), S indefinite, water depth to 18in (44cm).

Hottonia palustris (water violet)
Deciduous perennial forming masses of light green, deeply divided foliage held both below and above the water. Pale lilac flower spikes emerge above water in spring. Thin periodically. Propagate by stem cuttings in spring or summer. Zones 5–9. H 1–3ft (30–90cm), S indefinite, water depth to 18in (45cm).

Ceratophyllum demersum (hornwort)
Deciduous submerged perennial with slender stems and whorls of forked leaves. Tolerant of shade and deeper water than many submerged plants. Propagate by softwood cuttings in summer, or break young plantlets away from the main plant. Zones 8–10. S indefinite, water depth to 24in (60cm).

Lagarosiphon major, syn. *Elodea crispa*
Semi-evergreen perennial forming dense, submerged masses of branching, fragile stems covered in reflexed, linear leaves. Tiny, trans-lucent flower spathes develop in summer. Thin in summer and cut back in autumn. Propagate by stem cuttings in spring or summer. Zones 4–9. S indefinite, water depth to 3ft (1m).

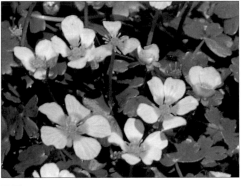

Ranunculus aquatilis (water crowfoot)
Annual or perennial, holding its white flowers and some of its leaves just above water. Best in large wildlife ponds or streams at a depth of 6–24in (15–60cm), where it can spread and root in mud bottoms. Propagate by fresh seed or by division in spring or summer. Zones 5–10. S indefinite, water depth to 3ft (1m).

FLOWING FOLIAGE
Leaves twist and spiral in water currents.

Myriophyllum verticillatum (milfoil)
Perennial with spreading stems and tightly packed, delicate, bright green leaves. Ideal for shallow water. Stems extend above the surface with spikes of inconspicuous, yellowish flowers. Propagate by stem cuttings in spring or summer. Zones 4–10. S indefinite, water depth to 18in (44cm).

Stratiotes aloides (water soldier, water aloe)
Semi-evergreen, free-floating perennial forming "pineapple-top" rosettes of spiky, dark olive-green leaves held partly below and partly above the water. Thin regularly. New plants form as small water buds on spreading stems: they may be separated in summer. Zones 6–9. H 16in (40cm), S indefinite, water depth to 3ft (1m).

Vallisneria spiralis (eelgrass, tape grass)
Submerged perennial, evergreen in the tropics, grown for its spiraling, strap-shaped, mid-green leaves, which can be 32in (80cm) long. Greenish flowers are produced year-round. Propagate by division in spring or summer or by separating runners that appear. Zones 8–10. S indefinite, water depth at least 12in (30cm).

ALSO RECOMMENDED

Callitriche hermaphroditica, syn.
C. autumnalis (zones 6–10)
Ceratopteris pteridioides (zones 9–10)
Egeria densa, syn. *Anacharis densa, Elodea densa* (zones 9–10)
Hygrophila polysperma rubra (zones 10–11)
Myriophyllum aquaticum (zones 6–11)

Potamogeton crispus (curled pondweed)
Perennial with seaweedlike submerged leaves, bearing crimson and creamy white flowers just above the water in summer. Spreads rapidly in mud-bottomed pools. Tolerates cloudy or shady water. Propagate by stem cuttings in spring or summer. Zones 7–10. S indefinite, water depth to 3ft (1m).

Utricularia vulgaris (greater bladderwort)
Deciduous, frost-hardy, free-floating perennial with feathery, bronze-green, bladderlike leaves that trap insects. Pouched, bright yellow flowers with red-brown streaks are held above the water in summer. Propagate by separating young plantlets in spring or summer. Zones 5–9. S 2–3ft (60–90cm), water depth to 3ft (1m).

Where specific page references are not given for descriptive plant entries found in other sections, brief details are given in the Plant Index *(see pp. 210–213).*

FLOATING-LEAVED PLANTS

Plants with foliage floating on the water surface are essential to maintain clear water. By blocking a proportion of sunlight they check the growth of algae, which thrive only in well-lit water. They also provide shade and shelter for pond life. Among those that are anchored by their roots in bottom soil or planting crates, the true water lilies *(Nymphaea)* are the most popular. In conditions where they are unsuitable, however, there are other more adaptable plants such as pond and fringe lilies *(Nuphar* and *Nymphoides)*, or plants such as water hawthorn *(Aponogeton distachyos)*. Other plants in this category, such as *Azolla filiculoides*, float completely, their suspended roots absorbing dissolved nutrients and any fish waste. Floaters tend to multiply rapidly and should be used and controlled with care. Some, such as water hyacinth *(Eichhornia) (see p. 26)* and water lettuce *(Pistia stratiotes)*, while not invasive in temperate climates, are so vigorous in tropical waters that their introduction may be prohibited in certain areas; for example, in parts of southern North America. In northen zones, the majority of floaters are winter killed. Where they are hardy, plants sink to the bottom in winter and float back to the surface in spring.

❋ ⬇

Azolla filiculoides, syn. *A. caroliniana* (fairy moss, water fern)
Tiny, free-floating perennial fern that forms clusters of soft leaves, each with a single fine root, that turn purplish-red in autumn. Useful for rapid, temporary cover in a new pond while other plants grow. Can be invasive: in summer, thin regularly. Zones 7–10. S indefinite.

❋ ⬇

Hydrocharis morsus-ranae (frogbit)
Perennial free-floater with rosettes of kidney-shaped, shiny leaves and papery white flowers with a yellow center. It prefers still, shallow water (it may root in mud), providing useful shelter for creatures, but is vulnerable to snail damage. New plantlets form on runners. Zones 7–10. S indefinite, water depth to 12in (30cm).

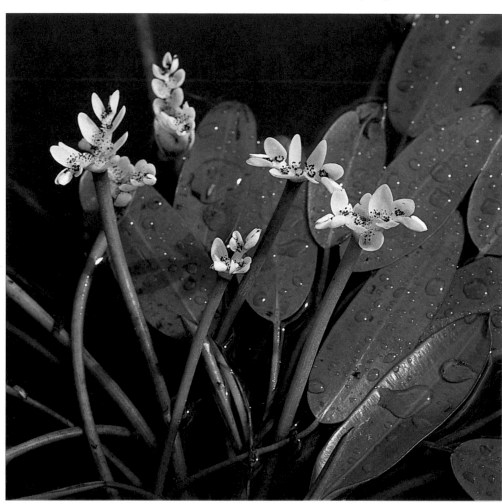

❋ ⬇

Aponogeton distachyos
(Cape pondweed, water hawthorn)
Deep-water perennial with floating, oblong, mid-green leaves. Heavily scented white flowers in forked racemes appear either in two flushes or throughout the summer. Propagate by fresh seed or by division in spring. Zones 9–10. S 4ft (1.2m), water depth to 2ft (60cm).

❋ ⬇

Marsilea quadrifolia (water clover)
Scrambling perennial fern with long, creeping roots and clover- or shamrock-shaped leaves. The leaves either float on the surface on stalks 3–6in (8–15cm) long, or stand above the water in muddy shallows. Propagate by division in either spring or summer. Zones 6–11. S indefinite, water depth to 24in (60cm).

Polygonum amphibium
(willow grass, amphibious bistort)
Amphibious perennial with long-stalked, floating leaves borne on stems that root at the nodes. In midsummer pink flowers are held above the water. Will also grow in boggy margins. Propagate by division. Zones 5–9. S indefinite, water depth to 18in (45cm).

Nuphar japonica (Japanese pond lily)
Deciduous perennial with heart-shaped floating leaves and round yellow flowers held just above the surface in summer. Grows in still or slowly moving water in full sun or partial shade. Can become invasive. Propagate and thin by division in spring. Zones 6–10. S 3ft (1m), water depth to 12in (30cm).

Salvinia auriculata (butterfly fern)
Free-floating tender perennial fern forming spreading colonies. The pale green or purplish-brown leaves are covered in silky hairs and tightly packed on branched stems. Remove faded foliage and thin when overcrowded by separating young plants in summer. Zones 10–11. H 1in (2.5cm), S indefinite.

Nymphoides peltata
(fringed water lily, water fringe)
Deciduous rhizomatous perennial with small, floating, mid-green leaves often splashed with brown. Small yellow flowers held 2–3in (5–8cm) above the water appear throughout summer. Propagate by division in spring. Zones 7–10. S 24in (60cm), water depth 6–18in (15–45cm).

Pistia stratiotes (water lettuce)
Deciduous free-floating aquatic with slightly overlapping, velvety, pale green leaves arranged like lettuce. Leaves are whitish-green on the underside. Produces tiny greenish flowers. Thin and separate new plantlets in summer. Zones 8–10. H 9–12in (22–30cm), S indefinite, water depth to 3ft (1m).

Victoria amazonica
(Amazon water lily, royal water lily)
Tropical perennial often grown as an annual with rimmed leaves up to 6ft (2m) across. The night-blooming flowers last two days; they open white then turn pink. Propagate by seed in winter or early spring. Zones 10–11. S 20ft (6m), water depth 2–3ft (60–90cm).

WATER LILIES

THE RANGE OF WATER LILIES *(Nymphaea)* available is increasing, with new cultivars continually being developed, many in North America. All have flowers that either float, or (particularly the tropical water lilies) stand just above the water surface. Many are delicately perfumed, and some change color as they open and mature. There are species and cultivars to suit most climatic conditions, size of pond, and planting depth, although all share a need for a sunny, sheltered position and still or nearly still water. Hardy water lilies will survive outside in zones 3–11, even if the surface of the pond is frozen. The old foliage sinks and dies in winter; new leaves appear in the following spring. Tropical water lilies are perennial in frost-free areas. They may bloom by day or by night. In cool climates they are commonly grown as annuals. If neglected, water lilies become coarse and congested, with few flowers. Removing fading leaves and flowers, and regularly lifting, dividing, and replanting *(see pp. 160–163)*, will preserve an elegant display. Water lilies may be propagated *(see p. 160)* by division, separating root buds or plantlets in spring or early summer; species may also be grown from seed.

Nymphaea 'Aurora'
Of all the lilies whose flowers change color, this has the widest range of shades. It is a small cultivar, with olive-green leaves mottled with red-purple. The semi-double flowers, cream in bud, open to yellow, then turn orange to flecked blood-red, with orange stamens. Hardy. S 30in (75cm), water depth 12–18in (30–45cm).

Nymphaea 'Blue Beauty'
A free-flowering cultivar with wavy-edged leaves that may be brown-flecked, with purplish undersides. The sweetly scented, semi-double, day-blooming flowers have rich blue petals and deep yellow stamens. Plant only once the weather becomes warmer in spring. Tropical. S 4–7ft (1.2–2.2m), water depth 1–2ft (30–60cm).

Nymphaea alba (common white water lily)
One of the few water lilies indigenous to Europe, *N. alba* is a prolific flowerer and is best in a large pond. Its round, dark green pads are 12in (30cm) in diameter. The semi-double flowers, 8in (20cm) across, are magnolia-white with yellow stamens. Hardy. S 5–6ft (1.5–2m), water depth 1–3ft (30–90cm).

Nymphaea capensis (Cape blue water lily)
This adaptable species will grow well in any size pond. Its large, wavy-edged leaves can be 16in (40cm) in diameter. The semi-double, star-shaped flowers, up to 10in (25cm) across, are light blue with yellow stamens, and held well above the water. Tropical. S 5–8ft (1.5–2.5m), water depth 1–2ft (30–60cm).

✽ ✦

Nymphaea 'Caroliniana Nivea'
This cultivar is suited to larger ponds, performing best when planted in a large crate or basket that allows a substantial root system to develop. The leaves are almost round; the flowers semi-double, star- to cup-shaped, fragrant, ivory-white, with yellow stamens. Hardy. S 4–5ft (1.2–1.5m), water depth 1–2ft (30–60cm).

✽ ✦

Nymphaea 'Escarboucle'
Excellent for most ponds in cool climates, and stays open later in the afternoon than most red-flowered cultivars. Brown-tinged young leaves mature to deep green; the semi-double flowers are bright crimson with golden stamens, their outer petals tipped white. Hardy. S 4–5ft (1.2–1.5m), water depth 1–2ft (30–60cm).

✽ ✦

Nymphaea 'Firecrest'
Needs ample space and a planting basket at least 2ft (60cm) wide and 1ft (30cm) deep. Its deep purple young leaves mature to green. The semi-double, star-shaped pink flowers, held just above the water, have orange inner stamens and outer stamens tipped with deep pink. Hardy. S 4ft (1.2m), water depth 12–18in (30–45cm).

✽ ✦

Nymphaea 'Froebelii'
A good choice for shallow water, ideal for barrels or small ponds. Bronzed young leaves mature to small, round or heart-shaped, pale green pads. The deep red flowers, 4–5in (10–13cm) across, are first cup-shaped, then star-shaped, with orange-red stamens. Hardy. S 3ft (1m), water depth 6–12in (15–30cm).

✽ ✦

Nymphaea 'Gladstoneana'
A vigorous, free-flowering cultivar that will grow large unless regularly thinned. The bronzed young leaves mature to almost round, dark green pads, with crimped edges. Flowers are semi-double, star-shaped, waxy-petaled, with bright yellow stamens. Tropical. S 5–8ft (1.5–2.4m), water depth 18–24in (45–60cm).

✽ ✦

Nymphaea 'Gonnère'
This magnificent white cultivar is ideal for any size of pond. Its slightly bronzed young leaves mature to round, pea-green pads up to 9in (22cm) across. The fully double, globe-shaped, fragrant white flowers, 4–6in (10–15cm) across, stay open until late afternoon. Hardy. S 3–4ft (1–1.2m), water depth 12–18in (30–45cm).

❋ ❀

Nymphaea pygmaea 'Helvola'
A small, free-flowering water lily ideal for small, shallow ponds or containers. The oval, heavily mottled, purplish leaves have purple undersides. The small, semi-double, clear yellow flowers are cup-shaped at first, opening to a star shape. Semi-hardy. Zones 6–11. S 2ft (60cm), water depth 6–9in (15–22cm).

❋ ❀

Nymphaea 'James Brydon'
A popular red-flowered cultivar for barrels or small to medium-sized ponds. Resistant to crown rot. Its purplish-brown young leaves mature to dark green pads. The double flowers, their petals suffused with brilliant rose-red, are 4–5in (10–12cm) across. Hardy. S 3–4ft (1–1.2m), water depth 12–18in (30–45cm).

❋ ❀

Nymphaea 'Lucida'
This free-flowering cultivar is suitable for any size pond. Its large leaves are heavily marked with dark purple, and the star-shaped flowers, 5–6in (12–15cm) in diameter, have red inner petals and outer petals of pale pink with deeper pink veins. Hardy. S 4–5ft (1.2–1.5m), water depth 12–18in (30–45cm).

❋ ❀

Nymphaea 'Laydekeri Fulgens'
One of the first cultivars to bloom in spring, flowering freely through the summer, and suitable for any size pond. The young leaves are blotched with purple, maturing to plain green. Semi-double, burgundy-red flowers have orange-red stamens. Hardy. S 4–5ft (1.2–1.5m), water depth 12–18in (30–45cm).

❋ ❀

Nymphaea 'Marliacea Albida'
Popular cultivar that reliably produces a high proportion of blooms for its limited spread of leaves. Slightly bronzed young foliage matures to deep green pads, tinged red-purple beneath. The cup-shaped, semi-double flowers are white with yellow stamens. Hardy. S 3–4ft (1–1.2m), water depth 12–18in (30–45cm).

❋ ❀

Nymphaea 'Marliacea Carnea'
A vigorous pink-flowered cultivar only suitable for medium-sized to large ponds. The purplish young leaves mature to large, deep green pads. The light pink, semi-double flowers with yellow stamens can be up to 8in (20cm) in diameter. Hardy. S 4–5ft (1.2–1.5m), water depth 12–18in (30–45cm).

Nymphaea 'Marliacea Chromatella'
One of the most reliable yellow water lilies for
any size pond. Also shade tolerant. Its coppery
young leaves, with purple streaks, mature to a
purple-mottled mid-green. Semi-double
flowers, 6in (15cm) in diameter, are borne in
abundance. Hardy. S 4–5ft (1.2–1.5m), water
depth 12–18in (30–45cm).

Nymphaea 'Odorata Sulphurea Grandiflora'
Cultivar whose yellow flowers tend to open
only from late morning to early afternoon, but
are reliably produced throughout summer. Its
dark green leaves are speckled with maroon; the
semi-double flowers are sweetly scented and
have yellow stamens. Hardy. S 3–4ft (1–1.2m),
water depth 12–18in (30–45cm).

Nymphaea 'Pearl of the Pool'
This cultivar flowers best when given a large
planting basket or crate. Its bronzed young
leaves mature to plain green pads, their lobes
sometimes overlapping. The star-shaped,
fragrant, pink flowers are 5–6in (12–15cm) in
diameter, with orange stamens. Hardy. S 4–5ft
(1.2–1.5m), water depth 12–18in (30–45cm).

Nymphaea 'Pink Sensation'
One of the finest pink cultivars, with flowers
that stay open late into the afternoon. Leaves
are purplish when young, later turning deep
green. The pink flowers open to a star shape,
5–6in (12–15cm) across, with yellow inner and
pink outer stamens. Hardy. S 4ft (1.2m), water
depth 12–18in (30–45cm).

Nymphaea 'Ray Davies'

A recently introduced cultivar suitable for small or medium-sized ponds noted for its evenly colored and shaped flowers. Its leaves are a glossy plain deep green and the fully double flowers are pale pink with a showy ring of golden stamens in the center. Hardy. S 3ft (1m), water depth 12–18in (30–45cm).

Nymphaea 'Rose Arey'

Best in a large planting container that will allow a substantial root system to develop. Its purple young leaves mature to green. Anise-scented, semi-double flowers open deep pink, paling with age, and have golden stamens, orange-pink toward the edges. Hardy. S 4–5ft (1.2–1.5m), water depth 14–24in (35–60cm).

Nymphaea 'Sunrise'

Although hardy, this cultivar needs a warm climate to flower well. Purple-mottled when young, the leaves mature to plain green, round to oval pads, up to 8in (20cm) across. The flowers are semi-double with long yellow petals and yellow stamens. Hardy. S 4–5ft (1.2–1.5m), water depth 14–18in (35–45cm).

Nymphaea 'René Gérard'

A large-leaved cultivar that looks best in medium-sized to large pools. Its bronzed young leaves mature to round, plain green pads, up to 12in (30cm) in diameter. The flowers are rose-red, their outer petals heavily flecked with pale pink; the stamens are yellow. Hardy. S 5ft (1.5m), water depth 12–18in (30–45cm).

Nymphaea 'Robinsoniana'

A free-flowering cultivar with contrasting flowers and foliage. Its light purple leaves have deep purple blotches and deep red undersides. Star-shaped flowers with cupped centers, 4½–5in (11–13cm) across, have orange-red petals and orange stamens. Hardy. S 4–5ft (1.2–1.5m), water depth 12–18in (30–45cm).

Nymphaea 'Saint Louis Gold'

Tropical cultivar with smaller but more richly-colored flowers than the similar 'Saint Louis'. The purple-blotched young leaves become large, plain green pads. Semi-double, fragrant flowers held above the water are first mustard-gold, fading to lemon. Tropical. S 8–10ft (2.4–3m), water depth 15–24in (37–60cm).

❋ ✿

Nymphaea 'Vésuve'

Cultivar with a long flowering season; in addition, its blooms are open for much of the day. The dark green leaves are almost circular, up to 10in (25cm) across. The star-shaped flowers are an even glowing cerise with orange stamens and inward-curving petals. Hardy. S 4ft (1.2m), water depth 12–18in (30–45cm).

❋ ✿

Nymphaea 'Virginalis'

One of the most reliably free-flowering white cultivars for a cool climate. The purple or bronzed young leaves mature to plain green pads with overlapping lobes. The cup-shaped, day-blooming, fragrant white flowers have yellow stamens. Hardy. S 3–4ft (1–1.2m), water depth 15–18in (37–45cm).

❋ ✿

Nymphaea 'Virginia'

A free-flowering cultivar with purplish deep green leaves and star-shaped, semi-double, very pale yellow (often near white) flowers 4–6in (10–15cm) across that are distinctively star-shaped, with many narrow chrysanthemum-like petals. Hardy. S 5–6ft (1.5–1.8m), water depth 14–20in (35–50cm).

❋ ✿

Nymphaea 'William Falconer'

A compact, vividly colored cultivar that is suitable for a medium-sized pond. Its leaves are maroon when young, maturing to dark green with heavy purple veining. The medium-sized, rounded, deep cherry red flowers open to reveal yellow stamens. Hardy. S 4ft (1.2m), water depth 18–30in (45–75cm).

❋ ✿ ◈

Nymphaea 'Wood's White Knight'

A vigorous, night-blooming cultivar for a large, tropical pond. The almost circular leaves, up to 15in (37cm) across, have unusual scalloped edges. The large, narrow-petaled flowers open wide around central yellow stamens, giving a daisylike effect. Tropical. S 8–10ft (2.4–3m), water depth 16–24in (40–60cm).

ALSO RECOMMENDED

N. 'Amabilis' Pink flowers. Hardy, S 5–7ft (1.5–2.3m), WD 12–18in (30–45cm).

N. 'American Star' Salmon flowers. Hardy, S 4–5ft (1.2–1.5m), WD 12–18in (30–45cm).

N. 'Attraction' *(see p. 37)*

N. caerulea Pale blue flowers. Semi-hardy, S 8–10ft (2.4–3m), WD 18–36in (45–90cm).

N. 'Charlene Strawn' Lemon flowers. Hardy, S 3–5ft (1–1.5m), WD 12–18in (30–45cm).

N. 'Charles de Meurville' Pink flowers. Hardy, S 4–5ft (1.2–1.5m), WD 12–18in (30–45cm).

N. 'Ellisiana' Red flowers. Hardy, S 3ft (90cm), WD 9–16in (22–40cm).

N. 'Emily Grant Hutchings' Deep pink flowers. Tropical, night-blooming. S 6ft (2m), WD 2–3ft (30–60cm).

N. 'General Pershing' Lilac flowers. Tropical, S 5–6ft (1.5–2m), WD 12–18in (30–45cm).

N. gigantea Purple-blue flowers. Tropical, S 6–9ft (2–3m), WD 18–36in (45–90cm).

N. 'Indiana' Apricot to orange flowers. Hardy, S 30in (75cm), WD 6–12in (15–30cm).

N. 'Louise' Red flowers. Hardy, S 4–5ft (1.2–1.5m), WD 12–18in (30–45cm).

N. mexicana *(see p. 26)*

N. 'Splendida' Pink flowers. Hardy, S 4–5ft (1.2–1.5m), WD 15–24in (37–60cm).

N. tetragona alba White flowers. Semi-hardy, S 2–3ft (60–90cm), WD 6–9in (15–22cm).

LOTUSES

WITH THEIR STRIKING LEAVES and exquisite midsummer flowers, lotuses *(Nelumbo)* are exceptionally beautiful plants, and have been cultivated for thousands of years. They require an open, sunny position, and many need at least semi-tropical conditions. Most lotuses are hardy in zones 5 through to 11, although in order to bloom well, they require several weeks of hot (90°F/32°C or higher), sunny weather in July. The rhizomatous roots may also be stored over winter *(see p. 158)*. Lotuses can be planted in water 6–24in (15–60cm) deep, and are thus suitable both for the margins and deeper, central areas of the average pond. However, the roots spread rapidly, and are best confined in planting baskets or crates. At first, the young leaves lie on the water surface; however, the stout leaf stalks soon thrust the foliage into the air. The leaves are large, bluish green, and platelike, with a waxy coating. The flowers, usually held just above the leaves, last for about three days, opening in the morning and closing by mid-afternoon. The petals fall to expose a delightful seedhead resembling a watering-can rose. Lotus species are grown from seed in spring; selections and cultivars must be propagated by division in spring.

Nelumbo nucifera 'Alba Grandiflora'
Vigorous deciduous perennial with wavy-edged leaves. Its large, white flowers have broad, oval petals and tufts of golden stamens. Sometimes referred to as the "magnolia lotus," 'Alba Grandiflora' is widely held to be the finest white-flowered cultivar. H 4–6ft (1.2–2m), S indefinite.

Nelumbo lutea (American lotus, water chinquapin)
Vigorous deciduous perennial with rounded leaves and yellow flowers, their petals fading gently toward the tips. The seedheads, 4in (10cm) in diameter, are a traditional food of native Americans. Grows well in shallow water. H 2½–5ft (0.7–1.5m), S indefinite.

Nelumbo nucifera (sacred lotus, Asian lotus)
Very vigorous deciduous perennial holding its leaves, which can be 3ft (90cm) across, very high above the water. The flowers have a pleasant fragrance and are large, opening rose-pink then fading to a pale flesh tone. The seed capsule turns from yellow to brown. H 5–7ft (1.5–2.2m), S indefinite.

Nelumbo nucifera 'Momo Botan'
Deciduous perennial, smaller than most lotuses, needing water no deeper than 12in (30cm). The peony-like double flowers are rose pink with yellow at the petal bases. It has a longer flowering season than most lotuses, and the flowers also stay open longer, sometimes all night. H 2–4ft (0.6–1.2m), S 3ft (1m).

Nelumbo nucifera 'Rosea Plena'
Vigorous, free-flowering deciduous perennial with leaves 18–20in (45–50cm) in diameter. The double, rose-pink flowers turn yellow toward the petal bases. While the flowers are large, up to 13in (33cm) across, the seed capsule is unusually small, only 1in (2.5cm) in diameter. H 4–5ft (1.2–1.5m), S indefinite.

Nelumbo 'Perry's Super Star'
Deciduous perennial with blue-green leaves. The sweetly scented flowers change from rich pink to yellow, culminating in a creamy white color with pink tips. They are very unusual in having six to eight green-tipped petals near the center of the flower. H 3–4ft (1–1.2m), S indefinite.

Nelumbo nucifera 'Mrs Perry D Slocum'
Deciduous perennial with glaucous leaves. It is exceptionally free-flowering with blooms that in many ways resemble those of the rose 'Peace'. The petals are pink-flushed yellow on the first day, pink and yellow on the second day, and cream-flushed pink on the third day. H 4–5ft (1.2–1.5m), S indefinite.

Nelumbo 'Shiroman', syn. var. *alba plena*
Vigorous deciduous perennial with leaves 24in (60cm) in diameter. The slightly fragrant, large, double flowers, 10in (25cm) across, are creamy white in color with golden stamens in the center. This rapidly spreading lotus should only be sited in a medium to large pond. H 3–5ft (0.9–1.5m), S indefinite.

Nelumbo nucifera 'Pekinensis Rubra'
(red lotus)
Deciduous perennial with leaves 20–24in (50–60cm) across. The slightly fragrant flowers, 8–12in (20–30cm) in diameter, are deep rose-red, later turning pink. The large, yellow seed capsules develop a green rim. H 4–6ft (1.2–2m), S indefinite.

Nelumbo 'Perry's Giant Sunburst'
Deciduous perennial with blue-green leaves, 17–21in (43–53cm) across. The pleasantly fragrant, large flowers are 10–14in (25–35cm) in diameter and have a rich creamy color, with buttery yellow stamens. They are held well above the leaves on robust, erect stalks. H 4½–5½ft (1.4–1.7m), S indefinite.

ALSO RECOMMENDED

N. 'Alba Striata' White-flowered, with jagged red petal margins.

N. 'Angel Wings' White-flowered.

N. 'Baby Doll' White-flowered.

N. 'Ben Gibson' Pink-flowered.

N. 'Charles Thomas' Pink-flowered.

N. 'Debbie Gibson' Cream-flowered.

N. 'Empress' White-flowered.

N. 'Kermesina' Rose pink- to bright red flowered.

N. *lutea* 'Flavescens' Yellow-flowered.

N. 'Maggie Belle Slocum' Pink-flowered.

N. *nucifera* 'Chawan Basu' Cream-flowered.

N. 'Sharon' Pink-flowered.

N. 'Shirokunshi' (tulip lotus) White-flowered.

N. 'Suzanne' Pink-flowered.

N. 'The Queen' Ivory-flowered.

MARGINAL PLANTS

Marginal plants inhabit shallow water, usually around the edges of a water garden. While most of their top growth is visible above the water surface, their bases and roots are under water, although many also grow well in marshy, saturated soil. Their vertical presence contrasts well with the flat water surface and the floating leaves of plants such as water lilies. Marginals planted around wildlife ponds can provide cover for birds, aquatic insects, and other small creatures. Generally used in informal ponds, marginals placed in baskets on shelves break the rigidity of formal edges. It is important to position marginals in the depth of water that best suits each individual plant. Some prefer a water depth of only 1–2in (2.5–5cm), while others tolerate a depth of up to 12in (30cm). Lotuses *(see pp. 188–189)* may also be used as marginals, given a minimum water depth of 6in (16cm). Many marginal plants grow extremely quickly, and where space is limited they should be contained in isolated planting beds or planting crates. Some of the more robust rhizomatous species, such as cattails *(Typha)*, develop sharply pointed roots that can pierce flexible liners. Planting crates will protect the liner.

Calla palustris (hardy call, water arum)
Deciduous or semi-evergreen perennial with long, creeping rhizomatous roots. In spring, white, arumlike flower spathes appear that echo the leaves in shape, followed by red or orange berries. Propagate by seed in late summer or by division in spring. Zones 3–8. H 10in (25cm), S 12in (30cm), water depth to 2in (5cm).

Alisma plantago-aquatica (water plantain)
Rhizomatous perennial with rosettes of oval leaves held on long stalks above the water. Dainty, pinkish white flowers open in summer. Self-seeds readily in wet soil. Propagate by seed in late summer or by division in spring. Zones 5–8. H 30in (75cm), S 18in (45cm), water depth to 10in (25cm).

Acorus calamus 'Variegatus'
(variegated sweet flag)
Deciduous rhizomatous perennial with irislike leaves, mid-green with cream stripes, with some wrinkling along the edges. Small conical flowers emerge just below the leaf tips. Propagate by division in spring. Zones 4–10. H 30in (75cm), S 24in (60cm), water depth to 9in (22cm).

Butomus umbellatus (flowering rush)
Perennial with bronze shoots that develop into thin, olive-green leaves. Rose-pink flowers are borne above the leaves on tall stems in summer. Best grown in open ground; if containerized it needs regular dividing and repotting. Propagate by division. Zones 3–7. H 2–4ft (60cm–1.2m), water depth 2–16in (5–40cm).

Cyperus papyrus (papyrus, paper reed)
Evergreen perennial sedge with stout, leafless stems, triangular in cross-section. Tufts of fine, pendulous leaves and flower sprays with as many as 100 rays develop in summer. Best sheltered from wind. Propagate by seed or by division in autumn. Zones 9–10. H 10–15ft (3–5m), S 3ft (1m), water depth to 10in (25cm).

Eriophorum angustifolium
(common cotton grass)
Evergreen marsh or marginal plant forming dense tufts of grasslike leaves. Flowers form as white "cotton balls." Best in acid conditions, such as peaty soil. Propagate by seed or by division in autumn. Zones 4–11. H 12–18in (30–45cm), S indefinite, water depth to 2in (5cm).

❋ 🔲 ♦ ♦

Iris laevigata 'Mottled Beauty'
Deciduous perennial forming clumps of sword-shaped, soft green leaves without a midrib. The white flowers are broad-petaled and beardless; the falls are spotted pale blue. Also grows well in moist soil. Divide rhizomes in late summer to propagate. Zones 4–9. H 2–3ft (60cm–1m), S indefinite, water depth 3–4in (7–10cm).

❋ 🔲 ♦

Glyceria maxima var. *variegata*
(variegated grass, sweet manna grass)
Deciduous perennial aquatic grass with leaves striped with creamy white, often flushed pink at the base. Flowers are heads of greenish spikelets in summer. Propagate by seed or by division in autumn. Zones 5–9. H 32in (80cm), S indefinite, water depth to 6in (15cm).

❋ 🔲 ♦ ♦

Houttuynia cordata 'Chameleon', syn.
H. cordata 'Variegata'
Spreading, often invasive perennial. Red stems bear aromatic leaves splashed with yellow and red. Insignificant flowers with white bracts are produced in spring. Propagate by lifting runners in spring. Zones 5–9. H 6–24in (15–60cm), S indefinite, water depth no more than 2in (5cm).

❋ 🔲 ♦ ♦

Iris laevigata 'Alba'
Deciduous perennial forming clumps of sword-shaped leaves with no midrib. Sparsely branched stems bear white, broad-petaled, beardless flowers. Grows in standing water or constantly moist soil. Divide rhizomes in late summer to propagate. Zones 4–9. H 2–3ft (60cm–1m), S indefinite, water depth to 3–4in (7–10cm).

❋ 🔲 ♦

Iris versicolor (blue flag, wild iris)
Deciduous clump-forming perennial with narrow, gray-green leaves. Each branched stem bears three to five violet-blue flowers. Falls are white veined with purple, yellow-blotched at the base. Also grows in wet soil. Divide rhizomes in late summer to propagate. Zones 2–8. H 2ft (60cm), water depth to 2–3in (5–7cm).

❄ ▦ ◍

Ludwigia palustris (water purslane)
Deciduous semi-hardy perennial that forms
mats of branched, creeping stems in shallow
water or mud. The leaves may become suffused
with purple, particularly in full sun. Tiny, bell-
shaped flowers appear in summer. Propagate by
seed in spring. Zones 4–10. H 20in (50cm),
S indefinite, water depth to 12in (30cm).

❄ ▦ ◍ ◍

Lysichiton camtschatcensis
Vigorous deciduous perennial with a stout
rhizome. White, arumlike spathes surrounding
erect spikes of small flowers appear in early
spring, before the bright green, paddlelike,
leathery leaves. Propagate by fresh seed in late
summer. Zones 6–8. H 30in (75cm), S 24–36in
(60–90cm), water depth 1in (2.5cm).

❄ ▦ ◍

Narthecium ossifragum (bog asphodel)
Deciduous perennial with rigid fans of reddish
green leaves and erect spikes of star-shaped,
yellow flowers in summer that mature to orange.
Needs acid conditions; grow in peaty soil or
pure sphagnum moss. Propagate by division or
by seed. Zones 4–9. H 8–12in (20–30cm),
S 8–12in (20–30cm), water depth 1in (2.5cm).

❄ ▦ ◍ ◍

Lysichiton americanus (yellow skunk
cabbage)
Vigorous deciduous perennial that grows well
in deep, moist soil and in still or moving water.
Yellow spathes appear in early spring, followed
by large leaves. Propagate by fresh seed in late
summer. Zones 4–8. H 4ft (1.2m), S 2½ft
(75cm), water depth 1in (2.5cm).

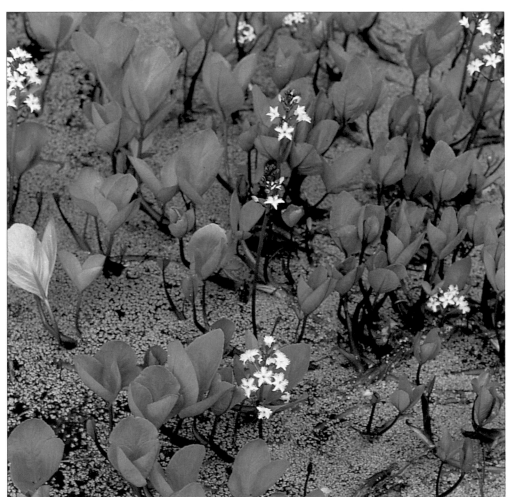

❄ ▦ ◍

Menyanthes trifoliata (bog bean,
buckbean, marsh trefoil)
Deciduous perennial with three-lobed, olive
green leaves on tall, sheathed stalks. White to
purplish flowers open from pink buds in late
spring. Divide congested plants or propagate
by stem cuttings in spring. Zones 4–8. H 9in
(23cm), S indefinite, water depth 2in (5cm).

Orontium aquaticum (golden club)
Deciduous rhizomatous perennial. The bluish green leaves have an attractive silvery sheen on the underside and will float in water. The pokerlike flowerheads stand well above the water. Propagate by fresh seed or by division in spring. Zones 6–11. H 12–18in (30–45cm), S 24in (60cm), water depth to 12in (30cm).

Phragmites australis 'Variegatus'
Variegated reed grass with leaves striped with bright yellow, fading to white and, in summer, heads of soft purple flowers. Also grows well in moist soil, but will be invasive. It is only suitable for large, natural poolsides. Propagate by division in spring. Zones 4–10. H 4–6ft (1.2–1.8m), S indefinite, water depth 3in (7cm).

Ranunculus lingua 'Grandiflorus' (greater spearwort)
Deciduous perennial with yellow flowers in late spring. Leaves are heart-shaped and long-stalked on nonflowering shoots; pointed and short-stalked on flowering ones. Propagate by fresh seed or by division in spring. Zones 4–8. H 2–5ft (1.5m), S 6ft (2m), water depth 3–6in (7–15cm).

Peltandra undulata, syn. *P. virginica* (green arrow arum)
Deciduous perennial with arrow-shaped, bright green leaves. Narrow yellow or white flower spathes appear in summer, followed by green berries. Propagate by seed or by division in spring. Zones 5–9. H 3ft (90cm), S 2ft (60cm), water depth 2–3in (5–7cm).

Pontederia cordata (pickerel weed)
Robust deciduous perennial that forms dense clumps of stems bearing smooth, narrowly heart-shaped leaves. In late summer, compact spikes of blue flowers develop from within a leaf at the stem tip. Propagate by fresh seed or by division in spring. Zones 3–6. H 30in (75cm), S 18in (45cm), water depth 5in (13cm).

❀ ❂ ♦

Sagittaria latifolia (American arrowhead, duck potato, wapato)
Deciduous perennial with soft green leaf-blades and whorls of white flowers in summer. Develops tubers at the ends of subterranean runners that may be separated from the parent for propagation purposes. Zones 4–11. H 5ft (1.5m), S 2ft (60cm), water depth 6in (15cm).

❀ ❂ ♦

Schoenoplectus lacustris subsp. *tabernaemontani* 'Zebrinus'
Perennial bulrush with a tough, creeping rhizome. Dark green stems have horizontal cream banding. Flowers are white and brown, in spikelike heads, in summer. Propagate by division in spring. Zones 4–11. H 5ft (1.5m), S indefinite, water depth 3–6in (7–15cm).

❀ ❂ ♦

Scrophularia auriculata 'Variegata' (water figwort)
Evergreen perennial with striking, cream-edged foliage. The greenish purple flowers may be removed to prevent rampant self-seeding. Propagate by division or by softwood cuttings in summer. Zones 5–9. H 3ft (90cm), S 2ft (60cm), water depth 3in (7cm).

❀ ❂ ♦

Saururus cernuus (lizard's tail, swamp lily, water dragon)
Deciduous perennial with erect stems carrying heart-shaped, bright green leaves. Spikes of waxy, fragrant flowers appear in summer. Looks best surrounded by water. Propagate by division in spring. Zones 4–9. H 9in (23cm), S 12in (30cm), water depth 4–6in (10–15cm).

❀ ❂

Thalia dealbata (hardy canna)
Evergreen perennial with long-stalked, blue-green leaves with a white, mealy coating. Spikes of tubular, violet flowers are carried above the leaves in summer, followed by decorative seedheads. Propagate from seed or by division in spring. Zones 6–11. H 5ft (1.5m), S 2ft (60cm), water depth to 6in (15cm).

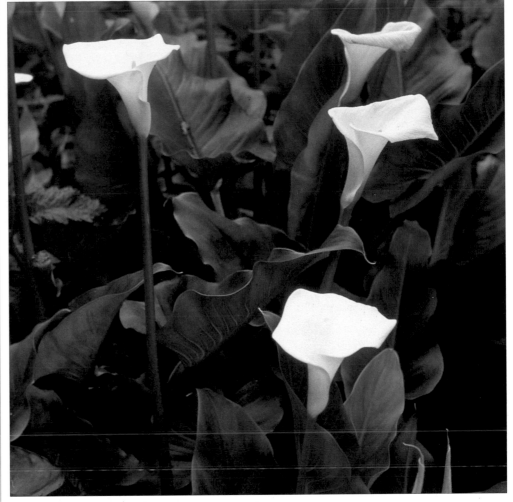

❄ ⊞ ◖

Typha latifolia 'Variegata'
Deciduous perennial forming large clumps of
wide, cream-striped leaves. Cylindrical
"bulrush" heads among the foliage comprise
light brown male flowers held above the dark
brown female flowers. Propagate by seed or
by division in spring. Zones 3–10. H 3–4ft
(1–1.2m), S indefinite, water depth 10in (25cm).

❄ ⊞ ⊡ ◊

Zantedeschia aethiopica 'Crowborough'
Semi-hardy tuberous plant (hardier under
12in/30cm of water), ideal in a formal setting,
with dark, glossy leaves. Large, fragrant, white
flower spathes with a central yellow spike appear
in summer. Propagate by offsets in winter.
Zones 5–11. H 1½–3ft (45cm–1m), S 14–18in
(35–45cm), water depth to 12in (30cm).

❄ ⊞ ◖

Veronica beccabunga (European brooklime)
Semi-evergreen perennial with white-centered
blue flowers and fleshy, creeping, rooting
stems; an excellent scrambling plant for the
water's edge. Replace old, straggly specimens;
propagate by cuttings in summer, or by seed or
division in autumn. Zones 5–7. H 4in (10cm),
S indefinite, water depth 3in (7cm).

❄ ⊞ ⊡ ◊

Zantedeschia aethiopica 'Green Goddess'
Semi-hardy tuberous plant with white-splashed
green, arumlike flower spathes in summer, each
with a central yellow spike. It is ideal for a
sunny corner of a formal pool. Propagate by
separating offsets in winter. Zones 8–11.
H 1½–3ft (45cm–1m), S 18–24in (45–60cm),
water depth 6–9in (15–22cm).

ALSO RECOMMENDED

Acorus gramineus 'Pusillus'
Caltha palustris (see p. 37)
Colocasia esculenta 'Fontanesii' (frost-
tender)
Equisetum japonicum
Houttuynia cordata 'Flore Pleno' (see p. 21)
Iris pseudacorus 'Variegata' (see p. 43)
Isolepis cernua
Juncus effusus 'Spiralis' (see p. 27)
Juncus ensifolius
Mentha aquatica (see p. 43)
Myosotis scorpioides (see p. 32)
Sagittaria sagittifolia (see p. 47)
Typha minima (see p. 32)

Where specific page references are not given for
plant entries found in other sections, brief details
are given in the Plant Index (see pp. 210–213).

MOISTURE-LOVING PLANTS

THERE IS A WIDE RANGE OF PLANTS that tolerate and positively thrive in moist soil. These moisture-lovers include not only those plants seen growing naturally by streams, boggy areas, and poolsides, but also many that, although traditionally raised in more normal soil conditions, will excel in this fringe environment, growing with a vigor and lushness they seldom exhibit in drier soil in high summer. Moisture-loving plants are often referred to and sold as "bog plants," but this is a misleading description. While boggy soil saturated with water is ideal for a large number of shallow-water aquatic plants (*see* Marginal Plants, *pp. 190–195*), nearly all moisture-lovers need good drainage and will not tolerate waterlogged soil. They can be used in surrounding beds to bridge the gap between aquatic plants contained in formal, enclosed pools and the rest of the garden, provided that they are given moisture-retentive soil and are well-watered in dry spells. They can be used to edge informal clay-bottomed or lined ponds, planted above the waterline but where the soil is still naturally damp. Many moisture-lovers are spreading and will mingle informally.

❋ ◊

Arisaema candidissimum
Tuberous perennial that appears in early summer; erect stems support hooded spathes that are pink-and-white striped inside, followed by large, three-lobed leaves that fade in autumn to a straw color, surrounding spikes of red fruits. Propagate by seed or offsets. Zones 7–9. H 6in (15cm), S 12–18in (30–45cm).

❋ ◊

Ajuga reptans 'Multicolor', syn. 'Rainbow', 'Tricolor'
Evergreen perennial with stems that spread to form a creeping mat. The blue spring flowers with purple bracts are carried on spikes 4–5in (10–13cm) above bronze-pink leaves splashed with gold. Propagate by division in spring. Zones 3–9. H 4–5in (10–13cm), S 18in (45cm).

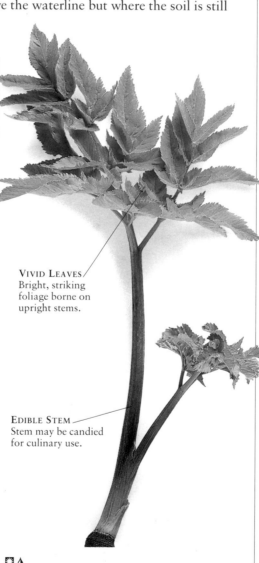

VIVID LEAVES
Bright, striking foliage borne on upright stems.

EDIBLE STEM
Stem may be candied for culinary use.

❋ ◊

Anagallis tenella 'Studland' (bog pimpernel)
Creeping perennial that roots freely as its stems spread. Mats of small, rounded leaves are brightened by a profusion of star-shaped, sweetly scented, deep pink flowers in spring. Plants are short-lived; propagate from soft tip cuttings in spring or early summer. Zones 5–7. H 2–4in (5–10cm), S 6–12in (15–30cm).

❋ ◊

Angelica archangelica (angelica)
Short-lived perennial, often grown as a biennial, that grows rapidly into a very large plant. It self-seeds freely; deadheading may prolong its lifespan. The bright green, deeply divided leaves are aromatic; yellow-green flowerheads appear in late summer. Propagate by seed. Zones 4–9. H 6ft (2m), S 3ft (1m).

❋ ◊

Aruncus dioicus (goat's beard)
Herbaceous perennial forming dense mounds of broad, fernlike leaves, bronze-green in spring, turning light green by summer. Large, creamy plumes of flowers gradually turn brown on the more feathery male plants; seed pods form on females. Propagate by seed or by division. Zones 3–9. H 5–6ft (1.5–1.8m), S 1m (3ft).

🏵 ◊

Chelone obliqua (turtle head, shellflower)
Herbaceous perennial with upright stems
supporting serrated, dark green leaves. In late
summer and autumn it produces terminal heads
of rich reddish purple, two-lipped flowers.
Propagate by seed or by division in spring or
autumn, or from soft tip cuttings in summer.
Zones 4–9. H 3ft (1m), S 20in (50cm).

🏵 ◊

Astilbe 'Venus'
Summer-flowering perennial with plumes of
shell pink flowers. The dark green foliage has
a coppery tint when young. The dried
flowerheads are attractive in winter, so should
not be removed until the following spring.
Propagate by division in spring or autumn.
Zones 3–8. H 3ft (1m), S 3ft (1m).

🏵 ▨ ◊ ◊

Carex elata 'Aurea', syn. *Carex stricta*
'Bowles' Golden' (Bowles' golden sedge)
Evergreen perennial with golden yellow tufts of
grassy foliage. Inconspicuous brown flowers
forming blackish spikelets are held among the
leaves in summer. Will also grow well in
shallow water. Propagate by division in spring.
Zones 5–9. H 15in–3ft (38cm–1m), S 3ft (1m).

🏵 ▨ ◊ ◊

Carex pendula (pendulous sedge)
Perennial with grasslike leaves. Tall, triangular
stems support graceful, pendulous spikes of
brown flowers, very striking when reflected in
still water. Will also grow well in very shallow
water and is ideal for the margins of a wildlife
pool. Propagate by division in spring. Zones
5–9. H 2–3ft (60–90cm), S 18in (45cm).

🏵 ◊

Cimicifuga simplex (bugbane)
Herbaceous perennial that will grow well in
light shade. This species is one of the last to
flower, sometimes well into late autumn. The
flowers are slightly fragrant, held in delicate
spikes on wiry stems; plants benefit from staking
in open sites. Propagate by seed or by division in
spring. Zones 3–8. H 4ft (1.2m), S 18in (45cm).

❇ ◊ ◊

Filipendula ulmaria 'Aurea'
Herbaceous perennial with beautifully divided
leaves, golden-green in spring, turning to pale
green. Branching heads of creamy flowers are
carried above the foliage in midsummer.
Deadhead promptly to encourage new growth.
Propagate in autumn by seed or by division.
Zones 3–9. H 2ft (60cm), S 18in (45cm).

❇ ◊ ◊

Cornus stolonifera 'Flaviramea'
Deciduous spreading shrub suited to moist or
well-drained soils, chiefly grown for its bright,
greenish yellow young stems, which can be
renewed by hard pruning in early spring.
Propagate from softwood cuttings in summer,
or hardwood cuttings in autumn or winter.
Zones 2–8. H 4–6ft (1.2–2m), S 12ft (4m).

❇ ◊ ◊

Crocosmia 'Lucifer'
Clump-forming cormous plant that grows in
moist or dry soils. Erect, swordlike, bright
green leaves surround purple, wiry stems that
support dense, branching spikes of brilliant
flame red flowers in midsummer. Propagate
by division in spring. Zones 5–9. H 4ft (1.2m),
S 10–12in (25–30cm).

❇ ◊

Filipendula purpurea
Herbaceous perennial forming informal clumps
of deeply divided leaves and dense clusters of
tiny, fragrant, rose-pink flowers in summer
followed by bronze-red seedheads. It is
susceptible to mildew if soil becomes dry.
Propagate in autumn by seed or by division.
Zones 4–9. H 4ft (1.2m), S 2–3ft (60–90cm).

❇ ◊ ◊

Filipendula vulgaris (dropwort)
Interesting perennial for the fringes of moist
soil with mat-forming, carrotlike foliage that is
edible. Flowers are borne in branching, creamy
heads, tinged pink on the undersides.
'Multiplex' is a fine, double-flowered cultivar.
Propagate in autumn by seed or by division.
Zones 3–8. H 2–2½ft (60–75cm), S 2ft (60cm).

❋ ◊ ◊ ◊

Gunnera manicata

Large perennial with enormous, jagged leaves borne on thick stems. Conical clusters of green flowers appear in spring followed by rust-brown seeds. Protect from wind and mulch for protection in winter in the northern part of its range. Zones 7–11. Propagate by seed or by division in spring. H and S 7–10ft (2.1–3m).

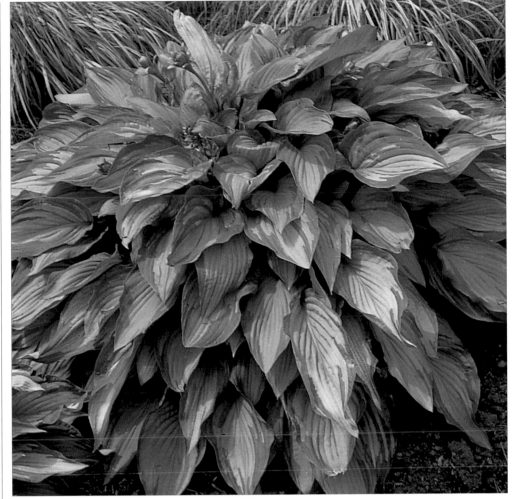

❋ ◊ ◊

Hosta fortunei 'Albo Picta'

Clump-forming perennial with spectacular leaves nearly 12in (30cm) long. These are pale green, with dark veins and creamy yellow centers fading to dull green. Pale violet flowers are borne on graceful stalks in early summer. Propagate by division in spring. Zones 3–8. H 2½ft (75cm), S 3ft (1m).

❋ ◊ ◊

Hemerocallis fulva 'Flore Pleno'

Herbaceous perennial forming mounds of light green, straplike leaves. In mid- to late summer it produces spikes of rich orange-buff, trumpet-shaped, double flowers, longer-lasting than the blooms of many other daylilies. Propagate by division in autumn or spring. Zones 3–9. H 3–4ft (1–1.2m), S 2½ft (75cm).

❋ ◊ ◊

Hosta fortunei 'Aureo-Marginata'

Herbaceous clump-forming perennial. This cultivar has large leaves that are smaller than many H. fortunei cultivars, but larger than many other hosta species. Pale violet, trumpet-shaped flowers are held well above the foliage in midsummer. Propagate by division in spring. Zones 3–8. H 2½ft (75cm), S 3ft (1m).

❋ ◊ ◊

Hosta 'Frances Williams'

Herbaceous clump-forming perennial. The large, heart-shaped, deeply ribbed and puckered leaves are glaucous blue, with a wide, creamy margin. In early summer, the pale lavender flowers make a cool contrast to the foliage. Propagate by division in spring. Zones 3–8. H 3ft (1m), S 5ft (1.5m).

✳ ◊ ◊

Inula hookeri

Herbaceous perennial that forms spreading clumps of branched stems. It has oval, light green to yellow leaves and a mass of woolly buds that open into slightly scented, greenish yellow, daisylike flowers in mid- to late summer. It can be invasive. Propagate by seed or by division. Zones 4–8. H 2½ft (75cm), S 3ft (1m).

✳ ◊ ◊

Iris ensata 'Blue Peter' (Japanese iris)

Rhizomatous herbaceous perennial with dense clumps of bold, sword-shaped leaves and blue flowers, 3–6in (8–15cm) across. Dislikes alkaline soil. Can be used as a shallow marginal if it is removed from saturated soil in winter. Propagate by division in late summer. Zones 4–9. H 2–3ft (60–90cm), S indefinite.

✳ ◊ ◊

Iris sibirica (Siberian iris)

Rhizomatous herbaceous perennial with sheaves of grasslike leaves. Each stem bears two or three dark-veined blue or blue-purple flowers, 2–4in (5–10cm) across. An adaptable plant that will also flourish in dry soil. Propagate by seed or by division in late summer. Zones 4–9. H 18in (45cm), S 3ft (90cm).

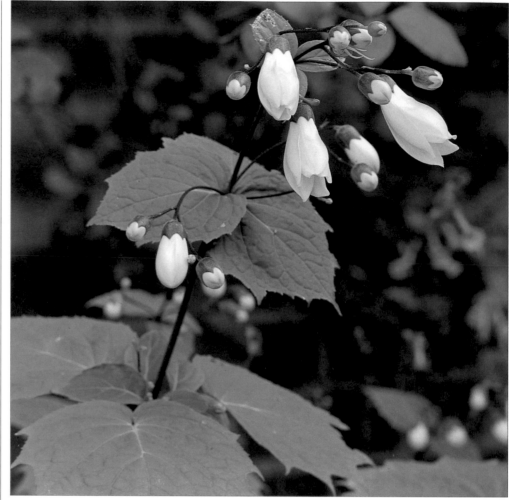

✳ ◊ ◊

Kirengeshoma palmata

Herbaceous perennial forming clumps of large, rounded hairy leaves with irregular edges. The funnel-shaped flowers, pale yellow and waxen, hang in loose sprays on purplish stems in late summer. Dislikes alkaline soil. Propagate by seed or by division in autumn or spring. Zones 5–8. H 3ft (1m), S 2ft (60cm).

✳ ◊

Leucojum aestivum (summer snowflake)

Bulb with glossy, strap-shaped, daffodil-like leaves. In springtime, sturdy green stems produce loose clusters of bell-shaped flowers resembling large snowdrops, with white petals tipped with green. Propagate by seed in autumn, or by division in autumn or spring. Zones 4–9. H 6–24in (15–60cm), S 6–12in (15–30cm).

✳ ◊

Ligularia 'Gregynog Gold'

Clump-forming herbaceous perennial with large, richly veined, deep green leaves. In mid- to late summer, daisylike, orange-yellow flowers are borne in large, pyramidal spikes. Tends to wilt quickly on bright, windy days or in dry spells. Propagate by seed or by division in spring. Zones 3–8. H 6ft (2m), S 2ft (60cm).

❄ ◊ ◊

Ligularia przewalskii
Elegant, clump-forming perennial with dark
green, deeply lobed basal leaves. The stems are
dark purple and carry narrow spikes of small,
ragged, daisylike yellow flowers in mid- to late
summer. Plants tend to wilt in bright sunshine.
Propagate by seed or by division in spring.
Zones 5–8, H 6ft (2m), S 3ft (1m)

❄ ◊ ◊

Lobelia 'Bees' Flame'
Clump-forming perennial with oval or
lanceolate, bronze-red leaves and tall, strong
spikes of large, velvety, luminous scarlet flowers
in late summer. Do not leave in wet soil over
winter, and provide a protective winter mulch in
cool temperate climates. Propagate by division
in spring. Zones 4–8. H 3ft (1m), S 12in (30cm).

❄ ◊ ◊

Lobelia 'Cherry Ripe'
Herbaceous clump-forming perennial with
spikes of scarlet flowers from mid- to late
summer. The fresh green leaves are often tinged
with bronze. Like 'Bees' Flame', this cultivar
should be given a protective winter mulch in
temperate climates. Propagate by division in
spring. Zones 4–8. H 3ft (1m), S 10in (25cm).

❄ ◊ ◊

Lobelia 'Will Scarlet'
Herbaceous clump-forming perennial with dark
green leaves tinged with red. It produces tall
spikes of bright scarlet, two-lipped flowers in
late summer. In temperate climates, protect
with winter mulch, or lift from wet soil and
overwinter in pots. Propagate by division in
spring. Zones 4–8. H 3ft (1m), S 12in (30cm).

❄ ◊ ◊

Lobelia x *gerardii* 'Vedrariensis'
Clump-forming herbaceous perennial. Produces
long-lasting, dense spikes of two-lipped flowers
on stout stems in late summer and early autumn
in varying tones of rich violet-purple. The basal
rosettes of oval leaves are dark green tinged
with red. Propagate by division in spring.
Zones 4–8. H 3ft (1m), S 12in (30cm).

✳ ◊ ◊

Lysimachia nummularia 'Aurea'
(creeping Jenny, moneywort)
Prostrate herbaceous perennial with bright
yellow flowers in summer. The rooting stems
produce soft yellow leaves that darken in late
summer or in shade. Can be invasive. Propagate
by division in spring or by seed in autumn.
Zones 4–10. H 1–2in (2.5–5cm), S indefinite.

✳ ◊ ◊

Mimulus cardinalis
Erect, branching perennial producing sprays
of snapdragon-like flowers from midsummer
onward. It can become untidy in late summer
and should be cut back to prompt new growth.
Propagate by seed or by division in spring, or
grow as an annual where winters are severe.
Zones 5–8. H 2–3ft (60–90cm), S 3ft (90cm).

✳ ◊ ◊

Mimulus luteus (yellow musk)
Spreading perennial with prolific snapdragon-
like yellow flowers, sometimes with brownish
red spots, produced from midsummer onward
above lush, hairy, mid-green foliage. A rampant
self-seeder, ideally suited for a large, informal
wildlife pond. May also be propagated by
division. Zones 5–8. H and S 18in (45cm).

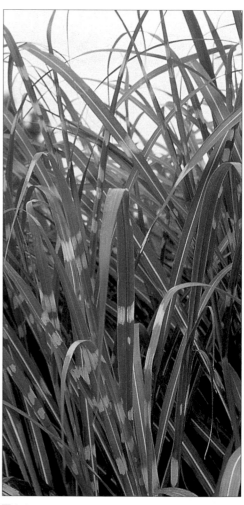

✳ ◊ ◊

Macleaya microcarpa 'Kelway's
Coral Plume'
Imposing herbaceous perennial with spikes
of cream or white flowers. Leaves are gray or
olive green above and downy white below.
Chop through roots to control spread. Divide in
spring or take root cuttings in winter. Zones
4–9. H 6–8ft (2–2.5m), S 3–4ft (1–1.2m).

✳ ◊ ◊

Miscanthus sinensis 'Zebrinus'
Clump-forming perennial grass that makes a
distinctive specimen plant. Tough stems and
leaves develop transverse yellow bands from
midsummer onward. The flowers are silky-
white fan-shaped heads borne in autumn.
Propagate by division in spring. Zones 5–9.
H 4ft (1.2m), S 18in (45cm).

Osmunda regalis (royal fern)
Elegant deciduous fern. Mature plants bear sterile fronds to 5ft (5m) that are pinkish when young and mature to bright green. Pale brown, fertile flower spikes appear at the tips of taller fronds. Protect the base with mulch in winter. Propagated by division in early spring. Zones 3–9. H 6ft (2m), S 3ft (1m).

Persicaria bistorta 'Superba'
Vigorous, clump-forming herbaceous perennial with dense, docklike basal foliage. Erect, broad, bottlebrushlike spikes of soft pink flowers are produced over a long period. Plants can become invasive. Propagate by seed or by division in spring or autumn. Zones 3–8. H 2–2½ft (60–75cm), S 2ft (60cm).

Parnassia palustris (grass of Parnassus)
Small perennial, often evergreen, with low tufts of heart-shaped, pale or mid-green leaves. Buttercup-like white flowers, with dark green or purplish green veins, are borne on erect stems in late spring and early summer. Not easy to establish in cultivated conditions. Sow seed in autumn. Zones 3–6. H 8in (20cm), S 2½in (6cm).

Persicaria campanulata (lesser knotweed)
Stout mat-forming herbaceous perennial with attractively crinkled, dark green leaves that are silver or buff on the underside. From mid-summer onward it produces a long-lasting display of small, pale pink or white, bell-shaped flowers. Propagate by seed or by division in spring or autumn. Zones 5–9. H and S 3ft (1m).

Petasites japonicus (butterbur)
Rhizomatous perennial with stout roots. Dense cones of small, greenish white, daisylike flowers are followed by impressive leaves, up to 3ft (1m) across. A dramatic specimen for informal ponds, but can be difficult to control. Propagate by division in spring or autumn. Zones 5–9. H 3ft (1m), S 5ft (1.5m).

❄ ◊ ◊

Phalaris arundinacea var. *picta*
(gardener's garters, ribbon grass)
Rhizomatous grass with broad, brightly white-striped leaves that turn biege in winter. Bears narrow clusters of flower spikelets in summer. Contrasts well with green or purple foliage, but can be invasive. Propagate by division in spring. Zones 4–9. H 3ft (1m), S indefinite.

❄ ◊ ◊

Primula beesiana
Perennial "candelabra" primrose with rosettes of oval, slightly toothed leaves, waxy white-powdered below. Midsummer-flowering in rose-purple with a yellow eye. Mixes well with other candelabras, particularly *P. pulverulenta*. Propagate by seed when fresh or in spring. Zones 6–8. H 2–3ft (60–90cm), S 1ft (90cm).

❄ ◊

Phlox paniculata 'Norah Leigh'
Herbaceous perennial with attractive cream leaves with a thin central zone of green. Pyramidal heads of fragrant, pale pink flowers appear in summer. Propagate by seed in autumn or spring, by division in spring, or from root cuttings in winter. Dislikes alkaline or clay soils. Zones 4–8. H and S 2ft (60cm).

❄ ◊ ◊

Physostegia virginiana subsp. *speciosa* 'Variegata' (obedient plant)
Erect perennial with toothed, cream-edged leaves and spikes of hooded, purple-pink blooms in late summer. These have hinged stalks, allowing the flowers to be moved into different positions. Propagate by division in spring. Zones 3–9. H 3ft (1m), S 2ft (60cm).

❄ ◊

Primula bulleyana
Compact herbaceous perennial with rosettes of oval or lance-shaped, dark green, toothed leaves. The candelabra flowers, deep orange or sometimes mauve, appear in early summer and maintain a vivid display for many weeks. Seeds readily, making good ground cover on moist soil. Zones 6–8. H 2ft (60cm), S 1ft (30cm).

❄ ◆ ◆

Primula florindae (giant cowslip)
Bold, clump-forming herbaceous perennial, one of the most vigorous waterside primroses. Established plants produce several stems with long, drooping heads of fragrant, white-powdered, sulphur yellow bells. Propagate by seed when fresh or in spring. Zones 6–8. H 2–3ft (60–90cm), S 1–2ft (30–60cm).

❄

Primula prolifera
Vigorous herbaceous perennial. Basal rosettes of rich green leaves surround tall, green flower stems with orange buds. The golden yellow, white-powdered flowers open in early summer. A good choice for mass planting by streams. Propagate by seed when fresh or in spring. Zones 6–8 H 3ft (90cm), S 2ft (60cm).

❄ ◆

Primula japonica 'Miller's Crimson'
Vigorous, clump-forming herbaceous perennial with pale green leaves that are oval to lance-shaped, toothed, and coarse. Sturdy spikes of intense crimson flowers appear in early summer. Unlike many selected cultivars, it breeds true from seed. May also be divided. Zones 5–8. H 1–2ft (30–60cm), S 1–1½ft (30–45cm).

❄ ◆

Primula pulverulenta
One of the most elegant candelabra primroses, although slightly smaller than many. This clump-forming species has red tubular flowers with purple-red eyes. The mid-green leaves are broadly lance-shaped and toothed. Propagate from seed when fresh or in spring. Zones 6–8. H 2ft (60cm), S 1–1½ft (30–45cm).

❄ ◆

Primula rosea
Clump-forming perennial that bears small, flat heads of rose-pink flowers in early spring. Less vigorous than most primroses and waterside plants; care is required to prevent it from being smothered. Propagate by seed when fresh or in spring. Zones 5–8. H 4–6in (10–15cm), S 6–8in (15–20cm).

※ ◊ ◊

Pulmonaria angustifolia subsp. *azurea*
(blue lungwort)
Herbaceous perennial that makes a slow-growing
ground cover in a wide range of conditions.
As rich blue flowers, sometimes pink-tinged,
appear, narrow, lance-shaped leaves open.
Propagate by division in spring or autumn.
Zones 2–8. H 9in (23cm), S 8–12in (20–30cm).

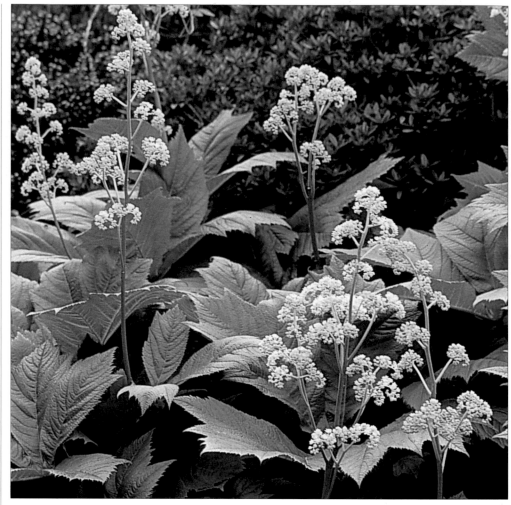

※ ◊ ◊

Rodgersia podophylla
Clump-forming perennial with large, attractive
leaves, bronze-veined when young, turning
green, then copper. The flowers are cream. A
good substitute for *Gunnera* in a small garden.
Must have shelter from wind. Propagate by
division in spring or by seed in autumn. Zones
5–8. H 4ft (1.2m), S 3ft (1m).

※ ◊

Rheum palmatum 'Atrosanguineum'
Stout, clump-forming cultivar grown for its
large, deeply cut leaves. Rich red-purple when
young, they retain this color on the undersides
in maturity. Spikes of small, rust-red flowers
appear in early summer. Grows best in deep,
moist soil. Propagate by seed in autumn or by
division in spring. Zones 5–9. H and S 6ft (2m).

※ ◊ ◊

Rodgersia sambucifolia
Rhizomatous perennial forming clumps of
emerald green, sometimes bronze-tinged leaves.
Astilbe-like heads of pink or white flowers
appear in summer. Ideal for woodland water
gardens or the side of a stream. Propagate by
division in spring or by seed in autumn. Zones
5–8. H 3–4ft (1–1.2m), S 3ft (1m).

※ ◊

Senecio smithii
Bushy herbaceous perennial with woolly stems
and long, serrated, leathery, dark green leaves.
Terminal clusters of white, daisylike flowers
with yellow centers are held above the foliage in
early summer, followed by attractive, fluffy
white seed heads. Propagate by division in spring.
Zones 7–9. H 3–4ft (1–1.2m), S 3ft (1m).

🌑 ◊

Trillium erectum (stinking Benjamin, birthroot, squawroot)
Clump-forming perennial wildflower with mid-green leaves borne in whorls of three. Maroon-purple spring flowers are unpleasant-smelling but attractive. Propagate by division in late summer or by seed in spring. Zones 5–7. H 12–18in (30–45cm), S 12in (30cm).

☀ ◊

Trollius europaeus (globe flower)
Compact herbaceous perennial resembling a large, double buttercup, with thick, fibrous roots and rounded, deeply divided, mid-green leaves. Solitary, many-petaled, lemon to mid-yellow flowers appear in spring. Propagate by division or by seed in early autumn. Zones 5–7. H 24in (60cm), S 18in (45cm).

🌑 ◊

Veratrum album (white false helleborine)
Clump-forming, potentially poisonous perennial with oval, deeply pleated, dark green leaves. These form arching mounds of foliage below dense terminal heads of pale green summer flowers. Ideal in a woodland setting. Propagate by division or by seed in autumn. Zones 5–9. H 6ft (2m), S 2ft (60cm).

🌑 ◊

Trollius pumilus
Small, tuft-forming perennial with fibrous roots and basal green leaves that are crinkled and finely divided. Solitary, cup-shaped flowers, yellow on the interior and dark wine-red or crimson outside, appear through late spring and early summer. Propagate by division or seed in early autumn. Zones 5–7. H and S 6in (15cm).

ALSO RECOMMENDED

Alnus incana
Arundo donax
Astilbe 'Fanal'
Brunnera macrophylla
Carex hachijoensis 'Evergold'
Darmera peltata (see p. 47)
Deschampsia cespitosa
Dryopteris filix-mas (see p. 39)
Eupatorium purpureum
Gentiana asclepiadea
Geum 'Borisii'
Gunnera tinctoria (frost-hardy)
Heuchera sanguinea
Hosta undulata var. *aureomarginata* (see p. 30)
Juncus ensifolius
Liatris spicata
Ligularia dentata 'Desdemona'

Ligularia 'The Rocket' (see p. 37)
Lobelia cardinalis (see p. 21)
Lobelia 'Cinnabar Rose'
Lysimachia nummularia
Matteuccia struthiopteris (see p. 36)
Metasequoia glyptostroboides
Miscanthus sinensis 'Gracillimus'
Persicaria amplexicaulis
Phalaris arundinacea var. *picta* 'Feesey'
Primula denticulata
Rheum palmatum
Onoclea sensibilis
Salix hastata 'Wehrhahnii' (see p. 20)

Where specific page references are not given to plant entries found in other sections, brief details are given in the Plant Index (pp. 210-213).

GLOSSARY

Words that appear in italics in a definition are also defined in the glossary.

ACIDIC (of soil, water) With a *pH* value of less than 7.

AGGREGATE Similar to *ballast*, a loose mixture of crushed stone and sand used to reinforce *cement*.

ALGAE Microscopic, non-flowering plants that lack true stems and roots.

ALGICIDE A product sold for controlling algae in ponds.

ALKALINE (of soil, water) With a *pH* value more than 7.

ALPINE A term loosely applied to rock-garden plants.

AMPHIBIOUS Able to live both on land and in water.

ANAEROBIC An environment low in or free of oxygen, conducive to certain bacterial activity.

ANNUAL Plant that flowers, sets seed, and dies within one growing season.

ANTHER The part of a stamen that produces pollen (the male cells).

AQUATIC PLANT Any plant that can grow with its roots surrounded by water, either free-floating or in saturated soil.

ARMORED CABLING Electric cable with reinforced protective covering for safety.

AXIL The upper angle formed where a leaf joins a stem, or where a stem joins a branch.

BACKFILL To fill in a hole around the object occupying it, for example, a rigid pool unit or a plant's root ball.

BALLAST A sand and gravel mix used in making *concrete*.

BARBELS The spines or bristles hanging down from the jaws of certain fish.

BARE-ROOT Plants sold with their roots bare of soil.

BASAL Growing at the base of a stem or from the *crown* of a plant.

BATTEN A narrow strip of wood.

BEARER A supporting beam or plank on which *joists* rest.

BEDDING MORTAR A mixture of sand and *cement* used for laying paving stones.

BENTOMAT A waterproof lining material containing *bentonite*.

BENTONITE A powder derived from fossilized volcanic ash which, when mixed with water and added to clay, swells into a water-resistant gel.

BIENNIAL A plant that flowers and dies in its second growing season.

BLEED (of plants) To lose sap from a cut or wound.

BLUE MOTTLING An indication on the surface that the soil below is waterlogged.

BOG GARDEN An area where the soil is permanently damp.

BOG PLANT Plants that will grow and thrive with their roots in wet soil; many will also grow in shallow water, and are more properly called *marginal plants*.

BOLSTER CHISEL A steel chisel with a wide blade used with a *club hammer* for cutting bricks, pavers, or blocks.

BRACT A modified leaf at the base of a flower. Bracts may resemble normal leaves, or be small and scalelike, or large and brightly colored.

BREEZE BLOCK An undecorative, molded concrete block.

BRICKLAYER'S TROWEL A pointed, flat-bladed trowel used to lift, shape, and apply mortar to brickwork.

BUD A condensed shoot containing an embryonic leaf, leaf cluster, or flower.

BUILDER'S SQUARE Wood triangle used to check the accuracy of right angles.

BULB A modified, usually underground, stem acting as a storage organ, generally comprising layers of tightly packed, fleshy scale leaves on a basal plate from which roots grow downward. An outer papery layer called the *tunic* may be present.

BULBIL A small, bulblike organ usually borne in a leaf axil or occasionally on a stem or in a flower head. Can be separated and used for *propagation*.

BULBLET A small bulb that develops from the basal plate of a mature bulb, usually outside the *tunic*. Can be separated and used for *propagation*.

BUTYL Strong, durable, waterproof liner made of rubber.

CALYX The collective term for the sepals; the outer whorl of usually green segments that enclose a flower in bud.

CARPENTER'S LEVEL A tool for checking horizontal levels.

CEMENT A fine, gray powder containing calcined limestone and clay that is mixed with sand and water to make *mortar* or *concrete* with the addition of *ballast*.

CHAMFER To bevel a right-angled edge or corner symmetrically.

CIRCUIT BREAKER An automatic switch that halts the flow of electricity in the event of a short-circuit, or if the current exceeds a pre-set safe value.

CLUB HAMMER A heavy, mallet-shaped hammer used with a *bolster chisel* to cut decorative bricks.

COARSE SAND A sand composed of hard, angular particles, used in specific mixes with cement and water for rendering walls and similar surfaces.

COCOON A protective envelope secreted by an insect *larva* in which a *pupa* develops.

CONCRETE A mixture of sand, *cement*, water, and small stones that sets to form an extremely strong, durable building material; often used to make foundations.

CONDUIT A tube or duct conducting water or enclosing cables.

CONIFER Cone-bearing tree, usually evergreen, but occasionally deciduous.

COPING The top course of stones or bricks in a wall; often flat or sloping stones that differ from those used in the wall for decorative effect or to allow rainwater to run off.

CORM A bulblike, underground organ, consisting of a swollen stem or stem base, often surrounded by a papery *tunic*.

COUNTERSUNK SCREW A screw with a head that lies flush with the surface when fully screwed down.

CROWN The basal part of an *herbaceous* plant where roots and stems join at soil level and from where new shoots are produced.

CULTIVAR A distinct plant variation that has originated in cultivation, not in the wild. An abbreviation of "cultivated variety," often itself abbreviated to "cv."

CULVERT An aperture in brickwork that allows water to flow out from a concealed header pool or tank.

CUTTING A portion of a plant (a leaf, stem, root, or bud) that is cut off to be used for propagation. A hardwood cutting is taken from mature wood of both deciduous and evergreen plants at the end of the growing season; a semi-ripe cutting is taken from half-ripened wood during the growing season, while a softwood, softwood stem, or tip cutting is taken from young, green growth during the growing season.

CV Abbreviation of *cultivar*.

DEADHEADING The removal of spent flowers or flower heads.

DECIDUOUS Plants that shed their leaves at the end of the growing season and renew them at the beginning of the next.

DECORATIVE BRICK A dense, hard, water-resistant brick, often dark in color and hence inconspicuous under water.

DELIVERY PIPE The pipe that runs from a pump to the water outlet in a recirculating feature.

DIBBER A tool used for making holes in soil into which seedlings or cuttings are inserted.

DIEBACK The progressive death of shoots from the tip downward as a result of damage or disease.

DIVISION A method of thinning or increasing plants by dividing them into pieces, each with a portion of the root system and one or more shoots (or dormant buds).

DORMANCY The state of temporary cessation of growth in plants, and slowing down of other activities, usually during winter.

DOUBLE FLOWER A flower with more than the normal number of petals in several rows, with few or no stamens visible or present.

ELBOW JOINT A length of connecting pipe bent to form a right-angle.

EPDM (thylene, propylene, diene, monomer) A synthetic rubber liner material with more stretch and greater UV resistance than PVC.

EVERGREEN Plants that retain their foliage for more than one growing season.

FALLS (fall petals of irises) The horizontal or more often, pendent petals at the base of the flower.

FAMILY In plant classification, a grouping together of related plant genera.

FLEXIBLE LINER A waterproof *butyl*, *EPDM*, *PVC*, or plastic material.

FLOW ADJUSTER An adjustable valve used to control water flow.

FOOTING A narrow trench *foundation*, usually for a wall.

FOUNDATION A solid base, often of *concrete*, on which a structure stands.

FROG The hollow in a brick.

FROND The leaflike organ of a fern. Some ferns produce both sterile and fertile fronds, the latter bearing spores.

FROST TENDER A plant vulnerable to frost damage.

FRY Young fish.

FUNGICIDE A substance for controlling diseases caused by fungi.

GALVANIZED Of metal objects such as nails, with a protective coating of zinc to protect them from rusting.

GENUS A category in plant classification between *family* and *species*, denoting a group of related species linked by a range of common characteristics. For example, all species of forget-me-not belong to the genus *Myosotis*.

GERMINATION The starting of a seed into growth.

GILL The breathing organ of a fish.

GLABROUS Completely smooth.

GLAUCOUS With a blue-green, blue-gray, gray, or white bloom.

GLOBOSE Shaped like a globe.

GROUND FAULT INTERRUPTER (GFI) An electrical device that shuts off power to a pump or other electrical device the instant it senses water in contact with the wiring.

HABIT Characteristic, natural form of growth of a plant – upright, prostrate, weeping, etc.

HARDPAN A virtually impermeable layer of compacted soil.

HARDWOOD CUTTING See *Cutting*.

HARDWOOD LUMBER Wood cut from deciduous trees.

HEAD The height of a water outlet above the level of the *reservoir pool*.

HEADER POOL The uppermost pool in a recirculating water feature.

HERBACEOUS A non-woody plant whose upper parts die down to a rootstock at the end of the growing season.

HOSE CONNECTOR A molded plastic joint used to join two pipes together.

HUMUS Decomposed *organic* matter that enriches soil.

HYBRID The offspring of genetically different parents, which are usually of distinct species.

HYPERTUFA A *concrete* mix incorporating some *organic* matter, encouraging mosses and algae to grow on its surface for an "antique" effect.

INFLORESCENCE A group of flowers borne on a single stem.

INVASIVE Tending to spread.

JOIST A wooden supporting beam that runs beneath and usually perpendicular to planks, used e.g. for flooring, decking, or bridges.

LARVA The active immature stage of some insects.

LEACHING The loss of nutrients from the *topsoil*, carried downward by water.

LEAF AXIL See *Axil*.

LOAM A term used for soil of medium texture, often easily worked, which contains more or less equal parts of sand, silt, and clay, and is usually rich in *humus*.

LOBE Of a leaf shape, where the margin is indented at one or more points.

LOG ROLL Edging material made from wooden stakes.

MARGINAL PLANTS Plants that grow partially submerged in shallow water or in boggy soil at the water's edge.

MARGINAL SHELF A shallow planting area created for marginal plants.

MEALY A sprinkling or covering of powder resembling meal.

MIDRIB The primary, usually central vein of a leaf or leaflet.

MOISTURE-LOVERS Plants that thrive in moist soil. Unlike bog plants, moisture-lovers need some soil drainage and do not tolerate waterlogged conditions.

MORTAR A mixture of *cement*, sand, and water used to bond bricks and stones, and for *pointing* and *rendering*.

MULCH Various materials, for example bark chips, applied in a layer to the soil surface in order to suppress weeds, conserve moisture, and maintain a cool, even root temperature.

NACREOUS A mother-of-pearl sheen.

NATIVE Plants originating in the country where they are grown.

NECTAR Sugary liquid secreted by flowers, which is often attractive to pollinating insects.

NEUTRAL (of soil) With a *pH* value of 7, i.e., neither acid nor alkaline.

NODE The point on a stem where leaves, shoots, or flowers arise.

NON-RETURN VALVE A valve that allows water to flow in one direction only.

OFFSET A young plant that arises by natural, vegetative reproduction, usually at the base of the parent plant.

ORGANIC 1) Chemically, referring to compounds containing carbon derived from decomposed plant or animal organisms. 2) Loosely applied to *mulches*, or similar materials derived from plant materials that have the effect of improving soil texture and quality.

ORNAMENTAL A plant grown for its decorative qualities.

OVERWINTER (of plants) Usually, to survive the winter by being given some protection against cold weather: for example, a *mulch*, or cover under glass.

PANICLE A branched *inflorescence* often consisting of several racemose branches (see *Raceme*).

PEA GRAVEL Fine, rounded gravel often used as a top-dressing for soil.

PERENNIAL A plant that lives for more than three seasons, commonly applied to herbaceous plants.

pH A measure of *acidity* or *alkalinity*.

PHOTOSYNTHESIS The production of organic compounds required for growth in plants by a complex process involving chlorophyll (the principal green plant pigment), light energy, carbon dioxide, and water.

PINNATE Leaves with leaflets arranged on either side of a central stem, usually in opposite pairs.

PLANTLET Usually used to describe a small plant produced naturally by the parent plant that can be detached and grown on separately as a method of propagation.

PLUMB-LINE A length of string with a metal weight attached, used to determine vertical alignment.

POINTING Filling the joints in brickwork and stonework with mortar.

POLLINATION The transfer of pollen from *anthers* to *stigmas*.

POLYETHYLENE A flexible waterproof liner material used for low-cost pond liners and other applications.

POTBOUND A plant whose growth is restricted by the size of its container; its roots become congested and tangled.

POTTING ON Transferring a young plant to a larger container once it has outgrown its module or original pot.

PREFORMED UNIT Ready-made, rigid moldings for pools and streams.

PRICKING OUT The transplanting of seedlings from their germinating bed, tray, or pot to positions where they have more room to grow.

PROPAGATION The increase of plants by seed (usually sexual) or by vegetative (asexual) means.

PUDDLING Coating with a mixture of wet clay that is impervious to water.

PUPA The inactive, immature stage of an insect, during which it metamorphoses into the adult stage, often in a *cocoon*.

PVC A strong, durable waterproof material made of polyvinyl chloride.

RACEME An unbranched flower cluster, usually with many stalked flowers borne on a long stem.

RECONSTITUTED STONE Natural stone *aggregate* cast in preformed shapes such as slabs or blocks.

REINFORCING FIBERS Synthetic fibers – based on polypropylene – which are mixed with cement-based materials to provide extra strength and elasticity.

RENDER To cover a surface with *mortar* or *cement* in order to produce a smooth finish.

RESERVOIR POOL A pool at the lowest point of a water feature.

RHIZOME A specialized, usually horizontally creeping, swollen or slender, underground stem that acts as a storage organ and produces aerial shoots at its apex and along its length.

ROOT BALL The roots and accompanying soil visible when a plant is removed from a container or lifted from open ground.

ROSETTE A circular cluster of leaves growing from the base of a shoot.

RUBBER MALLET See *Club hammer*.

RUNNER A horizontally spreading stem that runs above ground and roots at the *nodes* to form new plants.

RUST A fungal disease affecting plants.

SEALANT, SEALING COMPOUND A compound used to waterproof cement, wood, etc.

SEDGE A grasslike plant with triangular stems, usually growing in wet areas.

SELF-SEEDING Shedding fertile seeds that grow into young plants around the parent plant.

SEMI-DOUBLE FLOWER With two or three times the normal number of petals, usually in two or three rows.

SEMI-EVERGREEN Plants that retain some leaves or lose older leaves only in winter.

SEMI-RIPE CUTTING See *Cutting*.

SETT A granite paving block, often cuboid in shape.

SOFT SAND Fine sand.

SOFTWOOD CUTTING See *Cutting*.

SOFTWOOD LUMBER Wood cut from coniferous trees.

SPATHE A large *bract* that encloses an *inflorescence*.

SPAWN The mass of eggs deposited by fish or amphibians.

SPECIES A category in plant classification denoting closely related plants within a single *genus*.

SPHAGNUM Mosses common to bogs; their moisture-retentive character makes them ideal components of some growing media.

SPILL STONE A flat stone set at the point at which water falls from one level to another.

STAMEN The male organ of a flower.

STERILE Infertile, not bearing spores, pollen, or female reproductive organs (the pistil). Also, not producing flowers or viable seeds.

STIGMA The part of the female portion of the flower that receives pollen.

STOCK TANK DEICER A floating heater designed to keep water a few degrees above freezing in winter.

STRAIGHTSEDGE A straight length of timber on which to rest a carpenter's level.

SUBMERGED PLANTS Plants that for the most part have totally submerged foliage and, in many cases, emergent flowers whose leaves and stems release oxygen into the water as a by-product of photosynthesis.

SUBMERSIBLE PUMP A water-recirculating pump that is housed, and runs, under water.

SUBSOIL The layer of soil beneath the *topsoil*, usually less fertile and of poorer structure.

SUMP A pool or container into which water drains.

SURFACE PUMP A water-recirculating pump housed and running on dry land.

TAMP To compress firmly.

TERMINAL At the tip of a shoot, stem, or branch.

THINNING The removal of a proportion of a plant to improve the vigor and quality of the remainder.

TIP CUTTING See *Cutting*.

TOOTHED Small or narrow indentations around the margin of a leaf or flower.

TOPSOIL The top layer of soil, which contains plant nutrients.

TRANSFORMER An apparatus for reducing or increasing the voltage of electrical currents.

TRANSPIRATION Loss of water by evaporation from the leaves and stems of plants.

TRIFOLIATE With leaflets in threes.

TRUE Of plant breeding, plants that reliably produce offspring very similar to their parents when self-pollinated.

TUBER A thickened, usually underground, storage organ derived from a stem or a root.

TUNIC The papery outer layer of a *bulb* or *corm*.

TURION See *Winter bud*.

ULTRAVIOLET LIGHT (UV) Radiation with a wave-length less than that of visible light; a component of sunlight.

UNDERLAY Cushioning material laid under flexible liner as a form of protection.

UV FILTER AND MAGNET A combination filter system that prevents the buildup of minerals on which algae thrive.

VARIEGATED Marked with various colors in an irregular pattern, particularly of leaves with yellow or white markings.

VARIETY Botanically, a naturally occurring variant of a wild *species*.

WALL TIE A metal strip or wire figure-eight mortared into brickwork to cross the gap between double walls, giving them more stability.

WATER TABLE The level in soil below which water will not drain away; hence, the water level of natural ponds in the locality.

WICK EFFECT Tendency of water to move from a pond to surrounding soil, drawn by plants' root systems.

WINTER BUD A fleshy bud that detaches from the parent aquatic plant, overwintering at the bottom of a pond and growing into a new plant the following spring. Also called a turion.

WHORL A cluster of three or more flowers, buds, leaves, or shoots that are arranged around a stem at about the same level.

X Sign denoting a hybrid, produced from crossing two genetically distinct plants.

PLANT INDEX

A

Abies (firs) Tall, stately conifers with whorled branches and soft needles. *A. koreana*, the Korean fir (H to 30ft/10m), bears upright, violet-blue cones from early maturity.

Acer (maples) Deciduous or evergreen shrubs and trees for well-drained soil grown for their foliage or decorative bark; many, particularly the Japanese maples (*A. palmatum*), display brilliant autumn color.

Acorus Semi-evergreen marginal perennials grown for their often aromatic grass- or irislike foliage. Need an open, sunny position. Both *A. calamus* and *A. gramineus* can grow in moist soil to 6in (15cm) of water.
calamus 'Variegatus' 190

Ajuga Annuals and perennials for moist soil and sun or shade. Small, semi-evergreen *A. reptans* and its cultivars make excellent groundcovers.
reptans 'Multicolor' 196

Alchemilla Perennials bearing sprays of tiny, greenish yellow flowers in summer. *A. mollis* (H & S 20in/50cm) tolerates shade and moist, but not wet, soil.

Alder see *Alnus*

Alisma Deciduous perennial marginals grown for their handsome foliage and airy white flower clusters. Require a sunny position.
plantago-aquatica 190

Allium (ornamental onions) Perennials or bulbs needing sun and well-drained soil. Most have small flowers packed together in dense, spherical heads on stout stalks. Stalks and foliage are onion-scented when bruised.

Alnus (alders) Deciduous trees and shrubs that thrive in any soil and in wet conditions.

Amazon water lily see *Victoria amazonica*

American arrowhead see *Sagittaria latifolia*

American lotus see *Nelumbo lutea*

Amphibian bistort see *Polygonum amphibium*

Anagallis Annuals and creeping perennials grown for their flowers. Need an open, sunny position. All

enjoy moist soil, particularly perennial *A. tenella* (H 2–4in/ 5–10cm, S 6–12in/ 15–30cm), or bog pimpernel.
tenella 'Studland' 196

Angelica Summer-flowering, often short-lived perennials with flat-topped flower clusters. Some have culinary/medicinal uses.
archangelica 196

Anthemis Carpeting and clump-forming perennials, some evergreen, grown for their daisylike flower heads and fernlike foliage. Need sun and well-drained soil.

Aponogeton Tender perennial deep-water plants grown for their floating foliage and scented flowers. Need an open, sunny position.
distachyos 180

Arisaema Tuberous perennials grown for their large, hooded spathes. Need sun or partial shade and moist, humus-rich soil.
candidissimum 196

Artemisia Evergreen, semi-evergreen, or deciduous shrubs, sub-shrubs, and perennials grown for their silvery, aromatic foliage. All enjoy well-drained soil and a sunny position.

Aruncus Perennials forming mounds of broad, fernlike leaves and plumes of white flowers in summer.
dioicus 196

Arundo Large perennial grasses for full sun and moist or well-drained soil. *A. donax*, giant reed, can reach 20ft (6m) in height and will spread vigorously.

Asian lotus see *Nelumbo nucifera*

Asplenium Semi-evergreen or evergreen moisture-loving ferns. Most prefer partial shade and are suitable for woodland gardens, but *A. trichomanes* (H 6in/15cm, S 6–12in/15–30cm) tolerates full sun.

Astilbe Summer-flowering perennials preferring moist soil and, usually, partial shade. Will also tolerate full sun with moist soil. Flower heads remain handsome even when brown in winter.
'Venus' 197

Aucuba Bushy, evergreen shrubs for sun or shade and any but waterlogged soil, grown for their glossy foliage and fruits (formed only where plants

of both sexes grow).

Azalea see *Rhododendron*

Azolla Deciduous free-floating ferns. Can be invasive.
filiculoides 180

B

Banana water lily see *Nymphaea mexicana*

Betula (birches) Handsome deciduous trees, most upright and slender; *B. pendula* is the weeping birch. Prefer a sunny position and any moist but well-drained soil.

Birthroot see *Trillium erectum*

Blue flag see *Iris versicolor*

Bog arum see *Calla palustris*

Bog asphodel see *Narthecium ossifragum*

Bog bean see *Menyanthes trifoliata*

Bowles' golden sedge see *Carex elata* 'Aurea'

Brooklime see *Veronica beccabunga*

Brunnera Spring-flowering perennials, suited to light shade and moist soil.
macrophylla 39

Buckbean see *Menyanthes trifoliata*

Bugbane see *Cimicifuga simplex*

Butomus One species of hardy, rushlike marginal.
umbellatus 190

Butterbur see *Petasites japonicus*

Butterfly fern see *Salvinia auriculata*

C

Calla One species of perennial marginal plant.
palustris 190

Callitriche Perennial, submerged oxygenating plants needing full sun. *C. hermaphroditica* thrives in up to 20in (50cm) of still or moving water.

Caltha Deciduous perennials including some bog plants, grown for their yellow flowers. *C. palustris* is the marsh marigold; var. *palustris* (H 24in/60cm, S 18in (45cm) is more creeping in habit; 'Flore Pleno' has double flowers.
palustris 37

Camellia Evergreen shrubs and trees grown for their glossy leaves and

attractive flowers, borne from late winter to spring. Must have well-drained soil.

Canna Tender, rhizomatous perennials grown for their striking flower spikes. Require a warm, sunny position and humus-rich, moist soil. Some species, such as *C. flaccida* and *C. glauca* can be grown as marginal plants, but must be lifted and overwintered indoors.
glauca 25

Cape blue water lily see *Nymphaea capensis*

Cape pondweed see *Aponogeton distachyos*

Cardinal flower see *Lobelia cardinalis*

Carex (sedges) Evergreen, rhizomatous perennials that form dense, grasslike tufts. Several have variegated or golden foliage.
elata 'Aurea' 197
pendula 197

Cedrus (cedars) Evergreen conifers or shrubs for warm, well-drained sites in full sun. *C. deodara* (H to 80ft/25m) has gray-green leaves and glaucous cones; branch tips have an elegant, arching habit.

Centaurea Annuals and perennials for any well-drained soil grown for their flowers, which have slender ray petals around a thistlelike center.

Ceratophyllum Submerged perennials preferring sun, but tolerating shade better than most oxgenators.
demersum 178

Ceratopteris Tender, free-floating, spreading aquatic ferns needing full sun. Grown as annuals in the north.

Chelidonium (celandine) One species, *C. majus* (H 24–30in/60–90cm, S 12in/30cm), of hardy, yellow-flowered perennial that rapidly forms a groundcover, thriving in moist but not wet soil. The cultivar 'Flore Pleno' has double flowers.

Chelone Summer- and autumn-flowering, moisture-loving perennials.
obliqua 197

Cimicifuga Moisture-loving perennial wildflowers grown for their flowers, despite their unusual, slightly unpleasant smell.
simplex 197

Colchicum Spring- and autumn-flowering cormous perennials whose short-stalked, goblet-

shaped flowers usually appear before their straplike leaves. Need full sun and well-drained soil.

Colocasia Tender deciduous or evergreen perennials grown for their foliage. *C. esculenta* 'Fontanesii' (H 3½ft/1.1m, S 2ft/60cm) will grow in shallow water or wet soil, in sun or light shade.

Common cotton grass see *Eriophorum angustifolium*

Common white water lily see *Nymphaea alba*

Corkscrew rush see *Juncus effusus* 'Spiralis'

Cornus (dogwoods) Deciduous shrubs and deciduous or evergreen trees needing moist but well-drained soil. Trees, such as *C. controversa* (H & S 50ft/15m), are grown for their habit, foliage, and pink, cream, or white bracts; the shrubs are often regularly cut back to renew their colorful, red or yellow young stems.
stolonifera 'Flaviramea' 198

Crocosmia Cormous plants grown for their brightly colored flowers produced mainly in summer. Thrive in moist but well-drained soil and an open, sunny site.
'Lucifer' 198

Cryptomeria One species, *C. japonica*, a conifer with both tree and shrub forms (H 50–70ft/15–20m). Noted for its tolerance of heavy clay soils. There are several small cultivars with attractive foliage colors.

Curled pondweed see *Potamogeton crispus*

Cyperus Clump-forming sedges, grown for their slender leaves and flower spikelets. *C. papyrus* is tender, but *C. longus* (H 5ft/1.5m, S indefinite) and the smaller *C. latifolius* are hardy to zone 7. All prefer full sun and moist soil.
papyrus 190

D

Darmera A genus of only one species of moisture-loving perennial.
peltata 47

Daylily see *Hemerocallis*

Deschampsia Perennial grasses. *D. cespitosa* has dense, dark green leaves and pale brown flower

spikelets in summer. Tolerates sun or shade.

Dianthus (pinks, carnations) Evergreen or semi-evergreen perennials, annuals, and biennials grown for their mass of late spring to summer flowers, often scented. All need sun and well-drained soil.

Diascia Summer- and autumn-flowering annuals and perennials grown for their racemes of flowers in shades of pink. Need sun and moisture-retentive but well-drained soil.

Dierama (wandflowers) Tender evergreen, moisture-loving cormous plants with rows of pendent flowers on long, arching, wiry stems borne in summer.

Dropwort see *Filipendula vulgaris*

Dryopteris (wood ferns) Deciduous or semi-evergreen ferns. Must have shade and moist soil.
filix-mas 39

Duck potato see *Sagittaria latifolia*

E

Eelgrass see *Vallisneria spiralis*

Egeria Tender, semi-evergreen or evergreen floating or submerged aquatics. *E. densa* forms thick masses of long, wiry stems with small, whorled leaves; white flowers are held above water in summer.

Eichhornia Tender, evergreen or semi-evergreen aquatic plants, needing an open, sunny position in warm water.
crassipes 26

Elaeagnus Deciduous or evergreen shrubs and trees for well-drained soil. The usually fragrant flowers are followed in many cases by showy fruits. Can reseed excessively. Evergreen species such as *E. x ebbingei* (H & S 15ft/5m) make good hedges in sun or shade.

Epimedium Spring-flowering perennials, some evergreen. Make good groundcovers in partial shade and moist, humus-rich but well-drained soil. Tolerate dry shade once established.

Equisetum (horsetail) Primitive, rushlike, non-

GENERAL INDEX

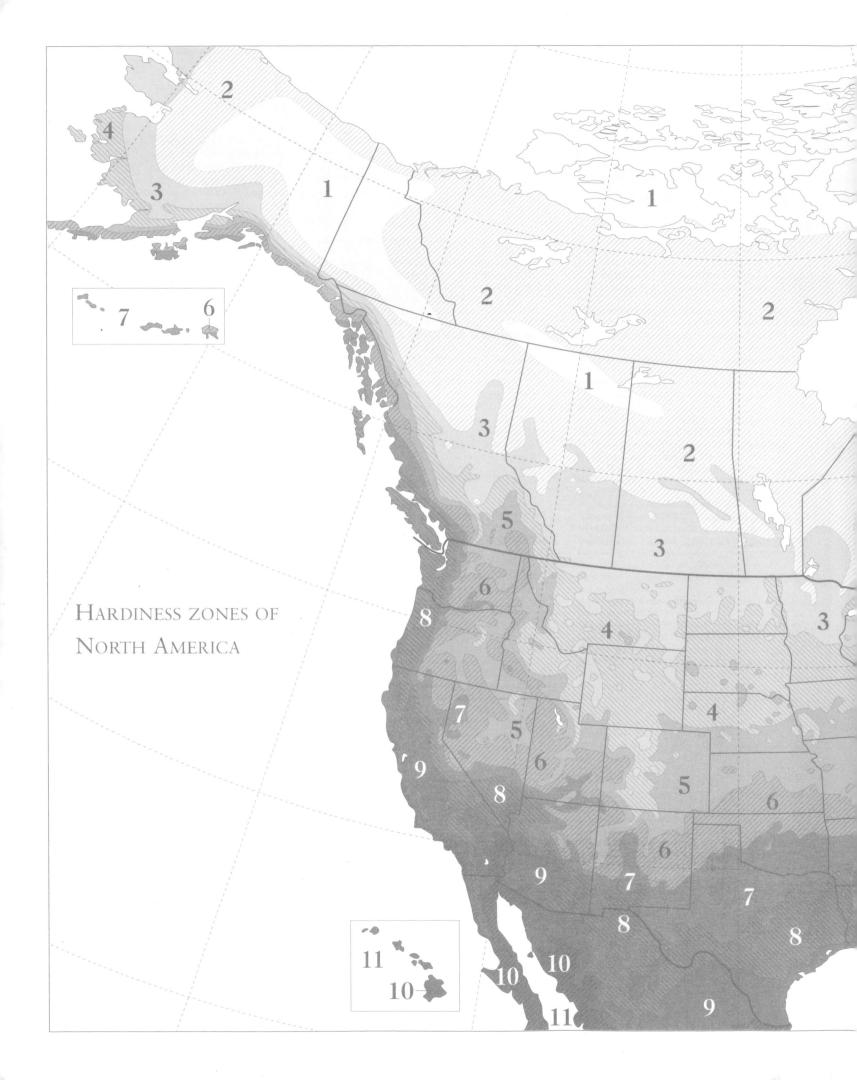

HARDINESS ZONES OF
NORTH AMERICA